Communications
in Computer and Information Science   1888

Rationale

The CCIS series is devoted to the publication of proceedings of computer science conferences. Its aim is to efficiently disseminate original research results in informatics in printed and electronic form. While the focus is on publication of peer-reviewed full papers presenting mature work, inclusion of reviewed short papers reporting on work in progress is welcome, too. Besides globally relevant meetings with internationally representative program committees guaranteeing a strict peer-reviewing and paper selection process, conferences run by societies or of high regional or national relevance are also considered for publication.

Topics

The topical scope of CCIS spans the entire spectrum of informatics ranging from foundational topics in the theory of computing to information and communications science and technology and a broad variety of interdisciplinary application fields.

Information for Volume Editors and Authors

Publication in CCIS is free of charge. No royalties are paid, however, we offer registered conference participants temporary free access to the online version of the conference proceedings on SpringerLink (http://link.springer.com) by means of an http referrer from the conference website and/or a number of complimentary printed copies, as specified in the official acceptance email of the event.

CCIS proceedings can be published in time for distribution at conferences or as post-proceedings, and delivered in the form of printed books and/or electronically as USBs and/or e-content licenses for accessing proceedings at SpringerLink. Furthermore, CCIS proceedings are included in the CCIS electronic book series hosted in the SpringerLink digital library at http://link.springer.com/bookseries/7899. Conferences publishing in CCIS are allowed to use Online Conference Service (OCS) for managing the whole proceedings lifecycle (from submission and reviewing to preparing for publication) free of charge.

Publication process

The language of publication is exclusively English. Authors publishing in CCIS have to sign the Springer CCIS copyright transfer form, however, they are free to use their material published in CCIS for substantially changed, more elaborate subsequent publications elsewhere. For the preparation of the camera-ready papers/files, authors have to strictly adhere to the Springer CCIS Authors' Instructions and are strongly encouraged to use the CCIS LaTeX style files or templates.

Abstracting/Indexing

CCIS is abstracted/indexed in DBLP, Google Scholar, EI-Compendex, Mathematical Reviews, SCImago, Scopus. CCIS volumes are also submitted for the inclusion in ISI Proceedings.

How to start

To start the evaluation of your proposal for inclusion in the CCIS series, please send an e-mail to ccis@springer.com.

Fernando Ortiz-Rodríguez · Sanju Tiwari ·
Patience Usoro Usip · Raul Palma
Editors

Electronic Governance with Emerging Technologies

Second International Conference, EGETC 2023
Poznan, Poland, September 11–12, 2023
Revised Selected Papers

Springer

Editors
Fernando Ortiz-Rodríguez (ORCID)
Tamaulipas Autonomous University
Reynosa, Tamaulipas, Mexico

Sanju Tiwari (ORCID)
Tamaulipas Autonomous University
Reynosa, Tamaulipas, Mexico

Patience Usoro Usip (ORCID)
University of Uyo
Uyo, Nigeria

Raul Palma (ORCID)
Poznan Supercomputing and Networking
Center
Poznan, Poland

ISSN 1865-0929   ISSN 1865-0937 (electronic)
Communications in Computer and Information Science
ISBN 978-3-031-43939-1   ISBN 978-3-031-43940-7 (eBook)
https://doi.org/10.1007/978-3-031-43940-7

This Springer imprint is published by the registered company Springer Nature Switzerland AG
The registered company address is: Gewerbestrasse 11, 6330 Cham, Switzerland

Paper in this product is recyclable.

Preface

Electronic Government, Electronic governance, and public administration are now in a deep digital transformation not only for Information, Communication, and Technology advancement but for all emerging technologies impacting them. Government services and processes are adopting technology to help the back office and the front office. This strategy may lead to efficient and sustainable government.

Emerging technologies are beginning to affect governments worldwide and research labs are working towards developing cutting-edge technology, often based on Artificial Intelligence techniques. The impact is in different domains such as health, education, tourism, manufacturing, and business.

This volume contains the main proceedings of the 2023 edition of the Second International Conference on Electronic Governance with Emerging Technologies (EGETC 2023). EGETC is established as a yearly venue for discussing the latest scientific results and technology innovations related to emerging technologies supporting electronic governance and aims to provide a forum for academics, scholars, and practitioners from academia and industry to share and exchange recent developments in the domain of e-government and e-governance of digital organizations. It also aims to shed light on emerging research trends and their applications. The event took place in the Supercomputing and Networking Center in Poznan, Poland from September 11th to September 12th, 2023.

The main scientific program of the conference comprised 16 papers: 15 full research papers and one short research paper selected out of 76 double-blind reviewed submissions with an average of three reviews per submission, which corresponds to an acceptance rate of 21%.

The General and Program Committee chairs would like to thank the many people involved in making EGETC 2023 a success. First, our thanks go to the four co-chairs of the main event, especially to our local chair Raul Palma and all reviewers for ensuring a rigorous review process that led to an excellent scientific program. Further, we are thankful for the kind support of all the staff of Springer. We finally thank our academic sponsor Autonomous University of Tamaulipas for their vital support of this edition of EGETC 2023.

The editors would like to close the preface with warm thanks to our supporting keynotes – Saraubh Gupta, Joint Secretary Ministry of Home Affairs Government of India, and Paul Timmers, European University Cyprus/University of Oxford–also to the program committee for their rigorous commitment to carrying out reviews, and finally, to our enthusiastic authors who made this event truly International.

September 2023

Fernando Ortiz-Rodríguez
Sanju Tiwari
Patience Usoro Usip
Raul Palma

Organization

General Chairs

Fernando Ortiz-Rodríguez   Universidad Autónoma de Tamaulipas, Mexico
Sanju Tiwari   Universidad Autónoma de Tamaulipas, Mexico
Patience Usoro Usip   University of Uyo, Nigeria
Raul Palma   Poznan Supercomputing and Networking Center, Poland

Program Chairs

Eric Pardede   Latrobe University, Australia
Anastasija Nikiforova   University of Latvia, Latvia
Miguel-Angel Sicilia   University of Alcalá, Spain
José Melchor Medina-Quintero   Universidad Autónoma de Tamaulipas, Mexico

Publicity Chairs

Fatima Zahra Amara   University of Khenchela, Algeria
Mounir Hemam   University of Khenchela, Algeria
Emmanouel Garoufallou   International Hellenic University, Greece
Samir Sellami   ENSET-Skikda, Algeria
Victor Lopez Cabrera   Universidad Tecnológica de Panamá, Panama
Sarra Ben Abbes   Engie, France
Rim Hantach   Engie, France

Tutorial

José L. Martínez-Rodríguez   Universidad Autónoma de Tamaulipas, Mexico
Antonela Carbonaro   University of Bologna, Italy
Antonio De Nicola   ENEA, Italy

Special Session

Rita Zgheib	Canadian University Dubai, Dubai
Gustavo de Assis Costa	Federal Institute of Education, Brazil
Praveen Kumar Shukla	Babu Banarasi Das University, India

Steering Committee

Shikha Mehta	JIIT Noida, India
Valentina Janev	University of Belgrade, Serbia
Ketan Kotecha	Symbiosis International University, India
M. A. Jabbar	Vardhaman College of Engineering, India
San Murugesan	BRITE Professional Services, Australia
Sven Groppe	University of Lübeck, Germany
Shishir Kumar Shandilya	VIT Bhopal University, India

Program Committee

Alexandros Gazis	Democritus University of Thrace, Greece
Amed Abel Leiva Mederos	Universidad Central de las Villas, Cuba
Anastasija Nikiforova	University of Tartu, Estonia
Carlos F. Enguix	Independent Researcher, Peru
Charalampos Alexopoulos	University of the Aegean, Greece
Csaba Csaki	Corvinus University - Corvinus Business School, Hungary
David Martín-Moncunill	Universidad Camilo José Cela, Spain
Edgar Tello Leal	Universidad Autónoma de Tamaulipas, Mexico
Emmanouel Garoufallou	International Hellenic University, Greece
Eloy Gil-Cordero	Universidad de Sevilla, Spain
Eric Pardede	La Trobe University, Australia
Esther García-Río	Universidad de Sevilla, Spain
Fernando Ortiz-Rodríguez	Universidad Autónoma de Tamaulipas, Mexico
Francisco Edgar Castillo Barrera	Universidad Autónoma de San Luis Potosí, Mexico
Gerard Deepak	Manipal Institute of Technology Bengaluru, India
Gerardo Haces	Universidad Autónoma de Tamaulipas, Mexico
Hugo Eduardo Camacho Cruz	Universidad Autónoma de Tamaulipas, Mexico
Jose L. Martinez-Rodriguez	Universidad Autónoma de Tamaulipas, Mexico
Jose Melchor Medina-Quintero	Universidad Autónoma de Tamaulipas, Mexico
Jude Hemanth	Karunya University, India

Contents

Deep Learning Models for Moving Vehicle Detection in Traffic Surveillance Video for Smart City Applications

K. Risha and D. Jude Hemanth$^{(\boxtimes)}$

Department of ECE, Karunya Institute of Technology and Sciences, Coimbatore, India
judehemanth@karunya.edu

Abstract. In the last few decades, CCTV surveillance has become a piece of unavoidable equipment in public places. The most important application is for traffic monitoring. Recently, accident cases have been rapidly increasing day by day. So, continuous analysis of vehicles is a challenging task. Developing an algorithm to find a specific vehicle or pedestrian is highly beneficial in such cases. Such a procedure can be done by video processing. Video processing and its applications have improved over the last few years. The advancements in this area are helpful in numerous fields. At the same time, the intervention of artificial intelligence also has a relevant role in this area. Machine learning has also become essential and valuable in various complex cases. Image classification using artificial intelligence provides a highly accurate result rather than any other classification method. This paper mainly compares different convolutional neural networks on moving objects detected by background subtraction and GMM with the morphological operation.

Keywords: Surveillance · Smart Cities · Video · Convolutional Neural Network · Transfer Learning

1 Introduction

Research in signal processing is developing every day. The fascinating branch of signal processing is image processing. Video processing is only a part of image processing. A video signal is a fusion of continuously captured images. The main difference between the processing of pictures and videos is the file size. The main drawback of the video file is its large size. Any operations which deal with videos are a time-consuming process. Specifically, it has been done by humankind. So, implementing a perfect algorithm to improve performance is appreciable, which is done in video processing. The process involved in video analysis is typical, which includes moving object detection, classification, and tracking. Several methods are available for this, and depending on the application, the choice of the method also varies.

The digital video contains various video frames which are arranged at a particular frame per second [1]. A video is a collection of fundamental parts like a scene, shot, or frame, which may or may not contain audio. A single picture shot of a movie camera

© The Author(s), under exclusive license to Springer Nature Switzerland AG 2023
F. Ortiz-Rodríguez et al. (Eds.): EGETC 2023, CCIS 1888, pp. 1–11, 2023.
https://doi.org/10.1007/978-3-031-43940-7_1

with various consecutive frames is called a frame [2]. In video processing, the input is usually some form of video, but the output may be video, image, or other data. The various phases of video processing are shown in Fig. 1.

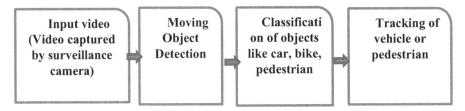

Fig. 1. Block diagram of the process involved in a Video analysis

In the case of video processing, the phases are typical, but the selection of stages depends on various factors. Figure 1 shows the different steps of video processing. The initial phase is the capturing of video with surveillance camera, and then the objects in motion are detected. In the next stage, the objects are classified and the last phase of video processing is tracking. The first three phases will usually be there; the fourth phase depends on application-moving object detection segments motile objects from the neighboring area [3]. The conclusion of moving object detection plays vital role in the video processing steps, such as classification and tracking.

The prime intention of moving object detection is to locate the mobile object in the focal point in a video [4]. It is a function that defines the physical shift of a particular thing or some objects in a specific region [5]. There are numerous approaches for finding moving objects. Still, recognition of an object is critical because this process is used in complicated situations like video classification and tracking, which have an unavoidable role in this field. Objects can be classified in traffic surveillance systems as motorbikes, cars, trucks, pedestrians, etc., in traffic videos. So, to track objects and inspect their character, the accurate classification of the mobile object is essential [6].

One of the small sections of artificial intelligence is deep learning, which follows the human brain's working principle for data processing and decision-making. In machine learning, there are different classes. Machine learning uses multiple layers to extract the most valuable features from the original input. In this, the networks can learn from unsupervised data. It is also known as deep neural learning or deep neural network [6]. Deep learning is a subset of machine learning in artificial intelligence (AI) that has networks capable of learning unsupervised data that is unstructured or unlabeled [7]. The term "deep" in deep learning indicates the multiple layers in the network. The networks are of an unbounded number of layers with a fixed size, which helps to optimize the error [8].

2   Existing Methods

There are various methods for this purpose, and some of them are described below:

In the first method, initially, preprocessing by using Robust PCA for background modeling and the output is given to the Faster R-CNN model. As a result, the overall efficiency of both detection and classification improved of moving objects [14]. The second method is a combination of background subtraction and CNNs. First, background subtraction is applied to find the moving target, and then CNN is used to classify the detected target into predefined classes [15]. The other method is extracting the video frames from a stationary camera and then using an algorithm to find the moving object. In the next stage, some preprocessing like background subtraction and filtering are done before the training and compiling of the CNN classifier [16].

3 Methods Used

In this paper, as an initial step, the methods used to determine the moving object are background subtraction and the Gaussian Mixture Model. In the case of the Gaussian mixture model, a set of video frames is used to initialize the foreground detector instead of a single frame in the case of background subtraction. The process in the Foreground Detector System compares the video frame with a preset environment to check whether each pixel is background or the foreground, then figure out a foreground mask. Finally, using background subtraction, foreground objects are segmented [9]. Usually, the foreground segmentation process output contains unwanted noise [10]. So, in the next stage, the result will be carried out through some post-processing.

In this paper, we use the morphological operation, such as an opening operation, i.e., erosion followed by a dilation, with the same structuring element for both operations. Opening removes small objects from the foreground of an image, placing them in the background [20]. Finally, the detected object is classified using different Convolutional Neural Networks. CNN indicates that the network employs convolution instead of multiplication in the layers. CNN is generally used in image processing. Convolutional Networks are regularized versions of fully connected networks, which result in being prone to overfitting data. Most image classification algorithms need various preprocessing methods, while CNN requires only a little preprocessing.

Our proposed work compares Convolutional Neural Networks such as Alex Net, Google Net, and Res Net in classifying the performance of moving object(s) after detection. We use both background subtraction and the Gaussian Mixture Model for moving object detection for the performance valuation; in each case, we use Morphological post-processing. As shown in Fig. 2, the video is captured initially for processing. In the second stage, convert the video into frames, then find the moving object present in the frame. The result involves some noise that morphological operations will reduce, and the objects are classified using different Convolutional Neural Networks.

3.1 Gaussian Mixture Model

Gaussian mixture models are based on a normal distribution with subpopulations within an overall population, which is a probabilistic model. In a mixed model, knowledge of a data point in which a subpopulation exists is unnecessary. It allows the model to learn naturally and is an unsupervised learning method because allocating a subpopulation is unnamed [11]. Various factors affect the accuracy of detection of moving objects, like (a) the brightness in the frame may change moderately in the outdoor region (e.g.: dawn

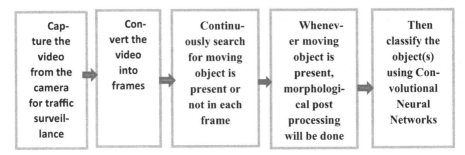

Fig. 2. Flowchart of the process

to dark, climate) or change abruptly in the indoor area (light on/off). (b)A new object can appear or disappear from the scene. To deal with all these problems, update the training set by adding new samples and removing the previous samples.

In the case of GMM, all pixels in a frame are typically distributed, which uses an iterative algorithm up to the local optimum. One of the applications of the Gaussian Mixture Model is clustering. This is also known as the soft clustering method. The posterior probability of each point decides which cluster that point belongs to. In this paper, the likelihood of every pixel is calculated to check whether each pixel is part of the foreground or background.

$P(X_t)$ denote the probability density function of Gaussian mixture comprising K component

$$P(X_t) = \sum_{i=1}^{K} W_{i,t}.\eta(X_t, \mu_{i,t}, \sigma_{i,t}) \tag{1}$$

where X_t: current pixel in frame t
K: the number of distributions in the mixture.
$W_{i,t}$: the weight of the kth distribution in frame t.
$\mu_{i,t}$: the mean of the kth distribution in frame t.
$\sigma_{i,t}$: the standard deviation of the kth distribution in frame t.
$\eta(X_t, \mu_{i,t}, \sigma_{i,t})$ is probability density function (pdf).

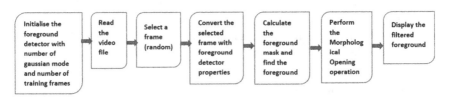

Fig. 3. Block diagram of the Gaussian Mixture Model for Moving Object Detection

Figure 3 shows the Gaussian Mixture Model block diagram for Moving Object Detection. For that, initialize the foreground detector with a certain number of video frames. Then, read the video file as input and select a frame to check whether a moving object is present. The chosen frame converts into foreground detector properties in the first stage. After that, calculate the foreground mask by using background subtraction. The result involves some noise that morphological operations can reduce. Finally, we get the moving object as the output.

3.2 Morphological Operation

The term morphology comes from the division of biology used for the form and structure of animals and plants. Mathematical morphology is used to extract appropriate image components for the representing shapes, like boundaries in image processing. Dilation and erosion are the basic morphological operations. The size and shape of the structuring element used for image processing determine the number of pixels added or removed from the objects in an image. Dilation and erosion apply to the binary image. Adding pixels to the boundaries is dilation, whereas the removing pixels from the boundaries is erosion.

Erosion is a morphological filtering operation in which image details smaller than the structuring element are removed [13]. In some image processing applications, the combination of dilation and erosion is used, for example, in opening and closing operations. An opening operation is typically splitting the small edges and removes thin projections to flatten the outer curve of an object. The definition of a morphological *opening* of an image is an erosion followed by a dilation, using the same structuring element for both operations. The morphological opening operation performs on the grayscale or binary image [12].

$$A \circ B = (A \ominus B) \oplus B \tag{2}$$

where,

symbol $\circ$ represents the Morphological opening operation.
symbol $\ominus$ represents erosion.
symbol $\oplus$ represents dilation.

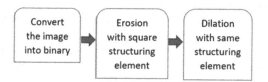

Fig. 4. Block diagram of Opening operation

As shown in Fig. 4, the block diagram describes how the input image first converts into a binary image for performing morphological operations. Then the binary image erodes with the structuring element. The eroded image dilates with the same structuring element. So, the result will be more precise.

3.3 Convolutional Neural Network

There are various classes of deep neural networks, and a convolutional neural network is one amongst them, representing CNN or ConvNet. CNN is an uninterrupted variant of a multilayer perceptron. A multilayer perceptron indicates fully connected networks, i.e., each neuron in one layer connects to every neuron in the next layer. The "full connectedness" of these networks avoids overfitting data. Convolutional networks are duplications of biological processes in that connectedness simulates the alignment of the animal visual cortex [8].

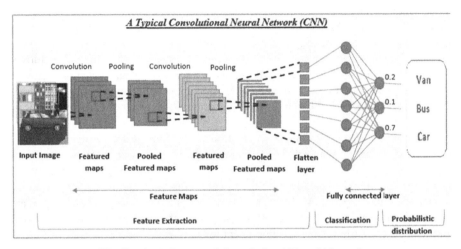

Fig. 5. Block diagram of Convolutional Neural Network

In Convolutional Neural Networks use convolution operations instead of matrix multiplication for at least one layer. Figure 5 shows the block diagram of Convolutional Neural Network. As shown in Fig. 5, CNN contains an input layer, multiple hidden layers, and an output layer, in which the hidden layer includes a sequence of convolutional layers [9]. The activation function is generally a RELU layer. It follows by further convolutions such as pooling layers, fully connected layers, and normalization layers referred to as hidden layers because their inputs and outputs mask by the activation function and final convolution [8]. CNN has many advantages over other fully connected networks with the same number of hidden units. The most important is training because CNN training is effortless and contains fewer parameters [8]. There are different architectures of ConvNets available.

Some commonly used Convolutional Neural Networks are:

i. Alex Net: It is CNN, which trains on more than a million images. In this paper, the network is eight layers deep.
ii. Google Net: In this, the network is 22 layers deep.
iii. Res Net: Residual Neural Network is 50 layers deep in this paper, and it gives the most accurate result in the case of moving object classification.

4   Experiment Results and Discussions

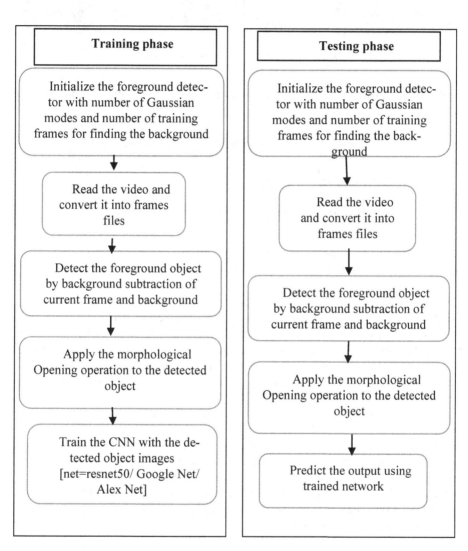

First, this paper discusses moving object detection by a conventional method like background subtraction and the Gaussian Mixture Model. The latter half compares the accuracy of the classification using different Convolutional Neural Networks after detection by both the above methods.

For the evaluation, we used three videos [19]. From that, around 2500 frames select for training purposes. The selected frames are of three types; only background, a single moving object in a frame and multiple objects in a frame. Figure 6 shows various structures randomly selected from the input video. The first image is the background. In the

Fig. 6. Different frames of testing video

second image, only one car is presented. In comparison, the third image contains three vehicles.

Fig. 7. Detected moving object(s) using Gaussian Mixture Model

Figure 7 contains various input frames in the RGB colour space. These frames are used for detecting the moving object in this paper and we considered all three possible conditions.

In the case of background subtraction, a single frame selects as a background, which usually does not contain any moving object other than noise. Then the frame with the moving object subtracts from the environment to get the target object. in the. In practice, the illumination in the scene could change either gradually or suddenly due to many reasons. Moreover, a new object could be brought into the scene or present object removed from the scene. In order to adapt to these variations, update the training set by add new samples and discard the old ones.

In GMM, every pixel in a frame is modeled into Gaussian or normal distribution. Initially, every pixel can be divided by its intensity RGB colour space. So, in case of GMM, some frames use as a background instead of a single frame in the background subtraction method. The foreground detector system object compares a colour or gray scale video frame to a background model to determine whether individual pixels are part of background or foreground. It then computes a foreground mask, by using background subtraction. After assigning background, moving object(s) detect using variance between background and foreground objects.

Fig. 8. Detected moving object(s) using Gaussian Mixture Model

The result will include a few unwanted things detached using morphological operations such as opening, that is, erosion followed by dilation, which results in an almost precise shape of the detected object. The structuring element used for both erosion and dilation are of same size and type. We use square as structuring element and size of the structuring element describes the area or space to be eroded or dilated in the image. The resultant image will be finer because of contrast enhancement in the connected region and removal of noise by removing the distant disjoint region. Figure 8 shows the intermediate result, i.e., the moving object detection result occurred using the above frames as input.

As is presented, initially, there is no moving object present. In the second case, a single moving vehicle is present, and two cars are present. In both cases, no other moving component is present after the applying the detection algorithm. The features after detection were used for the training purpose of Convolutional Neural Networks. At the testing time, various videos were used as input, and different frames were selected for classification. On CNN, initially specify the categories, i.e., label the output variables. Then set the image size as the input image size of the network. Resize and convert the image into RGB colour space of both the training and testing dataset. As a result, the computation time and complexity are less as compared with RGB image computation time.

Apply the training features to the training set. The fully connected layers are used and max pooling is used to avoid overfitting. Then, apply the network properties to test data. We use different networks such as Res Net, Google Net and Alex Net. In each case, all the other parameters are same. The activation is useful to get the network features easily for training and testing process. Finally, predict the image that builds a confusion matrix based on test label and predict the label. After all these procedures, the network is ready for prediction. Therefore, load a new image; in this case, it is a video frame. Then resize the image and apply the network properties for prediction, and the result will be displayed.

Table 1. Classification rate using ResNet

The moving Object Detection method used	In the absence of an object (%)	In the presence of a single object (%)	In the presence of multiple objects (%)
Background Subtraction	99	92	89
Gaussian Mixture Model	100	96	94

Table 1 compares the accuracy of classification using ResNet, which indicates that the accuracy is at the peak of the absence of an object and the presence of an object, 100 and 96 per cent, respectively. In contrast, accuracy is 94% for multiple object classification of moving object detection by GMM.

Table 2 compares the accuracy using GoogleNet. The accuracy is 95% and 90% for a single object and multiple objects correspondingly for GMM, whereas the values are 90% and 84% for background subtraction.

Table 2. Classification rate using GoogleNet

The moving Object Detection method used	In the absence of an object (%)	In the presence of a single object (%)	In the presence of multiple objects (%)
Background Subtraction	99	90	84
Gaussian Mixture Model	100	95	90

Table 3. Classification rate using AlexNet

The moving Object Detection method used	In the absence of an object (%)	In the presence of a single object (%)	In the presence of multiple objects (%)
Background Subtraction	99	90	82
Gaussian Mixture Model	100	92	86

Table 3 analyzes that accuracy is the least for AlexNet in both background subtraction and GMM in the single object and multiple objects. All three networks illustrate accuracy in the absence of a thing for GMM is 100%, and the same in background subtraction is 99%. According to the above three tables, ResNet shows the maximum classification accuracy, whereas GoogleNet is at the central position and AlexNet is at the bottom of the list.

In the case of background subtraction, the classification rate is less compared with GMM because of the presence of unwanted objects presented in the video. This paper mainly considers two conditions, i.e. presence of a single object and multiple vehicles. In the first case, we have a peak accuracy of 96%, and for the latter case, a minimum accuracy rate is 92%, which is between 94% and 86% for multiple objects. In the case of background subtraction, the classification rate for a single object is 92% is the maximum and 90 is the lowest,while for multiple cars, 89% is the highest and 82% is the lowest.

5   Conclusion

Recently, the attraction of researchers towards image processing has increased because of its satisfying results and applications. To conclude, the classification accuracy varies based on the moving object detection method used, the number of objects in the frame, and the Convolutional Neural Network used. The moving object detection by Gaussian Mixture Model results in better features for classification than the background subtraction method. In traffic surveillance video, among different Convolutional Neural

Networks, ResNet performed well compared with GoogleNet and AlexNet for moving object classification.

References

1. Wikipedia.org/Video processing
2. Shaikh, S.H., Saeed, K., Chaki, N.: Moving Object detection using background subtraction. https://link.springer.com/book/10.1007/978-3-319-07386-6
3. Hu, W., Tan, T., Wang, L., Maybank, S.: A survey on visual surveillance of object motion and behaviors. IEEE Trans. Syst. Man, Cybern.—Part C: Appl. Rev. **34**(3), pp. 334–352 (2004)
4. Karasulu, B., Korukoglu, S.: Performance Evaluation Software: Moving Object Detection and Tracking in Videos. Springer New York, New York, NY (2013)
5. Yilmaz, A., Javed, O., Shah, M.: Object tracking: a survey. ACM Comput. Surv. **38**(4), Article 13 (2006)
6. Ali, S.S., Zafar, M.F.: A robust adaptive method for detection and tracking of moving objects. In: International Conference on Emerging Technologies, pp. 262–266 (2009)
7. investopedia.com/terms/deep learning
8. wikipedia.org/wiki/Deep_learning
9. Risha, K.P., Kumar, A.C.: Novel Method of Detecting Moving Object in Video https://doi.org/10.1016/j.protcy.2016.05.235
10. MATLAB/R2012b/help/ Clustering Using Gaussian Mixture Models
11. brilliant.org/wiki/gaussian-mixture-model
12. www.mathworks.com/help/images/morphological-dilation-and-erosion
13. Digital Image Processing ,Rafel C Gonzalez, Richard E Woods
14. Tejada, E.D., Rodriguez, P.A.: Moving object detection videos using principle component pursuit and convolutional neural network. In: 2017 IEEE Global Conference on Signal and Information Processing (GlobalSIP), pp. 793–797 (2017). https://doi.org/10.1109/GlobalSIP.2017.8309069
15. Kim, C., Lee, J., Han, T., Kim, Y.-M.: A hybrid framework combining background subtraction and deep neural networks for rapid person detection. J. Big Data **5**(1), 1–24 (2018). https://doi.org/10.1186/s40537-018-0131-x
16. Alvi, N.Z., Singh, K., Chandel, G., Varshney, Y.V.: Convolution neural network based real time moving object detection. Int. J. Adv. Sci. Technol. **29**(10S), 8134–8143 (2020)
17. Kulchandani, J.S., Dangarwala, K.J.: Moving Object detection : Review of recent reseach trends. **IEEE *Xplore*:** 16 April 2015 **ISBN:**978–1–4799–6272–3
18. Albawi, S., Mohammed, T.A., Al-Zawi, S.: Understanding of Convolutional Neural Networks. **IEEE *Xplore*:** 08 March (2018)
19. Chauhan, R., Ghanshala, K.K., Joshi, R.C.: Conolutional Neural Network for Image Detection and Recognition. **IEEE *Xplore*:** 02 May (2019)
20. Ajit, A., Acharya, K., Samanta, A.: A Review of Convolutional Neural Networks. **IEEE *Xplore*:** 27 April (2020)
21. https://www.jpjodoin.com/urbantracker/dataset.html

Optimizing UAS Missions with Advanced Weather Monitoring and Analysis Software

Yuliya Averyanova and Yevheniia Znakovska(✉)

National Aviation University, Kyiv 03058, Ukraine
zea@nau.edu.ua

Abstract. UAS can be used for many applications in the frame of the concepts of Industry 4.0 and Society 5.0. But there is still a significant dependence of the UAS flights and mission realization on weather conditions. On one side the UAS operators are the user of meteorological information, on the other side, the UAS can be used for monitoring the weather conditions in addition to the primary mission. It allows to form the set of real-time data about the state of the atmosphere. The collected information can be used for early predictions and warnings of weather-related hazards and other meteorological purposes. In this context, it is important to process, extract, analyse, disseminate, and display a wide flow of information conveniently for the final user to help in his decision-making. In this paper, we are focusing on the development of software that can be used to support the decision-making of UAS operators and serve as a user-oriented platform for meteorological data representation, dissemination, and exchange.

Keywords: UAS · meteorology · decision-making · weather hazards · Industry 4.0 · IoT · Society 5.0 · Information technologies · software

1 Introduction

The progress of modern technologies, digitization, and automation of many human activities look toward the development of a smart and super-smart society. Some of the human-oriented aims of creating a smart society are to make growth in human quality of life and to develop nature-friendly technologies [1, 2]. The unmanned aircraft systems (UAS) in these concepts can play an important role as they can be used to increase productivity in the branches that include, but are not limited to - the delivery of goods, security, agriculture, distant and dangerous operations as rescue operations or monitoring dangerous areas, assist in realization of the Internet of Things (IoT) and everything [2–6]. The convenience to use UAS is their flexible mobility, ability to perform tasks at a precise position, economic efficiency, assistance in green technologies [7], and autonomous operation that can reduce human errors of substitute human when dangerous or routine operations.

The factors that can influence the efficiency of UAS operations or can make hazards to UAS flights and mission realization possible to divide into manmade intentional and those of natural origin [8]. An example of manmade is cyber threats [9, 10]. Modern UAS are considered as cyber and physical bodies as they involve physical body - unmanned aerial vehicles (UAV) and different facilities to support UAV operations. These facilities include a GPS receiver, control system, telecommunication facilities, special software, equipment for particular tasks and missions, etc. The restrictions and hazards of natural origin can be connected with weather and weather-related phenomena. Moreover, when drone operations for smart society it is mostly connected with flights in the boundary layer of the atmosphere. The boundary layer is characterized by increased variability of atmospheric characteristics [11]. The climate-change issues also make an impact on the UAS flight as the increase in average temperature over the globe causes the growth of convective events. In Fig. 1 the average monthly air temperatures in Kyiv city for twenty years period is shown. The data is taken from [12] and shows the average temperature for four months (March, June, September, and December). The straight line shows the averaging of the data. From Fig. 1 the clear gradual growth in temperature can be clearly noticed.

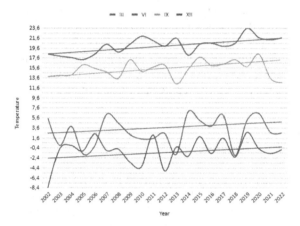

Fig. 1. Average monthly air temperatures in Kyiv city for twenty years.

Therefore, on the one side, the UAS is dependent on weather-related hazards and requires on-time and reliable information about the state of the atmosphere in the area of intentional flight. On another side, they can be used in the frame of the concept of Industry 4.0 and Society 5.0 for study and monitoring to be aware of the operative situation, to forecast changes as well as to make the interconnection between weather (including the state of water, soils, earth) and human and industrial activity. Then the information can be assessed to find effective solutions for the realization of the concept of Industry 4.0 and Society 5.0, creating IoT networks, the realization of concepts such as On-Demand Mobility (ODM) and Urban Air Mobility (UAM) [13, 14].

The effective realization of the mentioned concepts is based on the growth of information to be processed, evaluated, and use for particular purposes and operations. The increase in information volume, from one side help to take a substantiated decision. But from another side, it requires the.

– development of methods and algorithms for data processing, and data fusion;
– development of the mechanism to control information access and coordinate operations with information;
– development and certification of the sensors (including those for moving platforms);
– development of decision-support systems;
– development of the platforms to disseminate and exchange information;
– development interfaces and data format, including the unified format for data representation.

In this paper, we are focusing on the development of software that can be used to support the decision-making of UAS operators and serve as a user-oriented platform for meteorological data representation, dissemination, and exchange. As it can be important for increasing human performance and productivity of industrial processes [15].

The rest of the paper is organized as follows: Sect. 2 gives a brief overview of the literature, Sect. 3 defines the problem of the research, Sect. 4 presents the role of UAS for the innovative concepts and requirements, Sect. 5 demonstrates and discusses the developed decision support software, conclusions and plans on future research are presented in Sect. 6.

2   Brief Literature Review

The concept of Industry 4.0 was first mentioned in 2011 [16–18] as a new industrial revolution that I characterized by wide and extensive use of automation, digitalization of different fields of industry, intensive development of electronics based on miniaturization, and nanotechnologies exploring new materials. According to [19, 20] these were the results of the need to cut the period of development of innovations, to deliver unique services and goods, to make production more flexible, to provide decentralization in many areas, and to assist faster decision-making, to follow the requirements of sustainability and efficiency in resource utilization as well as to develop green and nature-friendly society. In paper [19] the fundamentals of Society 5.0 are discussed as the human-oriented smart society in all aspects of life. It is mentioned in the papers [17, 19] that the realization of the mentioned approaches is based on the gathering, processing, and use of a huge volume of real-world data. It is also indicated the necessity of the IT system to process and analyse the big array of the collected data. Therefore, the information and the lifecycle of the information from the collection of the data to the information that can be purposefully applied to particular operations in the real world are the key feature of Society 5.0.

The potentials of UAS technologies for Industry 4.0. Are discussed in papers [21–23]. The use of drones for monitoring and anomaly detection in the frame of concept 4. 0 is discussed in [24]. The application of drones for remote sensing is considered in the book [25]. The application of drones for meteorology and some related problems are discussed in [26]. The most crucial problems that should be taken into account when drones are used for meteorological purposes are revealed as differences in temperature measurement when up and down of the UAS due to inertia, the importance to calibrate sensors for measurement humidity, waste of time when data transmission due to communication and software. As was mentioned in the introduction section of the paper, the UAS flight and operations depend on the weather [27–29]. Paper [30] discusses the variation of the UAS characteristics on weather conditions. Paper [31] discuss the possibility to use the UAS to improve forecast and warning.

The variety of UAS applications shows the ability to use UAS in the frame of the concepts of Industry 4.0 and Society 5.0 to obtain operative meteorological information for improvements in operative meteorological information provision, weather forecasts [32], and application for IoT needs. In the paper [32] the drones that are specially designed for meteorological missions are discussed. Such measurements are sparsed in time and space. The principle of operative obtaining meteorological information using onboard systems of remote sensing and further flight trajectory correction is considered in [33]. Taking into account the variety of drone flights for different missions and their ability to measure the fundamental parameters of the atmosphere it is reasonable to consider the possibility to use commercial drones as multipurpose devices that can make meteorological measurements during mission realization and automatically collect and transmit measured data for further processing and analysing.

3 Problem Definition

UAS can be used for many applications in the frame of the concepts of Industry 4.0 and Society 5.0, creating IoT networks, and realization of concepts such as On-Demand Mobility (ODM) and Urban Air Mobility (UAM). The UAS flights and mission realization depend on the weather significantly. On the other side, the UAS can be used for multipurpose needs. One is the primary aim and another the monitoring the weather conditions. It allows to form the set of real-time data about the state of the atmosphere. The collected information can be used for early predictions and warnings of weather-related hazards and other meteorological purposes. In this context, it is important to process, extract, analyse, disseminate, and conveniently display information for information users. Therefore, the development of software that can be used to support the decision-making of UAS operators, and serve as a user-oriented platform for meteorological data representation, dissemination, and exchange is important for the effective realization of innovative concepts.

4   UAS as an Element for the Realization the Industry 4.0 Strategies

The diagram in Fig. 2 shows the variety of applications of UAS in the frame of the concepts of Industry 4.0 and Society 5.0, IoT, ODM, and UAM.

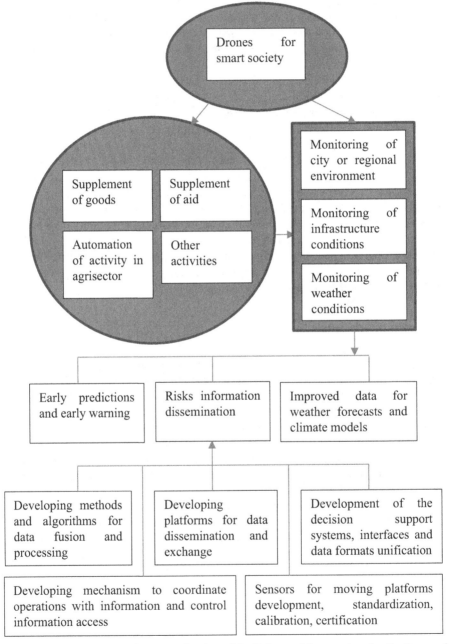

Fig. 2. UAS as an element for the realization of the Industry 4.0 strategies. Applications and needs.

In this diagram, it is possible to distinguish the primary applications of UAS in the context of new concepts. The arrows from the box "Drones for smart society" indicate these goals.

At the same time, additionally to the primary tasks the UAS can be additionally used for monitoring the nearby area. Such an approach allows sufficiently enlarge the area of observation and data collection, which, in turn, helps to improve awareness about the current state of the atmosphere, obtain real-time warning about possible warning, and improve weather forecast including an operative forecast of dangerous for UAS flight areas. The proposed utilization of the UAS as multifunctional devices lead to an increase in data streams. This, in turn, requires the consideration of the issues connected with data processing, data fusion, data coordination, development of the platforms to disseminate and exchange information, and development of the decision support systems (DSS) and interfaces for convenient perception.

5 Decision Support Software Based on Operative Meteorological Information

In paper [34] the DSS algorithm was developed to help UAS operators to take decisions when flight planning. The DSS was developed on the base of a risk-oriented approach and considers the restrictions not only for particular UAS types but for particular missions as well. In paper [35] the improved algorithm was proposed that also utilizes operative data from the own database. The database was formed using the data from the UASs that made flights in the nearby area or earlier in the same area. Exploring the abilities in data processing we improved the algorithms by adding a function of the short-term forecast of turbulence using the real-time data from UAS and the model [36]. The information about real wind and turbulence also can be extracted from the UAS gyroscope system. The measurements for real-time turbulence detection are based on the data from the gyroscope sensors. Significant and chaotic variations of UAS orientation and speed can indicate the place and presence of turbulence. The turbulence measurement can be represented with the diagram shown in Fig. 3.

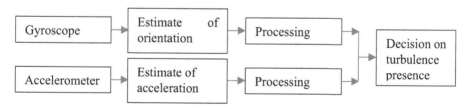

Fig. 3. The turbulence measurement diagram.

The interface of the developed software and simulation results are shown in Figs. 4 and 5 for two scenarios. The interface of the Decision-making support software is conditionally divided into four parts.

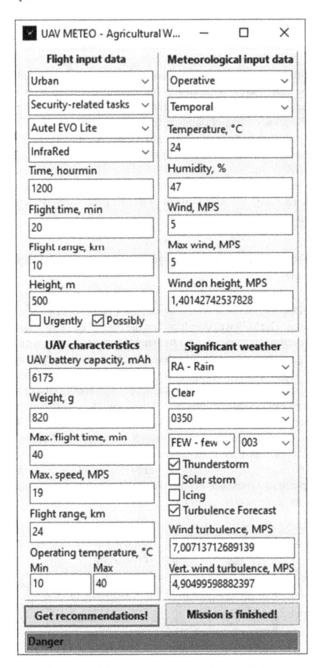

Fig. 4. Decision-making support software interface

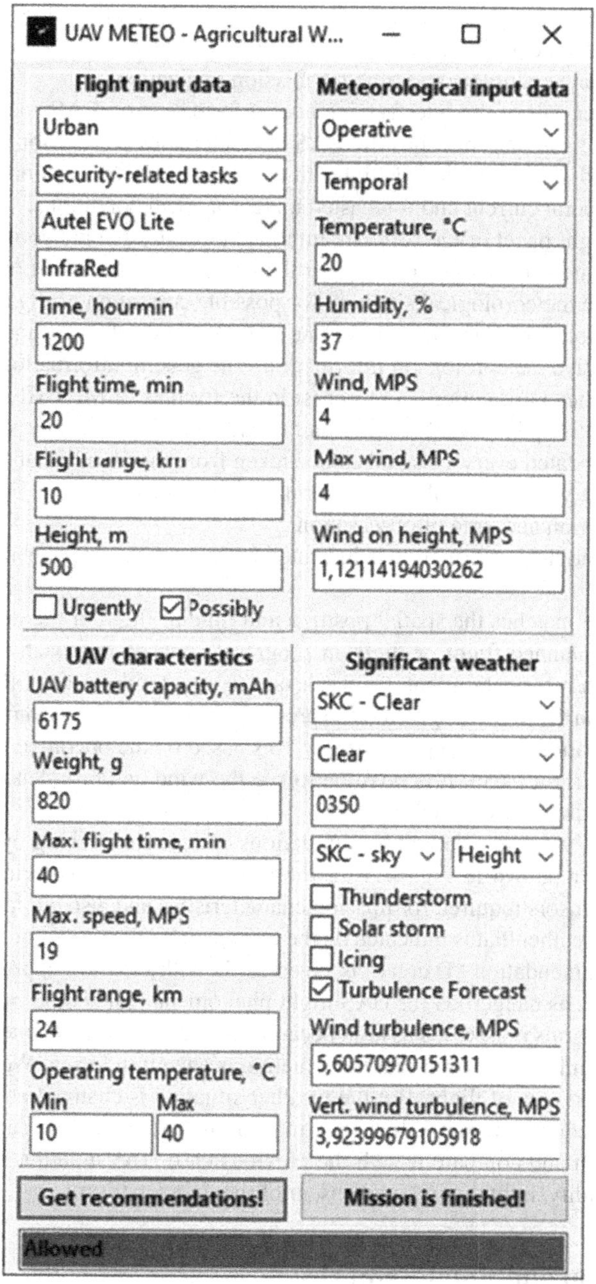

Fig. 5. Decision-making support software interface

The left upper part represents the initial data of the flight and mission. These include the mission itself, type of UAS, sensors required for mission realization, area of planned flight, planned range, altitude, and time for mission realization.

The left lower part of the interface includes information on UAS and its characteristics. Firstly, the software matches the UAS characteristics and sensor characteristics with the required characteristics of flight. In case of a positive decision, the software evaluates the general current and forecasted meteorological conditions.

The upper right panel of the software interface indicates the meteorological conditions. The software is developed to consider the general information about the weather and the operative meteorological situation for possible correction of flight trajectory or mission realization. The interface allows one to make a switch and choose to indicate general or operative meteorological information. The general information can be taken as aviation weather information and forecast in the formats of METAR and TAF [37]. This information is updated each hour or half of the hour. The operative meteorological information is updated every 10 s and can be taken from the cloud database. The cloud database is filled with meteorological information obtained from the UAS relating to their spatial position and time of observation.

The meteorological information is indicated in the lower right panel of the software interface.

The software matches the spatial position and time of flight of the other UAS with the area of the planned flight or flight in progress. Such an approach helps to avoid overloading with information that is not relevant to a particular area of flight. The recommendations on the flight are given when pressing the button "Get recommendations!". The recommendations can be updated every 10 s based on the operative information.

In the lower right panel, it is possible to see the wind and turbulence components calculated according to the model [36].

In this paper, we demonstrate two simulations of decision-making by the software. The first situation shown in Fig. 4 is for the mission of area monitoring for security purposes. The sensors required for mission characteristics and also are indicated on the left panel. The weather that is indicated on the right panel is operative for the considered case. The recommendation "Danger" is given as the risk-oriented approach considers the thunderstorm as dangerous for UAS flight phenomena that should be avoided. The risk of thunderstorms is assessed as high because it can lead to total damage of the UAV.

The next simulated decision-making situation is shown in Fig. 5. We introduce the same mission and area of flight. But the weather situation is changed and the software advice on the decision to make flight and mission is "allowed". We can examine the weather situation and compare it with the previous case. The situation was improved. The lower humidity, lighter wind, and absent of the thunderstorm.

6 Conclusion and Final Remarks

In this paper, we proposed and developed software that can be used to support the decision-making of UAS operators and serve as a user-oriented platform for meteorological data representation, dissemination, and exchange. The software can be used further as the basis for decision-making for autonomous flights. The results of the simulation of decision-making are based on real meteorological data and take into account the type of UAS, equipment for mission fulfilment (their weather restrictions and vulnerabilities), area of flight (urban, rural, category), and general and operative meteorological information. The function to forecast the turbulence using the operative data on wind, altitude, and topography (man-maid or natural) was added to increase the informativity and timely awareness about meteorological hazards along the planned flight area.

The software was developed to satisfy the demands of the concepts of Industry 4.0 and Society 5.0 to provide real-time and user-oriented information that is relevant to the particular flight area and mission.

It is evident that for flight operation a set of different data is used, for example, navigation, meteorological, control, operational, etc. Therefore, the algorithms for data fusion for further processing and use in the systems of autonomous flights should be developed.

Also, the use of certified meteorological sensors to combine commercial UAS in the network for operative monitoring of the weather situation.

Attention also should be paid to the development of information control and access mechanisms during the al information lifecycle.

References

1. Society 5.0. A People-centric Super-smart Society. 1st edn. Hitachi-UTokyo Laboratory (H-UTokyo Lab.), Tokyo, Japan (2020)
2. Alsamhi, S.H., et al.: Green internet of things using UAVs in B5G networks: a review of applications and strategies. Ad Hoc Netw. **117**, 102505 (2021)
3. Gupta, A., Afrin, T., Scully, E., Yodo, N.: Advances of UAVs toward future transportation: the state-of-the-art, challenges, and opportunities. Future Transp. **1**(2), 326–350 (2021)
4. Waharte, S., Trigoni, N.: Supporting search and rescue operations with UAVs. In: Proceedings of 2010 International Conference on Emerging Security Technologies, pp. 142–147 (2010)
5. Yinka-Banjo, C., Ajayi, O.: Sky-Farmers: applications of unmanned aerial vehicles (UAV) in agriculture. In: Dekoulis, G. (ed.) Autonomous Vehicles. IntechOpen (2020). https://doi.org/10.5772/intechopen.89488
6. Liu, Y., Dai, H.-N., Wang, Q., Shukla, M., Imran, M.: Unmanned aerial vehicle for internet of everything: opportunities and challenges. Comput. Commun. **155**, 66–83 (2020)
7. Hernández-Vega, J.-I., Varela, E.R., Romero, N.H., Hernández-Santos, C., Cuevas, J.L.S., Gorham, D.G.P.: Internet of things (IoT) for monitoring air pollutants with an unmanned aerial vehicle (UAV) in a smart city, pp. 108–120. Smart Technology, Springer (2018)
8. Averyanova, Yu., Blahaja, L.: A study on unmanned aerial system vulnerabilities for durability enhancement. In: Proceedings of the 5th International Conference on Actual Problems of Unmanned Aerial Vehicles Development (APUAVD-2019) October 22–24, pp. 40–43, Kyiv, Ukraine (2019)
9. Kim, A., Wampler, B., Goppert, J., Hwang, I.: Cyber attack vulnerabilities analysis for unmanned aerial vehicles. Am. Inst. Aeronaut. Astronaut. 1–30. (2012)
10. Sushchenko, O., Kuzmenko, N., Kuznetsov, B., Nikitina, T., Popov, A., Shmatko, O.: UAS Cyber Security Hazards Analysis and Approach to Qualitative Assessment. In: Shukla, S., Unal, A., Varghese Kureethara, J., Mishra, D.K., Han, D.S. (eds.) Data Science and Security. Lecture Notes in Networks and Systems, vol. 290, pp. 258–265. Springer, Singapore (2021)

11. Averyanova, Y., Znakovska, Y.: The spatial relationships of meteorological data for unmanned aerial system decision-making support. In: EGETC 2022: Electronic Governance with Emerging Technologies. Communications in Computer and Information Science, vol. 1666, pp. 64–80. Springer, Cham (2022) https://doi.org/10.1007/978-3-031-22950-3_6

12. Branch archive of Boris Sresnevsky: Central Geophysical Observatory. http://cgo-srezne vskyi.kyiv.ua/uk/diialnist/klimatolohichna/klimatychni-dani-po-kyievu. Accessed 29 May 2023

13. Narkus-Kramer, M.: On-demand mobility (ODM): a discussion of concepts and required research. In: Proceedings of 2013 Aviation Technology Integration and Operations Conference. Published Online (2013)

14. Thipphavong, D., Apaza, R., Barmore, B., Battiste, V., Burian, B., Dao, Q., et al.: Urban air mobility airspace integration concepts and considerations. In: Proceedings of Aviation Technology, Integration, and Operations Conference, pp. 1–16 (2018)

15. Havrylenko, O., Dergachov, K., Pavlikov, V., Simeon, Z., Shmatko, O., Ruzhentsev, N.: Decision Support System Based on the ELECTRE Method. In: Data Science and Security. Lecture Notes in Networks and Systems, vol 462, pp. 295–304. Springer, Singapore (2022) https://doi.org/10.1007/978-981-19-2211-4_26

16. Kube, G., Rinn, T.: Industry 4.0—the next revolution in the industrial sector. ZKG Int. **67**(11), 30–32 (2014)

17. Yang, F., Gu, S.: Industry 4.0, a revolution that requires technology and national strategies. Complex Intell. Syst. **7**, 1311–1325 (2021)

18. Mamad, M.: Challenges and benefits of industry 4.0: an overview. Int. J. Supply Oper. Manage. **5**(3), 256–265 (2018)

19. Lasi, H., Fettke, P., Kemper, H.G., Feld, T., Hoffmann, M.: Industry 4.0. Bus. Inf. Syst. Eng. **6**, 239–242 (2014)

20. Da Li, X., Xu, E.L., Li, L.: Industry 4.0: state of the art and future trends. Int. J. Prod. Res. **56**(8), 2941–2962 (2018)

21. Moreno-Jacobo, D., Toledo-Nin, G., Ochoa-Zezzatti, A., Torres, V., Estrada-Otero, F.: Evaluation of Drones for Inspection and Control in Industry 4.0. In: Ochoa-Zezzatti, A., Oliva, D., Perez, A.J. (eds.) Technological and Industrial Applications Associated with Intelligent Logistics. LNITI, pp. 579–595. Springer, Cham (2021). https://doi.org/10.1007/978-3-030-68655-0_29

22. Javaid, M., Khan, I.H., Singh, R.P., Rab, S., Suman, R.: Exploring contributions of drones towards industry 4.0. Industr. Robot Int. J.Robot. Res. Appl. **49**(3), 476–490 (2022)

23. Beke, É., Bódi, A., Katalin, T.G., Kovács, T., Maros, D., Gáspár, L.: The role of drones in linking industry 4.0 and ITS ecosystems. In: 2018 IEEE 18th International Symposium on Computational Intelligence and Informatics (CINTI), Budapest, Hungary, pp. 191–198 (2018)

24. Pensec, W., Espes, D., Dezan, C.: Smart anomaly detection and monitoring of industry 4.0 by drones. In: 2022 International Conference on Unmanned Aircraft Systems (ICUAS), Dubrovnik, Croatia, pp. 705–713 (2022)

25. Quattrociocchi, B., Calabrese, M., Iandolo, F., Mercuri, F.: Industry Dynamics and Industry 4.0: Drones for Remote Sensing Applications. Routledge, London (2022). https://doi.org/10.4324/9781003329046

26. Novotný, J., Bystřický, R., Dejmal, K.: Meteorological application of UAV as a new way of vertical profile of lower atmosphere measurement. Challenges Nat. Defence Contemp. Geopolitical Situation **2018**(1), 115–120 (2018)

27. Averyanova, Y., Znakovskaja, Y.: Weather hazards analysis for small UASs durability enhancement. In: 6th International Conference on Actual Problems of Unmanned Air Vehicles Developments (APUAVD) Proceedings, Ukraine, pp. 41–44 (2021)

28. Ranquist, E., Steiner, M., Argrow, B.: Exploring the range of weather impacts on UAS operations. In: 18th Conference on Aviation, Range and Aerospace Meteorology Proceedings, United States, pp. 1–11 (2018)
29. Averyanova, Y., Zaliskyi, M., Solomentsev, O., Sushchenko, O.: Turbulence detection and classification algorithm using data from AWR. In: Proceedings of the 2nd IEEE Ukrainian Microwave Week Proceedings, Kharkiv, Ukraine, pp. 518–522 (2022)
30. Ruzhentsev, N., Zhyla, S., Pavlikov, V., Volosyuk, V., Tserne, E., Popov, A.: Radio-heat contrasts of UAVs and their weather variability at 12 GHz, 20 GHz, 34 GHz, and 94 GHz frequencies. ECTI-EEC **20**(2), 163–173 (2022)
31. McFarquhar, G., Smith, E., Pillar-Little, E.A., Brewster, K., Chilson, P.B., Lee, T.R.: Current and future uses of UAS for improved forecasts/warnings and scientific studies. Bull. Am. Meteor. Soc. **101**(8), E1322–E1328 (2020)
32. Meteomatics. Mobile weather drones. https://www.meteomatics.com/en/meteodrones-weather-drones. Accessed 29 May 2023
33. Rudiakova, A.N., Averyanova, Y.A., Yanovsky, F.J.: Aircraft trajectories correction using operative meteorological radar information. In: Proceedings of International Radar Symposium IRS, pp. 256–259 (2020)
34. Averyanova, Y.A., Znakovska, Y.A.: Simulation of UAS operator's decision-making under different weather conditions. In: Proceedings of IEEE 4th International Conference on Modern Electrical and Energy System (MEES), Ukraine, pp. 1–4 (2022)
35. Ivanytskyi, M., Znakovska, Y., Averyanova, Y.: Meteorological information access and decision-making for UAS flight planning. In: 17th International Conference on the Experience of Designing and Application of CAD Systems (CADSM), Jaroslaw, Poland, pp. 28–32 (2023)
36. Fast Eddy Model. https://github.com/NCAR/FastEddy-model. Accessed 29 May 2023
37. International Civil Aviation Organization (ICAO). Manual on Remotely Piloted Aircraft Systems, Doc 10019, ICAO (2019)

Predictive Pricing Model for Shared Economy Ride Applications: Incorporating Latest Data and Factors

Harshit Shahi, K Aditya Shastry[(⊠)] [iD], Chethna Pathak, Abhiruchi Verma, and Nilesh Verma

Nitte Meenakshi Institute of Technology, Bengaluru 560064, India
`adityashastry.k@nmit.ac.in`

Abstract. The shared economy has transformed the way individuals travel, with apps for ridesharing such as Uber and Lyft acquiring immense traction over the past few years. However, due to the constantly changing and complicated nature of supply and demand, identifying the right pricing approach for cooperative economy trip apps may prove difficult. To tackle this issue, experts are looking into using data analytics and machine learning algorithms to create predictive pricing algorithms that can optimise the cost of shared trips according to a variety of parameters. The research presented here seeks to create a system of pricing for collaborative trips programmes, with an emphasis on estimating the cost of shared taxi apps and considering numerous elements and the most recent data available. We created a suggested pricing scheme and algorithm using personalised API information gathered by Uber that can optimise the cost of any Uber journey according to the data at hand. Furthermore, the research aims to develop an algorithm for detecting if a region is supporting or unsupportive of Uber's amenities, as well as to offer information on any modifications in Uber's continuing capabilities. The goals of this research are to improve the effectiveness and financial viability of Uber's shared economy ride services and offer knowledge about the ride-sharing economy's flexible pricing method. Tests revealed that the polynomial regression model outperformed the multiple linear regression, ridge regression, Lasso regression, and Elastic-Net regression models in terms of R-squared, Root Mean Square Error, and Mean Square Error.

Keywords: Regression · Uber Fare Price · Prediction · Shared Economy

1 Introduction

With the rise of app-based ridesharing like Uber and Lyft, the shared economy has revolutionised the industry of transportation in the past few years. These apps offer a novel and inexpensive way for individuals to explore the world, and the number of users is rising rapidly as a result. Sustainability and growth in the shared economy ride sharing industry hinge on finding the best pricing plan for ride sharing apps. This is difficult due to the fluid and intricate structure of supply and demand in the sharing economy. To

F. Ortiz-Rodríguez et al. (Eds.): EGETC 2023, CCIS 1888, pp. 24–37, 2023.
https://doi.org/10.1007/978-3-031-43940-7_3

combat this issue, scientists are investigating how data analytics and machine learning algorithms can be used to create predictive pricing models that can optimise the cost of rides shared by multiple passengers. The transport sector has always been of keen interest to academics and industry alike. This includes both older forms of public transportation like taxis and subways and more recent innovations like ride-hailing apps like Uber and Lyft. The Uber Developer set of APIs provides researchers with real-time operational data, including pricing and estimated arrival time, that can be used to conduct in-depth analyses of the transportation system [1–4].

The purpose of our research is to create a pricing model for ridesharing apps that takes into account a variety of parameters and the most up-to-date data in order to make price predictions for ridesharing cab apps. Using the individual API data from Uber, a suggested pricing model and algorithm will be developed that can optimise the price of any Uber ride given the current information. In addition, the goal of this study is to develop a formula for gauging the level of community support for Uber's infrastructure in a given location and to keep stakeholders apprised of developments in this regard. The key goals of the research are to increase Uber's shared economy ride applications' efficiency and profitability and to shed light on the shared economy's dynamic pricing mechanism. These findings have implications beyond only Uber, as they shed light on the pricing mechanism and the factors driving the demand and supply of shared rides, both of which are crucial to the success of the shared economy as a whole. This study adds to the growing body of literature exploring the intersection of the collaborative economy, data analytics, and machine learning algorithms, and could prove fruitful for researchers interested in these topics.

Using Uber's operational information, the research aims to forecast price in response to changes in demand at different locations, times of day, and days of the week. The researchers want to utilise time series analysis, statistical regression, and econometric prediction to look at how these factors affect how much Uber drivers get paid. The study will assess data collected during the workday and the middle of the week to reveal underlying patterns and trends. This will allow you to completely grasp the many ways in which prices and rider payments can vary. The results of this research will be useful for both the transportation industry and academics. The work's main objectives are to (1) predict the optimal price of any Uber ride using data from the dataset; (2) develop a suggestive algorithm for determining whether a given area is conducive to the facilities' existence; and (3) reflect any new developments in the services currently offered by Uber. The repository's Uber fare dataset [5] was used in experiments. The experimental findings showed that in terms of the performance metrics R-squared (R2), Root Mean Square Error (RMSE), and Mean Square Error (MSE), the polynomial regression (PNR) model outperformed the multiple linear regression (MLR), ridge regression (RLR), Lasso regression (LLR), and Elastic-Net regression (ENR) models.

The rest of the manuscript is laid out as follows. The relevant research in the field of estimating Uber fares is covered in Sect. 2. The results of the suggested work are shown in Sect. 4, which follows Sect. 3 on proposed work. At the end, the authors discuss the work's implications going forward.

2 Related Work

Taxicabs, subways, and newer taxi services like Lyft and Uber are all part of the New York City's transportation infrastructure, which is examined in [6]. Time series analysis and regression modelling are used to look at how components like location, the environment, and duration influence transaction values, all based on information pulled directly from Uber's APIs as it happens. The objective is to get knowledge that can be applied in the real world and is of interest to economists, transportation planners, and operations researchers.

In order to cut down on wasted trips, researchers [7] propose utilising machine learning to forecast the demand for ridesharing services. Using information gathered by RideAustin and DiDi Chuxing, the proposed algorithms were evaluated and found to reduce deadheading by a considerable amount on each journey, even when just a fraction of riders were given access to demand forecasts. Based on the premise of limitless access to short-term parking, the research demonstrates that giving drivers with demand forecasts can save deadheading miles by 68%–82% for RideAustin and 53%–60% for DiDi Chuxing.

The work [8] investigates the problem of forecasting surge pricing for ride-hailing services like Uber and Lyft in several cities across the world. An hour's worth of information is used to propose a log-linear model with regularisation and trend segmentation that can forecast surge multipliers for up to two hours into the future. In the majority of Pittsburgh, the model surpasses alternative approaches for predicting Uber surge ratios and can predict Lyft surge multipliers up to 20 min in time. The research also compares and contrasts the surge multipliers used by Uber and Lyft.

Pickup information such as time, date, and GPS coordinates are examined in this work [9] based on the Uber dataset for New York City. The authors used time series analysis and statistical regression to forecast Uber ride prices by analysing past information across geographies, climates, different time zones, and calendars. In the final component, the variables affecting Uber rates are identified through graph analysis, with particular emphasis on the characteristics that lead to swings in pricing.

The purpose of the research [10] is to use linear regression to analyse Uber Go, Go Sedan, and Uber Auto fares and to forecast which service will have the cheapest price. A smartphone application is developed that compares cab fare variations to assist consumers in choosing the service that offers the best combination of price and value. Labelled data is used in conjunction with the machine learning method of linear regression to create the model. The software has the potential to lessen transportation-related barriers, shorten waiting times, and save costs. The author's approach and findings can be used in the real world.

For short-term demand forecasting of ride-hailing services, the paper [11] proposes UberNet, a deep learning convolutional neural network (CNN). They use a wide range of both temporal and spatial information, including the climate, time of year, seasonal variations, economic and demographic variables that have been suggested as relevant to the forecast of passenger demand by the transportation management and travel behaviours.

3 Proposed Work

By taking a methodical approach, we were able to accomplish our research goals. Figure 1 shows this proposed approach.

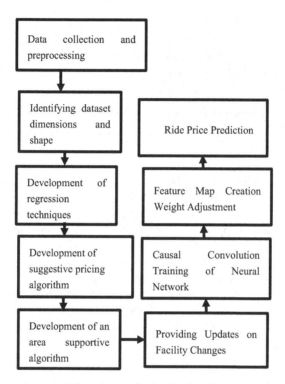

Fig. 1. Proposed approach for price prediction for shared economy ride applications

The work was divided into several tasks as shown below:

- Data Collection and Preprocessing: Data was gathered from a number of sources, including the Uber API, and then preprocessed. Incomplete values, anomalies, and discrepancies were removed from the data set during preprocessing and cleaning. The information for the dataset came from [5]. The characteristics of the Uber fare dataset are displayed in Table 1.
- Feature Selection and Engineering: Factors like time of day, location, distance, rider history, weather, and traffic conditions were chosen as characteristics that might impact the cost of sharing trips. By manipulating these variables, we were able to generate improved models for estimating the costs of carpooling.
- Machine Learning Algorithm Selection: Several regression algorithms (MLR, RLR, LLR, ENR, and PNR) were tested to see which one would provide the most accurate prediction of the ideal cost for shared trips. The data was prepared for training the algorithm, and then its effectiveness was measured with statistics like root-mean-squared error and correlation coefficient (R2).

Table 1.

Attribute	Description
Key	Unique trip ID
Fare-amount	Dollars per journey
Pickup-datetime	The day and time the metre was activated
Passenger-count	driver-entered passenger count)
Pickup_longitude	The longitudinal coordinate at which the metre was activated
pickup_latitude	the latitude at which the metre was positioned
dropoff_longitude	the longitude where the metre stopped working
dropoff_latitude	the longitude of the point where the metre was turned off

- To optimise the cost of any given Uber ride using the information at hand, a suggested price algorithm was developed. The method used took into account the most up-to-date information and variables that influenced the cost of carpooling.
- Developing a location Supportiveness Algorithm: An algorithm was built to establish whether or not a certain location was welcoming to Uber's infrastructure investments. As a result of the algorithm's analysis, Uber was able to pinpoint regions with the highest demand for and lowest supply of shared trips.
- Modifications to the continuing Uber-provided services were communicated through frequent notifications. This allowed for frequent modifications to the indicative pricing method, guaranteeing that the pricing framework always reflected the most up-to-date information.

The executed work, in its entirety, offered a thorough and data-driven method of creating a pricing scheme for collaborative economy rideshare apps. Insights into the dynamic pricing mechanisms of the shared economy were gained, and the effectiveness and competitiveness of Uber's shared economy ride apps were improved, thanks to the resultant suggestive pricing engine and region assistance methodology. The framework consists of two primary parts: training the neural network and causal convolution. The identified feature in the input is depicted on a feature map generated by the causal convolution, which takes an input and a filter and performs convolution to both. When training a neural network, the weights are adjusted by a process called gradient descent, which aims to minimise the network's RMSE during training.

The haversine formula was used to determine the distance between the pickup and drop-off points in order to execute the system. The location's longitude and latitude were retrieved via the geoapify API, and the distance between them was then utilised to calculate an estimated fare. A scatter plot was used to eliminate data outliers, ensuring that the information was accurate and usable. Using a bar graph, we were able to determine both the most popular day of the week and the busiest day of each month for travel. This helped the researchers identify trends in the information that might function as guideposts for future research. The best-fitting price forecasts were made using regression analysis, and these were tested to validate their accuracy in the real-world setting. The process of convolution of causes was used. A filter is applied by convolution to an input, leading to activation. By continually employing the identical filter, a feature map can be generated that displays the position as well as the strength of an identified feature in the input data.

Gradient descent was used for learning the neural network's parameters to minimise the RMSE. This requires a regularisation term and may be performed either deterministically or stochastically. The objective is to minimise root-mean-squared error (RMSE) across T training data sets, where yt(xt) is the output. The embedding of the weights is a q-dimensional space. These outcomes are within grasp if we put in the work.

- Effective price surge prediction and messaging to both drivers and passengers allows ride-hailing companies to make essential business choices. One of these is improved transportation efficiency and reliability thanks to better distribution of vehicles.
- Knowing the need for trips is strong may allow customers to cut wait times by either delaying their journey or opting for alternate modes of transportation; this benefits passengers as well as drivers.
- We tried various approaches to regression for forecasting fare costs. We found that New York City data was more pertinent to their needs, so we adjusted the settings to make it work with their prediction system and apply it to trips in India. The information is outdated and will require extensive cleaning until it gets utilised.

Following regression models were developed for predicting the prices.

1. Multiple Linear Regression (MLR) model: The first regression model we tried for predicting Uber fare prices was a multiple linear regression (MLR) model. Utilising a straight line, it calculates the estimated value of a dependent variable with a quantitative value in respect to two or more independent variables [12]. The MLR model is represented by Eq. (1).

$$Y = \beta_0 + \beta_1 X_1 + \beta_2 X_2 + \ldots + \beta_i X_i \tag{1}$$

where β_0 is the intercept, β_i is the slope of input attributes X_i, and Y is the predicted uber fare price

2. Ridge regression model: The subsequent type of model built was called the ridge regression model. To estimate the coefficients of multiple regression models when the variables that are uncorrelated are highly related, statisticians use a technique called ridge regression [13]. The ridge regression model is represented by Eq. (2).

$$L = \sum \left(\widehat{Yi} - Yi\right)^2 + \lambda \sum \beta^2 \tag{2}$$

The ridge equation is equal to the total of the errors plus the total of the squared portions of each coefficient, as indicated in equation (2).

3. Lasso regression model: The Lasso regression model, a regularisation technique, was the third model produced in this work. It is preferred over regression techniques because it yields more precise forecasts. Shrinkage is used in this model. Data values are "shrinked" when they are brought closer to the mean value. The lasso method prefers sparse systems (those with a small number of parameters) [14]. The Lasso

regression model, shown by Eq. (3), is used to forecast Uber fares.

$$L = \sum \left(\widehat{Y_i} - Y_i \right)^2 + \lambda \sum |\beta| \tag{3}$$

where the term $\left(\widehat{Y_i} - Y_i \right)^2$ represents the sum of errors and the term $\lambda \sum |\beta|$ denotes the sum of the absolute value of coefficients.

4. Elastic-Net regression model: This was the fourth model we created during our research. To regularise regression models, elastic net linear regression employs penalties from both the lasso and ridge approaches. The strategy combines the lasso and ridge regression techniques, gaining from their inadequacies to enhance the model's statistical regularisation [15]. The elastic net regression model utilised for uber price prediction is denoted by Eq. (4).

$$L = \sum \left(\widehat{Y_i} - Y_i \right)^2 + \lambda \sum \beta^2 + \lambda \sum |\beta| \tag{4}$$

As can be observed from Eq. (4), the elastic net regression is the sum of the ridge $(\left(\widehat{Y_i} - Y_i \right)^2 + \lambda \sum \beta^2)$ and the lasso regression $(\left(\widehat{Y_i} - Y_i \right)^2 + \lambda \sum |\beta|)$ models.

5. Polynomial regression model: Our proposed research concludes with the development of a polynomial regression model. By utilising a non-linear regression line, it is able to represent the complexities of non-linear correlations between variables [16]. Equation (5) demonstrates this.

$$Y = \beta_0 + \beta_1 X_1 + \beta_2 X_1^2 + \ldots + \beta_n X_n^2 \tag{5}$$

Various levels of the polynomial regression model were tested in this research.

4 Experiments and Results

The primary task entailed using the frontend's pickup and drop-off locations to determine the distance between them using the haversine equation. The geoapify API was used to retrieve the place's latitude and longitude coordinates. The team assessed the cost of the trip using the estimated distance.

The outliers in the data needed to be removed to allow for the information to be suitable for further study, something the scatter chart helped to detect. These questionable statistics, including those with negative price and distance numbers or distance values of 0, were labelled as anomalies. Figure 2 shows the scatter plot after removing these anomalies or outliers.

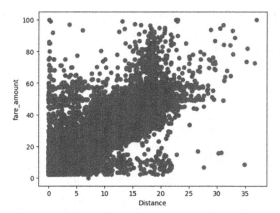

Fig. 2. Scatter plot before outlier removal

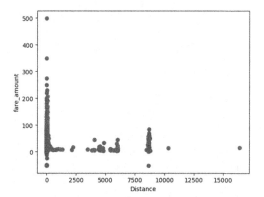

Fig. 3. Scatter plot after outlier removal

The removal of these outliers improved the suitability of the information for further examination, according to the scatter plot. This demonstrates that the information is more reliable and that additional investigations that were previously impractical due to the availability of incorrect values are now possible employing the information at hand. The correctness and dependability of the data, which are essential in any data analysis project, can be effectively ensured by utilising a scatter plot to identify and eliminate outliers as shown in Fig. 3.

In Figs. 4, 5 and 6, bar graphs are used to analyse the monthly number of trips made as well as the day of the week with the most excursions. The information was easily visualised using the bar graph, which demonstrated the rise of trips over a period of several months. With the help of this research, we were able to pinpoint the months when the amount of travels either considerably rose or fell, providing an indicator for additional investigation. Furthermore, we applied a similar strategy to examine the weekday with the most trips. Observations about variables like job schedules, patterns of traffic, or activities which might influence the amount of travels made on a given day might be gained by using this knowledge to spot trends in the data. In general, the usage of a bar graph gave researchers conducting data analysis a quick and easy approach to comprehend the information and detect patterns.

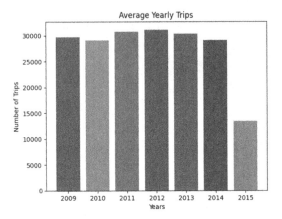

Fig. 4. Average yearly trips

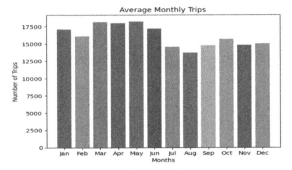

Fig. 5. Average monthly trips

On the test dataset, we compared the performance of various regression models. In Fig. 7, we can see the results of extensive testing of the polynomial regression model in terms of RMSE.

As a result of its superior performance on both the training and test data sets, the 5th order polynomial was selected. The relative R2 values between the various regression models are displayed in Fig. 8.

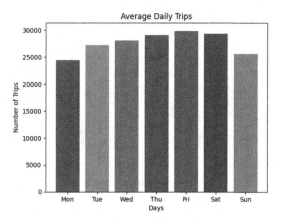

Fig. 6. Average daily trips

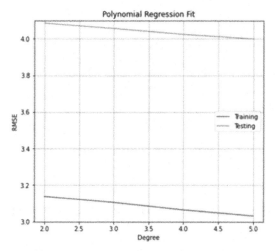

Fig. 7. Performance of polynomial regression model by varying its degrees with respect to RMSE

Residual sum of squares (RSS) comparison of regression models is displayed in Fig. 9.

Figure 10 illustrates the comparison of the regression models with respect to the MSE values.

Figure 11 demonstrates the comparison of regression models with respect to the RMSE metric.

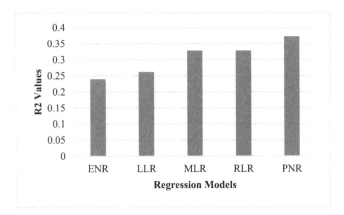

Fig. 8. R2 comparison of regression models for uber fare price prediction

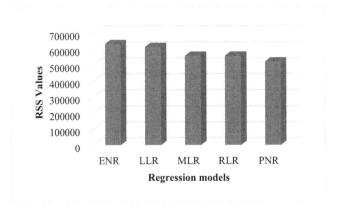

Fig. 9. RSS comparison of regression models for uber fare price prediction

Figures 8–11 show that polynomial regression models are the most effective at explaining the data. On this data set, the greatest results can be achieved with more complicated models such as polynomial (degree-5) ones. Even though Polynomial Regression (Order-5) was the most appropriate choice, the multiple regression algorithm can be used with confidence due to the fact that the scores are very similar and the method is more generalizable.

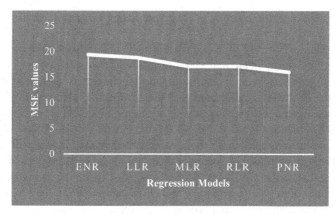

Fig. 10. MSE comparison of regression models for uber fare price prediction.

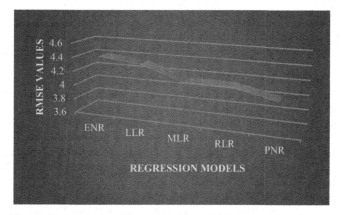

Fig. 11. RMSE comparison of regression models for uber fare price prediction

5   Conclusion and Future Scope

The research presented here proposes a predictive pricing system for ride-sharing apps that takes into account the most recent data and parameters. The goal of this research was to determine how best to minimise the total price of group travel by taking into account a wide range of factors utilising data analytics and machine learning. To make Uber's shared economy mode of transport more efficient and profitable, this investigation proposes a new pricing system and methodology that makes use of riders' individual API data. The research also sought to identify areas that are receptive to and unreceptive to Uber's offerings and to document any shifts in Uber's ongoing capacities. The results show that the polynomial regression model performed better than the other regression models. The suggested strategy might be applicable to other ride-sharing uses, and the findings of this study have real-world consequences for the variable pricing system used in the ride-sharing economy. In total, this research adds to the expanding body of research on shared economy pricing models and demonstrates the promise of combining data analytics with machine learning to create prediction price systems for ridesharing platforms.

More information that may affect pricing and demand for ride-sharing services might be incorporated into the model to make it more accurate. This information could include real-time traffic statistics, weather conditions, and special events. Secondly, the study's applicability to other ride-sharing apps and their respective abilities to predict pricing may be investigated. Further investigation into the model's probable influence on disadvantaged populations is warranted, as are the ethical considerations of using the model. As a conclusion, combining the recommended pricing model with additional capabilities like path optimisation, operator distribution and segmentation of customers might further enhance the effectiveness and customer experience as a whole of ride-sharing platforms. Both service providers and clients may stand to gain from applying the proposed methodology in shared economy ride services.

References

1. Fielbaum, A., Tirachini, A.: The sharing economy and the job market: the case of ride-hailing drivers in Chile. Transportation **48**, 2235–2261 (2021). https://doi.org/10.1007/s11116-020-10127-7
2. Mouratidis, K., Peters, S., van Wee, B.: Transportation technologies, sharing economy, and teleactivities: implications for built environment and travel. Transp. Res. Part D: Transp. Environ. **92**, 102716 (2021). https://doi.org/10.1016/j.trd.2021.102716
3. Lukasiewicz, A., Sanna, V.S., Diogo, V.L.A.P., Bernát, A.: Shared Mobility: A Reflection on Sharing Economy Initiatives in European Transportation Sectors. In: Česnuitytė, V., Klimczuk, A., Miguel, C., Avram, G. (eds.) The Sharing Economy in Europe: Developments, Practices, and Contradictions, pp. 89–114. Springer International Publishing, Cham (2022). https://doi.org/10.1007/978-3-030-86897-0_5
4. Khavarian-Garmsir, A.R., Sharifi, A., Abadi, M.H.H.: The social, economic, and environmental impacts of ridesourcing services: s Literature Review. Future Transport. **1**(2), 268–289 (2021). https://doi.org/10.3390/futuretransp1020016
5. https://www.kaggle.com/datasets/yasserh/uber-fares-dataset (Accessed 16 Mar 2022)
6. Chao, J.: Modeling and analysis of uber's rider pricing. In: Proceedings of the 2019 International Conference on Economic Management and Cultural Industry (ICEMCI 2019) (2019). https://doi.org/10.2991/aebmr.k.191217.127
7. Kontou, E., Garikapati, V., Hou, Yi.: Reducing ridesourcing empty vehicle travel with future travel demand prediction. Transp. Res. Part C: Emerg. Technol. **121**, 102826 (2020). https://doi.org/10.1016/j.trc.2020.102826
8. Battifarano, M.: Zhen (Sean) Qian, Predicting real-time surge pricing of ride-sourcing companies. Transp. Res. Part C: Emerg. Technol. **107**, 444–462 (2019). https://doi.org/10.1016/j.trc.2019.08.019
9. Sindhu, P., Gupta, D., Meghana, S.: IEEE Delhi Section Conference (DELCON). New Delhi, India **2022**, 1–7 (2022). https://doi.org/10.1109/DELCON54057.2022.9752864
10. Elizabeth Rani, G., Sakthimohan, M., Revanth Raj, R., Sri Ganesh, M., Shyam Sunder, R., Karthigadevi, K.: An automated cost prediction in uber/call taxi using machine learning algorithm. In: 2022 2nd International Conference on Advance Computing and Innovative Technologies in Engineering (ICACITE), Greater Noida, India, 2022, pp. 764–767, https://doi.org/10.1109/ICACITE53722.2022.9823852

11. Chen, L., Thakuriah, P., Ampountolas, K.: Short-term prediction of demand for ride-hailing services: a deep learning approach. J. Big Data Anal. Transp. **3**, 175–195 (2021). https://doi.org/10.1007/s42421-021-00041-4

12. Abdelshafy, M., Sarhani, M.: Prediction and Optimization of Uber Services: A Case Study of Morocco. In: Motahhir, S., Bossoufi, B. (eds.) Digital Technologies and Applications: Proceedings of ICDTA'23, Fez, Morocco, vol. 2, pp. 914–922. Springer Nature Switzerland, Cham (2023). https://doi.org/10.1007/978-3-031-29860-8_91

13. Banerjee, P., Kumar, B., Singh, A., Ranjan, P., Soni, K.: Predictive analysis of taxi fare using machine learning. Int. J. Sci. Res. Comput. Sci., Eng. Inform. Technol., 373–378 (2020). https://doi.org/10.32628/CSEIT2062108

14. Zhao, Z., You, J., Gan, G., Li, X., Ding, J.: Civil airline fare prediction with a multi-attribute dual-stage attention mechanism. Appl. Intell. **52**, 5047–5062 (2022). https://doi.org/10.1007/s10489-021-02602-0

15. Wang, C., Hao, P., Wu, G., Qi, X., Barth, M.: Predicting the number of uber pickups by deep learning. In: Conference: Transportation Research Board 2018At: Washington DC, United StatesVolume: 18–06738 (2018)

16. Khandelwal, K., Sawarkar, A., Hira, S.: Novel approach for fare prediction using machine learning techniques. Int. J. Next-Gener. Comput. (2021). https://doi.org/10.47164/ijngc.v12i5.451

Decision Making Using Statistical Methods for Opening a Training at Continuing Education Centers Under Smart Campus Applications

Burcu Akca, Onur Dogan$^{(\boxtimes)}$![ORCID], and Kadir Hiziroglu ![ORCID]

Department of Management Information Systems,
Izmir Bakircay University, 35665 Izmir, Turkey
{burcu.akca,onur.dogan,kadir.hiziroglu}@bakircay.edu.tr

Abstract. Continuing education centers play a crucial role in meeting the ever-growing demand for lifelong learning, providing opportunities for individuals to expand their knowledge and skills throughout their lives. Moreover, for educators, these centers offer a platform to share their expertise and contribute to the personal and professional development of learners. By teaching in continuing education programs, educators can not only make a positive impact on others but also generate additional income and broaden their career prospects. This study encompasses statistical analyses highlighting the importance of data-driven decision making in continuous education centers. Correlation and regression analyses were conducted on the data to examine the relationships between the number of participants in training programs and variables such as duration, fee, and popularity. According to the correlation analysis, weak positive relationships were observed between the number of participants and duration, fee, and popularity. The regression analysis aimed to determine how the number of participants is associated with factors: duration, fee, and popularity. The obtained coefficients represent the impact of these factors on the number of participants. Using the prediction formula derived from the regression analysis, the number of participants can be predicted based on specific values of duration, fee, and popularity. During the decision-making process, the expected income from the predicted number of participants is calculated to make a decision on whether to offer the training program. If the predicted income meets the instructor's expectations, the program can be opened. However, if the income expectation is not met, it may be more suitable not to proceed with offering the training. By making data-driven decisions, continuous education centers can effectively plan and guide their activities.

Keywords: Smart campus applications · Continuous education · Statistical decision-making

F. Ortiz-Rodríguez et al. (Eds.): EGETC 2023, CCIS 1888, pp. 38–46, 2023.
https://doi.org/10.1007/978-3-031-43940-7_4

1   Introduction

Smart campuses play a significant role in the transformation of educational environments today. These campuses aim to provide advanced services to students, academics, and staff through various smart applications and systems. Continuing education centers (CEC) utilize these smart campus applications to support the principle of lifelong learning and meet the educational needs of participants. For example, experts from different disciplines and sectors have the desire to pursue continuous education to keep up with rapid changes in the business world and enhance their careers [8]. This article will explore how decisions to offer education in continuous education centers can be made using statistical methods.

The overall structure of smart campus applications is also an important factor. These applications encompass technologies such as wireless networks, sensors, data analytics, and artificial intelligence. As a result, students and instructors can communicate more effectively, experience personalized learning experiences, and have easier access to educational resources. CEC can utilize the opportunities provided by these smart campus applications to optimize students' learning processes and enhance the quality of education. For instance, factors such as a student's interests and previous educational background can be evaluated through data analytics to create personalized learning programs.

The article aims to address the desire of professionals from various disciplines to receive education throughout their lives based on the principle of lifelong learning. For example, a professional working in the field of engineering may seek continuing education to keep up with technological advancements. Similarly, a person working in the healthcare sector may require continuing education to stay updated on medical innovations and learn about the latest treatment methods.

Education costs need to be taken into account, and it would be beneficial for CEC, educators, and participants to prioritize opening courses with high demand. In order to assess mean differences between two groups, a t-test is commonly used [14]. On the other hand, to examine the dependency or independence between variables, particularly for categorical data, the chi-square test is utilized. These statistical tests provide valuable insights into the relationships and differences within the data. F-test compares variances between groups, e.g., testing sales differences across time periods [10]. Hypothesis testing validates specific assumptions through one-tailed or two-tailed tests [11]. Regression analysis examines relationships between variables and analyzes the impact of one variable on another (Field, 2018). Analysis of variance (ANOVA) determines significant differences in means of different groups [7]. Factor analysis groups related variables to reduce data complexity or identify latent factors [15]. Cluster analysis groups data points with similar characteristics to identify meaningful patterns or segments [9].

In terms of the importance and contribution of this study, it is necessary to emphasize that similar studies are still not conducted sufficiently. The limited research in this field may lead to a lack of full understanding of the potential of smart campuses and continuous education centers. Therefore, this study integrates statistical methods in decision-making processes so that it enables continuous education centers to make informed choices regarding educational offerings. By analyzing relevant data and employing statistical techniques, these centers can assess the demand for specific courses or programs, identify emerging trends in the job market, and align their educational offerings with industry needs. Statistical methods provide valuable insights into student preferences, performance indicators, and the effectiveness of educational interventions, enabling continuous education centers to make data-driven decisions that foster lifelong learning.

2 Related Work

This section discusses the studies conducted on the evaluation of lifelong learning activities in Turkish universities. The studies focus on various topics such as disadvantaged groups, communication effectiveness, educational programs, and perceived competence of teachers, highlighting the awareness of academics regarding the importance of lifelong learning and exploring ways to enhance the efficiency of smart campuses and continuous education centers using statistical methods.

Some studies address the lifelong learning activities of Turkish universities in terms of disadvantaged groups, female participants, and educational content. Çankaya [5] conducted a study focusing on the evaluation of lifelong learning activities in Turkish universities for disadvantaged groups. The study utilized qualitative research methods and analyzed data obtained from university websites. The analysis involved examining web documents related to various disadvantaged groups, such as female unemployed individuals, male unemployed individuals, unemployed individuals with disabilities, young unemployed individuals, and former convicts. Additionally, Candır Şimşek [4] conducted qualitative research to explore the views of women participating in educational programs at Istanbul University's CEC. The study found that the participants were generally satisfied with the quality of the educational programs but identified some shortcomings in the instructors and suggested improvements to the physical environment of the center. Furthermore, Ayvacı and Özbek [2] conducted a content analysis of the training programs offered at continuous education centers affiliated with universities in Turkey. The analysis revealed that the most commonly provided training topics were management and leadership, health and sports, foreign languages, and computer and technology. These studies provide valuable insights into the lifelong learning activities of Turkish universities and shed light on the experiences of disadvantaged groups, female participants, and the educational content offered.

Fadıloğlu Zengel [17] examined the communication activities of continuous education centers in Turkish universities, and it was found that the communication effectiveness on their websites was inadequate. Yıldırım and Akçay [16] evaluated the administrative effectiveness of lifelong learning services in universities, and emphasized the need for improvements in organizational structure and processes. Arslan [1] conducted at Uludag University, where lifelong learning and continuous engineering education programs were structured, stated that experts developed the programs according to the needs of the industrial sector and subject to continuous improvement. In a study evaluating the perceived competence of primary school teachers towards lifelong learning [3], it was found that teachers' perceived competence was at a moderate level, and factors such as gender and age did not have a significant impact on perception. Samancı and Ocakcı [12] highlighted lifelong learning-oriented education policies in the European Union and Turkey in their study, emphasizing the significant contribution of lifelong learning to the personal development of individuals and societal progress.

The following statistical methods are used in the literature:

- *t-test*: This method is used to determine the mean difference between two groups. It is typically employed when the samples have a normal distribution and similar variances [14].
- *Chi-square test*: This test is used to examine the dependency or independence between two variables, especially when analyzing categorical data.
- *F-test*: This test is used to compare variances between two or more groups. It can be applied, for example, to test differences in sales between different time periods [10].
- *Hypothesis testing*: This method is used to test the validity of a specific assumption. It involves one-tailed or two-tailed hypothesis tests, depending on the research question [11].
- *Regression analysis*: This analysis is employed to examine the relationship between two or more variables and analyze the impact of one variable on another [6].
- *Analysis of variance (ANOVA)*: ANOVA is used to determine if the means of different groups are significantly different from each other [7].
- Factor analysis: This method is used to group related variables together, typically for the purpose of reducing data complexity or identifying latent factors [15].
- *Cluster analysis*: This technique is employed to group data points with similar characteristics together, allowing researchers to identify meaningful patterns or segments [9].

The findings from studies discussed above indicate a significant awareness of lifelong learning activities in universities and a high level of consciousness among academics in this field. However, it is important to highlight the limitations of these articles. It should be noted that decisions such as whether to open or close educational programs are not made using data-driven decision-making methods, and there is a need for further research in this area. This study aims to address this gap and emphasize the importance of data-driven decision-making processes. The purpose of this study is to contribute to the use of data analytics and statistical methods to enhance the effectiveness of lifelong learning activities in universities. In this way, by building a stronger foundation in decision-making processes, the quality and effectiveness of lifelong learning activities can be improved. Additionally, this study emphasizes the need for universities to embrace a data-driven decision-making approach in lifelong learning and focus on further research in this field.

3   Statistical Methods

Correlation analysis and regression analysis are two commonly used statistical techniques in research to examine the relationships between variables.

Correlation analysis evaluates the degree and direction of the linear relationship between two variables. One widely used measure of correlation is the Pearson correlation coefficient (r) [13]. The Pearson coefficient ranges from -1 to +1, where a positive value indicates a positive correlation, a negative value indicates a negative correlation and a value close to zero suggests no significant correlation. The significance level of the correlation coefficient helps determine whether the observed correlation is statistically significant.

Regression analysis, on the other hand, explores the relationship between a dependent variable and one or more independent variables. It aims to predict or estimate the value of the dependent variable based on the known values of the independent variables. The most common form of regression analysis is linear regression, which assumes a linear relationship between the variables [15]. It estimates the coefficients and the equation of the regression line that best fits the data.

Both correlation analysis and regression analysis are valuable tools for understanding and analyzing relationships between variables in research studies. They provide insights into the strength, direction, and significance of associations, as well as the ability to predict or estimate values based on these relationships.

4   Case Study

The total number of trainings included in this study is 62. Table 1 presents the independent variables and the corresponding values as examples. The training programs vary in terms of participation numbers, duration, fees, and popularity. The term "popularity" represents the total number of searches obtained from Google Trends or a similar source. Popularity is evaluated as a criterion based on the internet search numbers of the relevant training programs. The "Health Law Mediation Special Specialization Training" program has the highest fee (2400 Turkish Lira - TL) among all the programs listed. The "Functional Medicine Trainings Module-1- Our Hormones" program has the highest duration (45 h) among all the programs listed. The "Occupational Health and Safety Certificate Program (Training 1)" has the highest number of participants (541) among all the programs listed. The "Ethical Approach Training in Traditional and Complementary Medicine (GETAT) Clinical Research" program has the highest popularity rating (1662) among all the programs listed.

Table 1. A sample of training topics and independent variables

No	Topic	Participation number	Duration (hours)	Fee (TL)	Popularity
1	Consumer Law Mediation General Specialization Training	180	45	1050	510
2	Health Law Mediation Special Specialization Training	84	62	1150	537
3	Intellectual and Industrial Property Law Mediation Specialization Training	60	66	1250	947
4	Commercial Law Mediation General Specialization Training (Training 1)	326	74	1500	633
5	Commercial Law Mediation General Specialization Training (Training 2)	55	74	2000	633
6	Health Law Mediation Special Specialization Training	39	62	2400	590
7	Ethical Approach Training in Traditional and Complementary Medicine (GETAT) Clinical Research	41	10	300	1662
8	Occupational Health and Safety Certificate Program (Training 1)	541	16	500	2968
9	Occupational Health and Safety Certificate Program (Training 2)	396	16	150	2968
10	Occupational Health and Safety Certificate Program (Training 3)	279	16	120	2968
11	Functional Medicine Trainings Module-1- Our Hormones	45	45	4500	534
12	Certificate Program for Ethics Committee Members and Member Candidates in Clinical Research	27	10	500	1926

4.1 Correlation

A correlation analysis was conducted to determine the relationships. Table 2 gives the correlation results. The correlation coefficient between the "Partici-pation number" and "Duration" was found to be 0.272, indicating a moderate and positive relationship. The correlation coefficient between the "Participation number" and the "Fee" was calculated as 0.061, indicating they have almost no relationship. Finally, the correlation coefficient between the "Participation number" and popularity was found to be 0.722, indicating a strong and positive relationship. In other words, as the "Popularity" increases, the "Participation number" generally tends to increase.

4.2 Regression

The regression analysis was performed to analyze the data. In this analysis, "Participation number" was used as the dependent variable, and the independent variables were "Duration", "Fee", and "Popularity". Before the regression,

Table 2. Correlation results

X	Y	Coefficient	Type	Strength
Duration	Participation number	0.272	Positive	Moderate
Fee	Participation number	0.061	Positive	Weak
Popularity	Participation number	0.722	Positive	Strong

independent variables should be normalized. Equation 1 shows the regression formula with the normalized coefficient. As a result of the regression analysis, coefficients representing the effect of these independent variables on the dependent variable were obtained. For example, an increase of one hour in duration is associated with an increase of 1.901 (almost 2) participants.

$$\text{Participation Number} = 0.111 + (1.901 \times Duration) + (-0.023 \times Fee) \\ + (0.107 \times Popularity) \tag{1}$$

4.3 Decision Making

The decision of whether to open the training or not is based on comparing the instructor's earnings expectation and expected revenue from the predicted number of participants. When calculating the instructor's earnings expectation, there is a 40% deduction for tax and university share. The regression formula can be used to predict the number of participants. Figure 1 provides two examples.

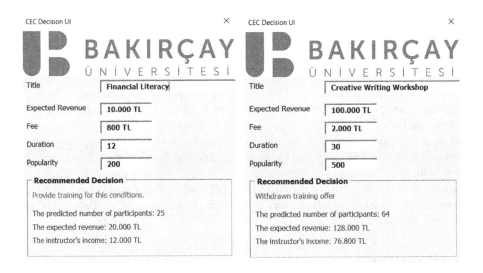

Fig. 1. User interface for two examples (TL: Turkish Lira)

The expected revenue for the "Financial Literacy" training is stated as 10,000 TL. The training has a duration of 12 h, a fee of 800 TL, and a popularity rating of 200. The predicted number of participants, conducted through regression analysis, is 25. Based on the predicted number of participants, the expected revenue is calculated to be 20,000 TL, with the instructor's income amounting to 12,000 TL. It should be noted that the training income is determined by multiplying the estimated number of participants by the fee and applying a 40% deduction. Because the instructor's income is met, the system recommends providing the training.

In another scenario, the expected revenue for the "Creative Writing Workshop" is mentioned as 100,000 TL. The workshop is scheduled for 30 h, with a fee of 2,000 TL and a popularity rating of 500. Through regression analysis, the predicted number of participants is determined to be 64. Using the predicted number of participants, the expected revenue is calculated to be 128,000 TL, with the instructor's income amounting to 76,800 TL after the 40% deduction is applied. These conditions are not enough to meet the instructor's expectations from this training. Therefore, the system does not recommend offering to open the workshop.

5   Conclusion and Discussion

This study highlights the importance of data analysis and statistical methods in continuing education centers. The analysis aims to evaluate the relationships between the number of participants and the duration, cost, and popularity of education programs.

The correlation analysis revealed positive relationships for three variables. The "Participants number" and "Duration" have a moderate relation with 0.272. A weak relationship of 0.061 was found between the "Participants number" and "Fee", indicating no relationship between them. However, authors believe that if the number of training was more, it would have a relation. Because of that, it was included in the study. Lastly, a strong relationship of 0.722 was observed between the "Participants number" and "Popularity". As the level of popularity increases, there is a tendency for the number of participants to increase.

Regression analysis was conducted to examine the impact of "Duration", "Fee", and "Popularity" factors on the number of participants in education programs. The obtained coefficients represent the effect of each factor on the number of participants. For example, it can be a 1.9 (near to 2) increase in the number of participants.

The findings of this study provide guidance for continuous education centers to make informed decisions and plan their activities based on data analysis. The predicted number of participants and expected revenue calculations can be used in determining whether to open education programs. If the expected revenue meets the income expectations of the instructor, the system facilitates the decision-making process of opening a new education by calculating whether the expected revenue is met or not.

References

1. Arslan, R.: Uludağ üniversitesi'nde hayat boyu öğrenme ve sürekli mühendislik eğitimi uygulamaları. Uludağ Üniversitesi Mühendislik Fakültesi Dergisi **14**(1) (2009)
2. Ayvacı, H.S., Ozbek, D.: Türkiye'deki üniversitelerin sürekli eğitim merkezlerinde gerçekleştirilen eğitimlerin tematik analizi. J. Instruct. Technol. Teacher Educ. **10**(1), 52–71 (2021)
3. Bozat, P., Bozat, N., Hursen, C.: The evaluation of competence perceptions of primary school teachers for the lifelong learning approach. Procedia Soc. Behav. Sci. **140**, 476–482 (2014)
4. Candir Simsek, H.: Evaluation of continuing education center activities in terms of female participants: a qualitative research at Istanbul university continuing education center. J. Social Policy Conf. **83**, 365–391 (2022)
5. Cankaya, I.: Sürekli eğitim merkezlerinin faaliyetlerinin dezavantajli gruplar açisindan incelenmesi. Turkish Acad. Stud.-TURAS **1**(1), 44–56 (2020)
6. Field, A.: Discovering statistics using ibm spss statistics 5th ed (2018)
7. Howell, D.C.: Statistical methods for psychology. Cengage Learning (2012)
8. Johnson, L., Levine, A., Smith, R., Stone, S.: The 2010 Horizon Report. ERIC (2010)
9. Landau, S., Leese, M., Stahl, D., Everitt, B.S.: Cluster analysis. John Wiley & Sons (2011)
10. Montgomery, D.C., Peck, E.A., Vining, G.G.: Introduction to linear regression analysis 5th ed (2012)
11. Salkind, N.J., Frey, B.B.: Statistics for people who (think they) hate statistics: Using Microsoft Excel. Sage publications (2021)
12. Samanci, O., Ocakci, E.: Hayat boyu öğrenme. Bayburt Eğitim Fakültesi Dergisi **12**(24), 711–722 (2017)
13. Stevens, J.P.: Applied multivariate statistics for the social sciences. Routledge (2012)
14. Swinscow, T.D.V., Campbell, M.J., et al.: Statistics at square one. Bmj London (2002)
15. Tabachnick, B.G., Fidell, L.S., Ullman, J.B.: Using multivariate statistics, vol. 6. pearson Boston, MA (2013)
16. Yildirim, R., Akcay, R.C.: Sürekli eğitim merkezi öğretim elemanlarına göre yaşam boyu öğrenme hizmetleri yönetsel etkililiğinin değerlendirilmesi. Dumlupınar Üniversitesi Eğitim Bilimleri Enstitüsü Dergisi **1**(1), 40–63 (2017)
17. Zengel, G.: Türkiyedeki üniversitelerin sürekli eğitim merkezlerinin web sitelerinin ikna edici iletişim açısından incelenmesi. Master's thesis, Sosyal Bilimler Enstitüsü (2021)

Evolutionary Algorithms in Crisis Management of Supply Chains to Enhance Global Food Security During War in Ukraine

Skitsko Volodymyr[ID] and Voinikov Mykola[✉][ID]

Kyiv National Economic University named after Vadym Hetman, 54/1 Beresteysky Prospect,
Kyiv, Ukraine
mykola.voinikov@gmail.com

Abstract. This paper discusses the use of evolutionary algorithms to optimize food safety, particularly in the case of the ongoing war in Ukraine. Traditional optimization methods appear to be increasingly ineffective due to the complexity of the search space and the massive volume of data available. Notably, the paper recognizes that decision-making efficiency is time-sensitive in emergencies, and evolutionary algorithms, due to their dynamic nature, can generate solutions within a reasonable timeframe. Inspired by biological evolution, evolutionary algorithms can adapt and explore a diverse search space, allowing for more informed decision-making, enhanced operational efficiency, and increased food security. The paper delves into evolutionary algorithms' theoretical foundations and principles, including genetic algorithms, evolution strategies, and differential evolution. It also discusses mathematical models for transportation optimization using evolutionary algorithms, providing examples of multi-index transportation problems and multi-objective traveling salesman problems. By leveraging these advanced methods, organizations can process and analyze their data more efficiently, leading to improved decision-making, enhanced operational efficiency, and increased food security. The paper provides insights into how these algorithms can be applied in logistics to improve food security, highlighting their potential applications and challenges.

Keywords: Global Food Security · Logistics · Evolutionary Algorithms · Transportation Problem · Traveling Salesman Problem

1 Introduction

1.1 Overview of Global Food Prices and the Application of Evolutionary Algorithms

Global food security, a concept deeply intertwined with the overall well-being of humanity, has become a subject of pressing importance in today's complex and rapidly changing world. It encapsulates the principle that all individuals, at all times, should have physical, social, and economic access to sufficient, safe, and nutritious food to meet their dietary needs and preferences for an active and healthy life.

F. Ortiz-Rodríguez et al. (Eds.): EGETC 2023, CCIS 1888, pp. 47–59, 2023.
https://doi.org/10.1007/978-3-031-43940-7_5

This fundamental issue has been thrown into sharp relief by ongoing global events, such as the war in Ukraine, which presents a significant challenge to maintaining global food security. War disrupts supply chains, undermines agricultural production, and creates a hostile environment for the transportation and distribution of food supplies. Ukraine is one of the world's largest grain exporters, and the war has implications for global food supplies and prices, affecting countries far beyond its borders. The ramifications of Russia's invasion of Ukraine remain markedly evident, with food prices escalating and subsequently catalyzing a global crisis [1].

Even before the Russian invasion of Ukraine, global food systems had been under pressure from various compounding challenges: the relentless impacts of climate change, numerous geopolitical conflicts, and the profound disruptions caused by the COVID-19 pandemic. These variables have incited instability in food prices and accessibility, leading to an escalation in food insecurity, notably among at-risk groups in poor nations. Consequently, the global count of individuals suffering from hunger has skyrocketed, reaching an alarming 828 million in 2021 [2].

Recognizing logistics as a key factor in global food security is critical for solving this issue. Improving logistical efficiency and overcoming high transportation costs, process coordination failures, delivery delays, risks, emergency planning, and other adverse circumstances can significantly enhance food security. By leveraging economic and mathematical techniques and models, logistics can be optimized to mitigate high food prices and ensure supplies reach those in need both strategically and spontaneously, addressing unexpected needs for food delivery.

Modern technologies have led to an unprecedented surge in data collection capabilities. Businesses across the globe are now able to gather and analyze vast amounts of data, leveraging it to inform their decision-making processes using economic-mathematical methods and models [3]. This data-driven approach can revolutionize food security strategies, enabling more informed decisions, predicting food supply needs, and optimizing resource allocation and operations.

However, the exponential growth in data volume has presented a new set of challenges. The massive volume of data consumers, such as businesses and governments, now have access to has made algorithm efficiency a critical issue. Traditional search and optimization methods, once considered state-of-the-art, are now proving ineffective due to the increasingly complex search space. This issue is particularly prominent in dynamically fluctuating environments, such as logistics within conflict zones or emergency transportation planning. These scenarios arise abruptly, requiring immediate and efficient planning as the cost of delay may be too high.

In response, the scientific community has been actively exploring new data processing and analysis methods. Among these, evolutionary algorithms have emerged as a promising solution. Evolutionary algorithms are a subset of evolutionary computation, a family of algorithms for global optimization inspired by biological evolution [4]. These algorithms reflect the process of natural selection, where the fittest individuals are selected for reproduction to produce the offspring of the next generation.

Evolutionary algorithms excel when the optimization problem is multifaceted, features numerous objectives, the fitness landscape is 'rugged,' hosts local optima, or when scant knowledge is available about the underpinning optimization problem. In addressing global food security, especially amidst the Ukrainian conflict, these evolutionary algorithms can be crucial for optimizing numerous facets of food distribution. This includes forecasting food shortages, identifying optimal distribution routes, or strategizing emergency transportation. The time-sensitive nature of logistics, particularly in conflict or crisis scenarios, makes evolutionary algorithms a particularly apt choice. By harnessing these advanced techniques, organizations are empowered to process and analyze their data with enhanced efficiency, thus facilitating improved decision-making, amplified operational efficiency, and bolstered food security.

In this paper, we will not present specific mathematical formulas. Instead, we provide the problem formulations to illustrate the advantages, disadvantages, and peculiarities of employing evolutionary algorithms to tackle such multifaceted logistical challenges. We aim to demonstrate how these algorithms can improve decision-making, enhance operational efficiency, and bolster food security even under the most demanding circumstances.

Furthermore, this research is designed to elucidate the current application of these algorithms and lay the groundwork for future works in this direction. By exploring these methodologies in the context of global food security, we hope to inspire future investigations, stimulate dialogue, and catalyze developments that will continue to optimize logistics, especially in crisis settings. We believe this foundation will spark innovative solutions and foster advancements that could further refine and amplify the impact of evolutionary algorithms in improving global food security.

1.2   Theoretical Foundations and Principles of Evolutionary Algorithms

Evolutionary algorithms are a family of optimization techniques based on the principles of biological evolution, such as natural selection and genetic inheritance [4]. These algorithms are used to find solutions to complex, multi-dimensional problems that may be difficult or impossible to solve using traditional methods. The power of evolutionary algorithms lies in their ability to explore a large and diverse search space and to adapt their search strategy over time based on the quality of solutions found.

Evolutionary algorithms possess several common characteristics that define their approach. Firstly, they operate on a population of potential solutions rather than focusing on individual entities. These populations are initialized randomly and undergo an evolutionary process. Secondly, a fitness function evaluates the quality of each solution within the population by measuring its performance in the specific problem context.

Additionally, evolutionary algorithms incorporate a selection mechanism to determine which solutions will form the next generation. Typically, solutions with higher fitness scores are more likely to be selected. Genetic operators such as mutation (introducing random changes) and crossover (combining components from different solutions) are employed to generate new solutions. These genetic operators bring about variation and enable the exploration of different regions within the search space. The iterative nature of evolutionary algorithms involves repeating the process of selection, crossover, and mutation for multiple generations, progressively refining the quality of solutions within the population.

Lastly, evolutionary algorithms exhibit stochastic behavior, incorporating randomness into their operations. This stochasticity allows for a thorough search space exploration and helps prevent premature convergence to suboptimal solutions. Inspired by the principles of biological evolution, including survival of the fittest, genetic inheritance, and variation, evolutionary algorithms offer a high degree of flexibility and adaptability. Consequently, they are well-suited for tackling complex optimization problems across diverse domains.

To sum up, let us look at a standard evolutionary algorithm's structure [6]:

1. Initialization: In this first step, as mentioned before, we randomly generate an initial population of individuals. Depending on the problem, we can represent these individuals as vectors, matrices, or other suitable data structures. The size of the population often depends on the problem's complexity and the available computational resources. This step is crucial because it provides the raw material for the evolutionary process.
2. Evaluation: After generating the initial population, we assess each individual's fitness. We use a fitness function specific to the problem to quantify the optimality of a solution. The fitness function helps us rank individuals based on their suitability as solutions.
3. Selection: During selection, we choose individuals for reproduction based on their fitness. The fittest individuals have a higher chance of selection, ensuring their traits pass on to the next generation. We can use various selection strategies, such as roulette wheel selection, tournament selection, and elitism. Each strategy balances the exploration and exploitation trade-off differently.
4. Recombination and Mutation: In this step, we generate new individuals by combining the characteristics of selected individuals through recombination or crossover. We also introduce diversity into the population by randomly modifying parts of the individual through mutation. This mutation allows us to explore new regions of the solution space.
5. Replacement: After recombination and mutation, we update the population. We replace some or all of the population with newly created individuals. The replacement strategy can significantly impact the performance of the evolutionary algorithm. Some strategies replace the worst individuals, while others replace a random subset. Elitist strategies always keep the best individuals from the current population.
6. Termination: The algorithm continues to iterate through the steps until it meets a termination condition. This could be when we find a solution that meets minimum criteria, reaches a predetermined number of generations, exhaust the allocated computational resources, or when the fitness of the highest-ranking solution plateaus. At this point, the algorithm stops and returns the best solution(s) found.

With all common characteristics, there are several types of evolutionary algorithms, each with its unique characteristics and mechanisms. The most common types include genetic algorithms, evolution strategies, and differential evolution. Let us take a closer look at each type [5, 6]:

– Genetic algorithms use candidate solutions called chromosomes, made up of decision variables called genes. These genes represent values to be optimized. While modern genetic algorithms often use direct mapping to an optimization domain, they historically used binary strings or different types of encoding, a practice still occasionally used. Genetic algorithm implementations vary but commonly use a mutation operator that alters each decision variable with a certain probability. Recombination is typically implemented using two-point or multi-point, or uniform crossover. Selection in genetic algorithms can take various forms, with rank-based or tournament selection preferred due to better exploration maintenance.

- Evolution strategies use problem-dependent representations and apply mutation and selection as search operators. Like other evolutionary algorithms, they execute these operators in cycles, each known as a generation. The process continues through successive generations until it meets a specific termination condition. In evolution strategies, strategy parameters guide the mutation of every decision variable. These parameters, which often adapt during an evolution strategy run, shape the characteristics of the probability distributions that generate new decision variable values.

- Differential evolution is a form of an evolutionary algorithm that uses an adaptive search mechanism independent of probability distributions. It employs a unique mutation operator inspired by the Nelder Mead simplex search method, which involves selecting, scaling, and adding vector differences from the population. After mutation, the crossover operator recombines the mutated search point with another, replacing it if the new solution has an equal or more excellent objective value. The algorithm is mainly self-adapting, with moves becoming smaller as the population converges, a phenomenon known as contour matching. Differential evolution is relatively easier to implement than other algorithms due to fewer parameters.

In conclusion, evolutionary algorithms offer a powerful approach to solving complex optimization problems that may be difficult or impossible to solve using traditional methods. By leveraging the principles of biological evolution, these algorithms can adapt and explore a large and diverse search space, providing a high degree of flexibility and adaptability. With the several types of evolutionary algorithms available, researchers and practitioners can choose the one that best suits their problem context. In the next chapter, we will look at applying evolutionary algorithms in logistics to improve food security.

2 Mathematical Models for Transportation Optimization Using Evolutionary Algorithms

2.1 Efficient Transportation Planning with Multi-index Transportation Problem

The transportation problem is a unique variant of the linear programming problem. The goal is to minimize the cost of transporting a specific commodity from multiple starting points or origins (such as factories or manufacturing facilities) to various endpoints or destinations (like warehouses or stores) [7]. Each origin has a finite supply, which refers to the maximum quantity of products that can be dispatched. Conversely, each destination has a demand that must be met, indicating the minimum quantity of products that must be delivered. The expense of shipping from an origin to a destination is directly proportional to the number of units transported.

The objective of the transportation problem is to develop a transportation plan that fulfills the demand by utilizing the available supply, all while minimizing the associated costs [7].

The transportation problem remains pertinent today, driving optimal resource allocation across various domains. In manufacturing, it informs effective goods distribution. In information technologies, it aids the development of efficient communication networks, and in cloud computing, it assists in the balanced sharing of hardware and software resources. Thus, its significance continues in these fields.

Problem Statement. Envision a scenario where numerous manufacturers exist for manufacturing provisions, which are subsequently packaged at various warehouses and delivered to different endpoints. Moreover, the process allows for the utilization of diverse types of vehicles and goods. In a war situation, an additional risk factor must be incorporated into the strategy to preserve provision and lives by avoiding potentially hazardous routes. The primary objective here is to mitigate risks while minimizing the overall cost of transportation. To this end, applying the multi-index transportation problem [8] can prove beneficial. This model provides an optimized solution for complex logistical challenges, ensuring efficient, cost-effective, and safer transport operations, even under unpredictable circumstances like warfare, by including additional indexes and risk matrixes to the objective function.

Several indices are identified in the context of the transportation problem: manufacturers, goods, warehouses, vehicle types, and endpoints. Meanwhile, the objective function is characterized by two key components: cost and risk. These two parameters collectively define the optimal transportation strategy, serving as the benchmarks against which potential transportation configurations are evaluated. The indices encompass the problem's multivariate aspects, incorporating the transportation network's diverse elements.

Given the complexity of the task with its multiplicity of potential solutions, traditional optimization methods may fail to deliver optimal efficiency. In such circumstances, applying evolutionary algorithms emerges as a viable approach. Implementing solutions for the transportation problem using genetic algorithms, evolution strategies, and differential evolution would involve creating a representation of the problem, defining the fitness function, and implementing the specific mechanisms of each method.

Genetic Algorithms. In addressing the complexities of multi-index transportation problems, where strategic decision-making is vital for optimizing logistics and distribution networks, the utility of genetic algorithms has been distinctly pronounced. A substantial body of academic literature, including but not limited to studies [9, 10], and [11], serves as an empirical testament to the effectiveness of genetic algorithms.

Representation: Each chromosome could represent a solution to the problem, with genes representing the quantity of a specific good type that must be transported from a particular manufacturer to a selected endpoint via a specific warehouse using a defined type of vehicle.

Fitness Function: The fitness function would correspond to the objective function derived from the transportation problem, thereby aiding in identifying and selecting the most suitable transportation strategy.

Selection, Crossover, and Mutation: Standard genetic algorithm operators can be used. For instance, one could use tournament selection, one-point crossover, and a mutation that randomly alters the quantity of product transported.

Advantages: Genetic algorithms are versatile method that can be applied to various problems. They are also easy to understand and implement.

Disadvantages: Genetic algorithms can sometimes get stuck in local optima, especially for complex problems. They also require careful tuning of parameters such as the mutation and crossover rates.

Unique Aspects: Crossover allows genetic algorithms to combine good parts of different solutions.

Evolution Strategies. Evolution strategies are predominantly effective in handling continuous optimization problems. Consequently, their application to transportation problems has not been extensively explored. Despite this, the adaptive nature of these strategies implies a potential for customization and experimentation within this domain, thus warranting further scholarly investigation.

Representation: Similar to genetic algorithms, each individual represents a solution to the problem.

Fitness Function: Identical to genetic algorithms.

Mutation and Recombination: In evolution strategies, the mutation is typically more significant than recombination. A mutation could involve adding a normally distributed random value to the quantity of product transported. Recombination could be intermediate (averaging the values of two parents) or discrete (randomly choosing values from either parent).

Advantages: Evolution strategies are particularly good at continuous optimization problems. They also have a self-adaptive feature where the mutation strength can change over time, potentially improving the search process.

Disadvantages: Like genetic algorithms, evolution strategies can get stuck in local optima. They also typically require more function evaluations than genetic algorithms or differential evolution.

Unique Aspects: The emphasis on mutation and the self-adaptive feature are unique aspects of evolution strategies.

Differential Evolution. Differential evolution has already been applied in logistics previously, for example, in the study [12] which tackles station-to-door transport inefficiencies in urban logistics. Still transportation problem is poorly explored, solving with differential evolution.

Representation: Similar to genetic algorithms and evolution strategies, each vector represents a solution to the problem.

Fitness Function: Identical to genetic algorithms and evolution strategies.

Mutation and Crossover: Differential evolution uses a unique form of mutation where a new vector is formed by adding the weighted difference between two vectors to a third vector. Crossover is then used to combine this new vector with the original vector.

Advantages: Differential evolution is good at global optimization and can handle noisy or approximated fitness functions. It also requires fewer parameters than genetic algorithms or evolution strategies.

Disadvantages: Differential evolution can be slower than genetic algorithms or evolution strategies, especially for significant problems. It also may not perform well on discrete or combinatorial problems.

Unique Aspects: The unique form of mutation in differential evolution allows it to potentially explore the search space more effectively.

Key Considerations. It is worth noting that the successful application of evolutionary algorithms in solving a multi-index transportation problem hinges primarily on effectively addressing two crucial aspects: initialization of the initial population and management of constraints to ensure the consistent feasibility of solutions.

The first step, initialization of the initial population, is pivotal in preventing premature convergence of solutions. The characteristic of uniqueness is essential because the redundancy of solutions can lead to a local extremum rather than striving toward a globally optimal solution [6]. Thus, employing an effective strategy to initialize a range with unique solutions is integral to mitigating the risk of early stagnation in the search space. An example of the process of population initialization with feasible solutions can be found in the study [11].

When implementing evolutionary algorithms for supply chain optimization, a crucial consideration pertains to the algorithm's ability to manage problem-associated constraints. Constraint handling for transportation problems is a rather challenging field. Therefore, it is essential to devise an appropriate constraint-handling mechanism that can maintain the feasibility of solutions without drastically increasing the computational overhead or limiting the diversity of the population.

In this regard, one might explore techniques such as feasibility-preserving crossover and mutation operations, adaptive penalty functions, or constraint-dominated selection strategies, ensuring the evolved solutions remain within the problem's feasible region [6, 10].

Consequently, the authors [10] put forward a penalty-based approach for managing the feasibility of solutions. In contrast, the authors in reference [11] suggest a technique that restores a solution to the feasible area through an iterative process of adding or subtracting units until the solution becomes feasible.

The effectiveness of employing evolutionary algorithms to solve a multi-index transportation problem relies heavily on the robust initialization of the initial population and proficient management of constraints. Both these factors synergistically contribute to the exploration and exploitation balance of the algorithm, subsequently impacting the quality of the solution and efficiency. Given these elements' complexity and significance, they warrant comprehensive research and thoughtful consideration in designing and implementing evolutionary algorithms for solving multi-index transportation problems.

Leveraging multi-index transportation problems with multiple objectives enables efficient management of essential provision transportation, which is pivotal to ensuring global food security. This particularly applies to transporting grains, a staple food source integral to numerous global economies. By integrating this method into logistics operations, the transportation efficiency of these crucial commodities can be enhanced, thus contributing to the broader goals of global food security.

2.2 Optimizing Route Planning with Multi-objective Traveling Salesman Problem

The traveling salesman problem [13, 14] is a classic problem in computer science and operations research. In this problem, a hypothetical salesman must travel between several cities, visiting each city once and returning to the city where he started to minimize the total distance traveled. Each city is connected to others by a path with a different length. The challenge lies in finding the shortest route that allows the salesman to visit each city exactly once and return to the origin city.

The traveling salesman problem has numerous applications in various fields, including planning and logistics [13]. In these applications, the 'city' can represent customers and soldering points, and the 'distance' can represent travel times and costs. The problem also has applications in astronomy, where astronomers observing multiple sources aim to minimize the time spent moving the telescope between sources. Additional constraints, such as limited resources, risk level, or time windows, may also be imposed in many applications.

Problem Statement. Envision a scenario wherein the objective is to facilitate the transportation of essential commodities to zones embroiled in conflict. This task transcends the boundaries of a conventional traveling salesman problem, morphing into a multifaceted, multi-objective challenge that necessitates meticulous planning and strategic decision-making.

This problem can be viewed as a variant of the traveling salesman problem, known as the multi-objective traveling salesman problem [15]. While in the standard traveling salesman problem, the goal is to find the shortest possible route, in the multi-objective traveling salesman problem, we have multiple objectives to optimize simultaneously, which often conflict. For instance, the route that minimizes time may not be the one that minimizes cost or risk. Therefore, the solution to the multi-objective traveling salesman problem is typically a set of Pareto-optimal routes, each representing a different trade-off among the objectives.

There are three objectives to the problem. First, we aim to minimize the time to deliver the goods, as swift delivery is often crucial in conflict zones where resources may be scarce. Second, we aim to minimize the cost of transportation, which includes factors such as fuel costs, vehicle maintenance, and labor costs. However, unlike typical transportation problems, a third critical objective comes into play in this scenario: minimizing risk. This risk pertains to the potential harm that could befall the salesmen or the goods during transportation. The risk could stem from various factors, such as the volatility of the conflict, the safety of the chosen routes, the security measures in place, and the reliability of the vehicles used for transportation.

To achieve these objectives, we need to consider a multitude of variables. These may include the number and capacity of available vehicles, the availability and skill set of the salesmen, the quantity and nature of the goods to be transported, the distances between the origins and destinations, the current state of the roads, the intensity of the conflict in different zones, and the availability of security escorts, among others.

The example underscores the importance of leveraging advanced optimization techniques, such as the multi-index traveling salesman problem and evolutionary algorithms, to navigate the complexities and uncertainties of such high-stakes logistical challenges.

Genetic Algorithm. The employment of genetic algorithms for addressing the multi-objective variant of the traveling salesman problem represents a propitious methodology, as evinced by pertinent research literature [16].

Representation: Each chromosome could represent a possible route, with each gene representing a city in the problem. The sequence of genes thus signifies the order of city visits.

Fitness Function: The fitness function would correspond to the total distance or time of travel of the route, aiming to minimize this value.

Selection, Crossover, and Mutation: Standard genetic algorithm operators can be used. Tournament selection, order-based crossover (to maintain the validity of solutions), and a swap mutation (randomly swapping two cities) can be employed.

Advantages: Genetic algorithms are versatile and can be applied to various problems. They are also intuitive to understand and implement.

Disadvantages: Genetic algorithms can sometimes get stuck in local optima, especially for complex problems. They also require careful tuning of parameters like the mutation and crossover rates.

Unique Aspects: The crossover operation allows for combining portions of good solutions from the population.

Evolution Strategies. Evolution strategies have been less frequently applied to traveling salesman problem due to their focus on continuous optimization. However, their adaptive nature hints at potential experimentation within the traveling salesman problem's context.

Representation: Similar to genetic algorithms, each individual represents a possible route.

Fitness Function: Identical to genetic algorithms.

Mutation and Recombination: The mutation could involve swapping two cities in the route. Recombination could be performed by choosing portions of the route from two-parent solutions.

Advantages: Evolution strategies' self-adaptive feature could potentially improve the search process over time.

Disadvantages: Like genetic algorithms, evolution strategies can get stuck in local optima. They also typically require more function evaluations than genetic algorithms or differential evolution.

Unique Aspects: The emphasis on mutation and the self-adaptive feature are unique to evolution strategies.

Differential Evolution. The application of differential evolution to traveling salesman problem is not typical due to its nature of handling continuous variables. However, the global optimization strength of differential evolution suggests potential experimentation in traveling salesman problem.

Representation: Similar to genetic algorithms and evolution strategies, each vector represents a possible route.

Fitness Function: Identical to genetic algorithms and evolution strategies.

Mutation and Crossover: Differential evolution uses a unique form of mutation and crossover, which might need to be adapted for traveling salesman problem. An adapted mutation could involve creating a new route by swapping cities based on the weighted difference between two routes.

Advantages: Differential evolution is robust in handling noisy or approximated fitness functions. It also requires fewer parameters than genetic algorithms or evolution strategies.

Disadvantages: Differential evolution can be slower than genetic algorithms or evolution strategies, especially for large problems. It may not perform as well on discrete or combinatorial problems like traveling salesman problem.

Unique Aspects: The unique form of mutation in differential evolution allows it to potentially explore the search space more effectively.

Key Considerations. To adapt evolutionary algorithms to tackle the traveling salesman problem specifically, the design of the potential solution is crucial. A solution can be a specific ordering of all the cities, representing a complete tour.

Let us look at the main key points for adapting evolutionary algorithms for the traveling salesman problem throughout the algorithm's functioning.

The initialization phase calls for the incorporation of domain-specific knowledge or well-established heuristics. For instance, algorithms based on the principles of nearest neighbor or other analogous greedy strategies can be deployed to generate preliminary solutions. The likelihood of these initial solutions being in proximity to the optimum solution is higher as compared to those generated randomly. This phenomenon can be attributed to the problem-specific approach of these strategies.

The fitness function for the presented problem is characterized as a composite of risk measurement, cost, and time dedicated to a particular route. Such an approach ensures a comprehensive assessment of the viability and effectiveness of the proposed solution.

A specialized design of the crossover operation is vital to prevent the generation of invalid tours. The ordered crossover [6] is commonly used for its effectiveness in this regard. It formulates offspring solutions by incorporating a subset from a parent tour and fills in the remaining cities in the sequence they appear in the alternate parent. This process guarantees that every city is visited precisely once, thereby maintaining the integrity of the solution.

Of the unique challenges posed by the traveling salesman problem, an additional stopping criterion could be the stagnation of the quality of the best solution over multiple generations. This plateau may indicate that the algorithm has reached a state of local optimum, thereby necessitating termination. Identifying such stagnation serves as a dynamic indicator of the progress and effectiveness of the algorithm, prompting its termination at the right time. Also, to improve the performance of such algorithms, it can be combined with local search techniques or heuristics. For example, a local search algorithm can be applied after each generation to refine the solutions.

It is important to note that the choice of parameters can significantly influence the performance of the evolutionary algorithms [6]. Therefore, carefully tuning these parameters is often necessary to achieve good results.

In conclusion, evolutionary algorithms offer a promising approach to solving the multi-objective traveling salesman problem in complex scenarios such as transporting goods to conflict zones. By effectively balancing multiple conflicting objectives and considering many variables, they can help develop efficient and robust route plans that minimize time, cost, and risk.

3 Conclusions

In this paper, we have explored the application of evolutionary algorithms to enhance global food security during war, with a particular focus on transportation optimization. The ongoing war in Ukraine has created significant challenges for maintaining global food security, as supply chains are disrupted, agricultural production is undermined, and food transportation and distribution are threatened. We have discussed the potential of evolutionary algorithms to optimize various aspects of food distribution, such as predicting food shortages and identifying optimal distribution routes. By leveraging these advanced methods, organizations can process and analyze their data more efficiently, leading to improved decision-making, enhanced operational efficiency, and increased food security.

We have also discussed evolutionary algorithms' theoretical foundations and principles, including their common characteristics and mechanisms, such as population-based search, fitness evaluation, selection, and genetic operators. We have highlighted the advantages of evolutionary algorithms, such as their adaptability, flexibility, and ability to explore a large and diverse search space. Additionally, we retain examined several types of evolutionary algorithms, such as genetic algorithms, evolution strategies, and differential evolution, each with its unique characteristics and mechanisms.

Furthermore, we have explored two specific optimization problems related to global food security, the multi-index transportation problem and the multi-objective traveling salesman problem. We have discussed the challenges associated with these problems and how evolutionary algorithms can be applied to address them. In particular, we have examined the importance of population initialization and constraint management for the multi-index transportation problem and the multi-objective traveling salesman problem, respectively.

In conclusion, evolutionary algorithms offer a powerful approach to solving complex optimization problems related to global food security. By leveraging the principles of biological evolution, these algorithms can adapt and explore a large and diverse search space, providing a high degree of flexibility and adaptability. With the several types of evolutionary algorithms available, researchers and practitioners can choose the one that best suits their problem context. Applying evolutionary algorithms to transportation optimization problems, such as the multi-index transportation problem and the multi-objective traveling salesman problem, can enhance food security strategies, leading to better decision-making, improved operational efficiency, and, ultimately, increased food security.

References

1. Jungbluth, F., Zorya, S.: Ensuring food security in Europe and Central Asia, now and in the future. World Bank Blogs. 2023, February 3. https://blogs.worldbank.org/europeandcentra lasia/ensuring-food-security-europe-and-central-asia-now-and-future
2. Food and Agriculture Organization of the United Nations, the International Fund for Agricultural Development, the United Nations Children's Fund, the UN World Food Programme, & the World Health Organization. 2022, July 6. UN Report: Global hunger numbers rose to as many as 828 million in 2021. World Health Organization. https://www.who.int/news/item/06-07-2022-un-report--global-hunger-numbers-rose-to-as-many-as-828-million-in-2021

3. Chen, H., Chiang, R.H., Storey, V.C.: Business intelligence and analytics: from big data to big impact. MIS Q. **36**(4), 1165–1188 (2012). https://doi.org/10.2307/41703503

4. Vikhar, P.A.: Evolutionary algorithms: a critical review and its future prospects. In: International Conference on Global Trends in Signal Processing, Information Computing and Communication (ICGTSPICC), Jalgaon, India. 2016, pp. 261–265 (2016). https://doi.org/10.1109/ICGTSPICC.2016.7955308

5. Corne, D.W., Lones, M.A.: Evolutionary algorithms. In: Martí, R., Panos, P., Resende, M.G.C. (eds.) Handbook of Heuristics, pp. 1–22. Springer, Cham (2018). https://doi.org/10.1007/978-3-319-07153-4_27-1

6. Luke, S.: Essentials of Metaheuristics, 2nd edn. Lulu, p. 242 (2013)

7. Haley, K.B.: The solid transportation problem. Oper. Res. **10**(4), 448–463 (1962)

8. Haley, K.B.: The multi-index problem. . Oper. Res. **11**(3), 368–379 (1963)

9. El-Shorbagy, M., Mousa, A., ALoraby, H., AboKila, T.: Evolutionary algorithm for multi-objective multi-index transportation problem under fuzziness. J. Appl. Res. Indust. Eng. **7**(1), 36–56 (2020). https://doi.org/10.22105/jarie.2020.214142.1119

10. Falcone, M., Lopes, H., Coelho, L.: Supply chain optimisation using evolutionary algorithms. IJCAT. **31**, 158–167 (2008). https://doi.org/10.1504/IJCAT.2008.018154

11. Skitsko, V., Voinikov, M.: Solving four-index transportation problem with the use of a genetic algorithm. Logforum **16**(3), 397–408 (2020). https://doi.org/10.17270/J.LOG.2020.493

12. Li, Z., et al.: Two-stage dynamic optimization on station-to-door delivery with uncertain freight operation time in urban logistics. J. Urban Plann. Develop. **148**(3) (2022). https://doi.org/10.1061/(ASCE)UP.1943-5444.0000853

13. Reinelt, G.: The Traveling Salesman: Computational Solutions for TSP Applications, p. 23. Springer, Heidelberg (1994). https://doi.org/10.1007/3-540-48661-5

14. Lawler, E.L., Lenstra, J.K., Rinnooy Kan, A.H.G., Shmoys, D.B.: The Traveling Salesman. John Wiley and Sons (1986)

15. Lust, T., Teghem, J.: The Multiobjective Traveling Salesman Problem: A Survey and a New Approach. In: Coello Coello, C.A., Dhaenens, C., Jourdan, L. (eds) Advances in Multi-Objective Nature Inspired Computing. Studies in Computational Intelligence, vol 272. Springer, Berlin, Heidelberg (2010). https://doi.org/10.1007/978-3-642-11218-8_6

16. Bryant, K., Benjamin, A.: Advisor, Genetic Algorithms and the Traveling Salesman Problem. Department of Mathematics (2000)

Modeling Nations' Decarbonisation Potential

Olena Zhytkevych[1](✉) ⓘ, Andriy Matviychuk[2] ⓘ, and Tetiana Kmytiuk[2] ⓘ

[1] Ukrainian American Concordia University, Office 1-4, 8/14 Turheniivska Str, Kyiv 01054, Ukraine
elena.zhitkevich@gmail.com
[2] Kyiv National Economic University Named After Vadym Hetman, 54/1 Peremogy Ave, Kyiv 03057, Ukraine

Abstract. Global industrialization and excessive consumption of fossil fuels have led to an increase in greenhouse gas emissions and, as a result, rising global temperatures and environmental problems. Growing challenges are setting the world community on the path to reducing carbon emissions as much as possible. Adopted in 2015, the Paris Agreement placed an obligation on the signatory countries to change their development trajectory in order to limit global warming. Responding to this need, the aim of this research is to explore the possibility of applying artificial intelligence techniques in economic decisions to model and analyze decarbonisation capabilities of nations effectively and efficiently.

We proposed and validated 11 indicators to define clusters among of 39 countries with similar decarbonisation capabilities over ten-year period. As a result, eight distinct clusters were obtained. The cluster analysis has been conducted in dynamics and identified leader and other clusters, the countries of which should follow leaders by changing their indicators' values in order to improve their decarbonisation positions in the map. These changes will be associated with transformations of carbon-intensive to zero-carbon economies.

We believe that clustering countries by their decarbonisation capabilities have implications for designing zero-carbon policies towards shifting an economy's sectors to renewable energy consumption or/and supply.

Keywords: Carbon Dioxide Emission Target · Decarbonisation · Clustering · Self-Organizing Map · Neural Network

1 Introduction

1.1 Background

As noted in [1], the continues military conflict caused by Russia's full-scale invasion of Ukraine is effecting large damage to the environment, this war has adverse affects on Ukrainian and the global climate causing major carbon dioxide (CO_2) and other greenhouse gas emissions (GHG) into the atmosphere. Russia's war against Ukraine is ongoing and according to the State Environmental Inspectorate of Ukraine, as of February 18, 2023, 14 million square meters were polluted with remnants and rubble from destroyed facilities and ammo [2].

F. Ortiz-Rodríguez et al. (Eds.): EGETC 2023, CCIS 1888, pp. 60–77, 2023.
https://doi.org/10.1007/978-3-031-43940-7_6

After the end of the military aggression of the Russian Federation, the Ukrainian economy and its decarbonisation strategy should be restored or/and developed optimally by taking into account economic, safety and energy factors, resource provision and implementations of the best global practices and emerging technologies. Hence, careful assessment of the decarbonization capabilities of Ukraine and implementations of the best global practices toward low-carbon economy and technologies are required.

The development of mechanisms for innovative recovery and growth of the national economy towards low-carbon economy in the conditions of dynamic development of industries and post-war adverse consequences need experts' knowledge blended with tools which can generate the most efficient and effective results. Responding to this need, the aim of the research is to explore the possibility of using clustering as a tool in economic decisions to model and analyze decarbonisation capabilities of nations, in particularly Ukraine.

2 Related Works

The recent studies on usage of clustering for decarbonisation nations were not many, especially those that focused on decarbonisation at national and international levels at once, however this line of research is very popular nowadays. In particular, a number of works are devoted to the study of various aspects of solving the problem of decarbonization and the possibility of achieving net zero emissions in industrial clusters of developed countries, such as the United Kingdom [3–6], Spain [7], etc.

In our study [8] we investigated the correlation and non-extensive properties of time series of the global carbon emissions, as well as emissions by countries such as the US, China, Germany, Great Britain, India and others, and constructed the corresponding indicators of crisis phenomena in the economy, clearly reflecting the collective dynamics of the entire research base during events of this kind.

In the papers [9, 10], approaches to predicting energy indicators are proposed, which are based on various clustering methods that determine representative observations based on a set of attributes – specific fuel demands and the productivity from renewable technologies. This technique is found to require three orders of magnitude less computation time than the traditional technique to achieve a comparable level of accuracy.

The work [11] identified clusters of CO_2 emissions across 72 countries based on three key determinants (non-renewables, population, and real GDP) using data for 2015. It was established that in most cases, a 2-cluster solution appears to be optimal. However, we believe that these may lead to significant discrepancies in clustering outcomes since the time factor (dynamic impact) was neglected in this work.

In the similar way we also clustered 39 countries based on 11 indicators that measure both direct and indirect CO_2 emissions, differentiating countries by their economic and population growth, energy consumption, and CO_2 emission level, obtaining 8 stable clusters for 2012–2021 of observations [12]. This made it possible to analyze the general development trajectories of countries in creating climate-resilient economies, to identify the leading countries in this regard, and to set benchmarks for improving catching up countries' own internal decarbonization activities based on leader nations' strategies and borrowing their best practices.

Clustering methods have found their application in other problems related to the energy sector, in particular, the assessment energy performance using volatility change based symbolic transformation [13], modeling and short-term prediction of heating, ventilation, and air conditioning system with a clustering algorithm [14], spatial clustering for district heating integration in urban energy systems [15], pattern analysis of electricity consumption [16–18] and others.

The main gaps recognized in the review of related works are the following:

1. there is a lack of clustering usage in decarbonisation assessment even though this approach is not a very new;
2. the mentioned papers have some limitations (limited scope, list of countries studied or/and time period of research) which may lead to distorting final results;
3. often the process of collecting and choosing the set of potential influence factors are subjective – many of these factors might not be determined by any objective circumstances and can be chosen by experts and researchers, depending on their experiences, patterns of evaluation process, priorities, etc. All these may contribute to a significant imprint of subjectivity in determining the level and targets of carbon dioxide emissions and, therefore, require to minimize experts influence.

Consequently, this paper's objective is to develop the efficient and effective classification of countries based on their decarbonisation characteristics, which are grouped as economic growth, energy consumption and CO_2 emission levels during last decade.

The following tasks were undertaken to achieve this objective:

– Introduce the methodology for the clustering process, which includes defining and analyzing the data for each nation with further selection of the databases and their indicators that have had an impact on CO_2 emission levels over the 10-year period.
– Validate the list of indicators that affect CO_2 emissions for analyzed countries.
– Conduct cluster segmentation and examine examples of national CO_2 emission levels in dynamic.
– Represent main conclusions by research question and further discussions about practical implications and limitations.

3   Methodology

3.1   Clustering Method

Clustering is a technique of data mining which operates on large amounts of data and it is unsupervised learning. The cluster analysis is considered to be an important tool for exploratory data analysis to summarize main characteristics of data.

There is a wide range of cluster analysis methods: K-means [19], K-medoids [20], Principal Component Analysis [21], Spectral Clustering [22], Dendrogram Method [23], Dendrite Method [24], Self-Organizing Maps – SOM [25, 26], Density-Based Spatial Clustering of Applications with Noise – DBSCAN [27], Hierarchical DBSCAN – HDBSCAN [28], Ordering Points to Identify the Clustering Structure – OPTICS [29], Uniform Manifold Approximation and Projection – UMAP [30], Balanced Iterative Reducing and Clustering Using Hierarchies – BIRCH [31], etc.

Each of these methods has its advantages and areas of application and tasks, where it reveals itself in the best way. Experimental studies on comparative analysis of the effectiveness of various clustering methods are described, in particular, in scientific works [32–39].

Taking into account the capabilities of each of the mentioned methods and the specifics of this study, the Kohonen self-organizing maps toolkit was used to cluster countries by the level of CO_2 emission, which, in addition to forming homogeneous groups of researched objects, provide a convenient tool for visual analysis of clustering results. In particular, in contrast to other clustering methods, the location of an object on the Kohonen map immediately indicates to the analyst how developed the investigated property is compared to others, because the best and worst objects according to the analyzed indicator are located in opposite corners of the self-organizing map [40].

The result of constructing the Kohonen map is a visual representation of a two-dimensional lattice of neurons that reflect the organizational structure of the countries of the world, forming clusters in which countries are similar to each other according to the group of indicators of evaluating the CO_2 emission level (see Fig. 1).

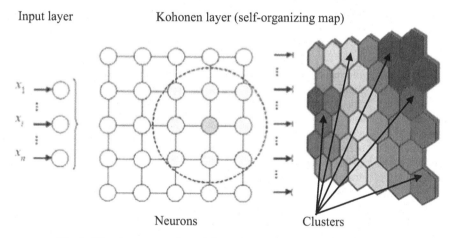

Fig. 1. Visual representation of clusters on the self-organizing map [41].

3.2 Secondary Data Analysis

In the process of clustering countries by decarbonisation factors, it is critically important to identify what indicators affect the amount of CO_2 emissions, hence it requires appropriate analysis of numerical statistical databases.

In the study, all data has been obtained from open sources, various databases online which provide free access to the information about potential influence factors (indicators) of CO_2 emission levels in order to form the input data set. The comparison of the databases is represented in Table 1 below.

Table 1. Comparison of databases.

Database	Scope (number of factors)	Time coverage	Data completeness	Geography coverage
World Development Indicators provided by the World Bank [42]	large variety of indicators (energy, climate change and economic indicators, etc.)	1960–2022	some gaps in the period of 2020–2022 and data provided not for all countries	264
Energy Statistics Database provided by the United Nations Statistics Division [43]	comprehensive energy statistics on the production, trade, conversion and final consumption of primary and secondary, conventional and non-conventional, and new and renewable sources of energy	1990–2021	some gaps in the period of 2020–2021 and data provided not for all countries	86 and more
Greenhouse Gas Inventory Data from the United Nations Framework Convention on Climate Change database [44]	information on anthropogenic emissions by sources and removals by sinks of the following GHGs: carbon dioxide (CO_2), methane (CH_4), nitrous oxide (N_2O), etc	1990–2020	some gaps in the period of 2019–2020 and data provided not for all countries	45
Statistics provided by the International Renewable Energy Agency [45]	comprehensive statistics on a range of topics related to renewable energy, such as climate change, energy transition, finance and investment, etc	mostly 2012–2022, but some reports provide statistics from earlier years	mostly completed	224

(*continued*)

Table 1. (*continued*)

Database	Scope (number of factors)	Time coverage	Data completeness	Geography coverage
European statistics provided by the Eurostat [46]	economy and finance, population and social conditions, industry, trade and services, transport, environment and energy, etc	mostly 2010–2021, but some reports provide statistics from earlier years	no data gaps	27 European Union countries (from 2020), and 19 Euro area countries (from 2015), and limited data for non EU countries
World Energy & Climate Statistics – Yearbook 2022 by the Enerdata [47]	comprehensive global energy transition statistics on production, consumption and trade of oil, gas, power and renewables, CO_2 emissions from fuel combustion	1990–2021	minimum data gaps	43
Statistical Information provided by the State Statistics Service of Ukraine [48]	demographic and social statistics, economic statistics, multidomain statistical information, etc	mostly 1995–2021, but some reports provide statistics from earlier years	mostly completed	1

The database comparison, based on our critical review helped us to select the appropriate ones for further data collection by following criterion: data relevance, completeness and coverage at national and international levels. The existence of gaps in data (missing indicators) may increase the risk of getting not accurate identification of CO_2 emission levels, so we tried to avoid the databases with data gaps, at the same time we kept focus on geographical and time coverage.

Taking into account the analysis of the databases, it was reasonable to merge two reports – the World Bank's report "World Development Indicators" [42] and the Ener data's "World Energy & Climate Statistics – Yearbook 2022" [47]. Since the report "World Energy & Climate Statistics – Yearbook 2022" contains important indicators for our further clustering and covers 43 countries (some countries from European Union, CIS, America including North & Latin America, Asia, Pacific, Africa and Middle-East) it has been used for analysis of economic and demographic data.

The following task was to validate the list of indicators by justifying the set of factors from the selected databases for the clustering. It is obvious that the identification of the level of CO_2 emission is multifactor and continue to develop over time. Hence, the set of dominant factors should explain current and potential economies abilities to reach zero carbon emissions, such as their economic growth, energy consumption, international trade, urbanization, etc. So, the fundamental effect of urban population growth and international trade and energy resources consumption on the environment should be considered in the process of designing policies to mitigate environmental pollution, in particular, GHG emissions.

The indicators should cover a wide range of important evaluation parameters, as well as satisfy the conditions of completeness, effectiveness and minimizing criteria, following methodological basic assumption: the number of evaluated parameters must be sufficient and limited to ensure the efficiency of management decisions. The selection process of key indicators included the following steps [12]:

- choose the maximum possible set of characteristics (among 29 factors from selected databases) of the objects of study that affect CO_2 emission levels;
- form a set of those features that precisely describe the most important activities in the context of the analysis. For this purpose, the selected 11 indicators have been grouped by the similarity with each other into 3 subsets (Table 2).

This grouping indicators into three subsets helped us to classified input data set. Since our study extended the tendency of recent research on the energy and environmental linkage by further disaggregating renewable energy components, economy growth and urbanization, including distinctive individual influence of energy product consumption (without production), economic growth rate and current CO_2 emissions on the evaluating CO_2 emission levels, so three subsets of indicators were formed and represented below in Table 2.

As a result of the analysis of the most significant data indicators in context of their impact on economic, climate and energy capabilities of a country, 11 indicators were selected out of the 29 given (see the last 3 columns of Table 2). The selection and validation processes were based on the criteria of completeness, effectiveness and minimizing of indicators and their possibility of strong impact on identification the CO_2 emission level of each individual country.

Hereby, the first subset has been composed by GDP per capita growth and urban population. Urbanization is a key factor that stimulates economic development through the varying social and structural reforms but GDP per capita growth and GDP per capita are mutually exclusive. Since we focus on dynamic change factors, so the GDP per capita growth should be selected.

Second subset includes information on energy products, electricity and renewable energies and it has been composed by: energy intensity of GDP; electricity consumption; electrification; share of renewables in electricity production; share of wind and solar in electricity production; coal and lignite consumption; oil products consumption; natural gas consumption.

Table 2. Grouped validated indicators.

Full set of indicators of selected datasets	Validated indicators		
	Subset of economic and demographic growth factors	Subset of primary consumption energy products and energy transformation	Subset of GHG emissions
natural gas production; natural gas consumption; electricity production; GDP per capita growth; GDP per capita; electricity consumption; electrification; urban population; total energy primary production; total energy primary consumption; oil products production; oil products consumption; share of renewable in electricity production; share of wind and solar in electricity production; energy intensity of GDP; coal and lignite production; coal and lignite trade; coal and lignite consumption; electricity balance of trade; natural gas balance of trade; oil products balance of trade; crude oil; NGL production; crude oil; NGL trade; total balance of trade; CO_2 emissions; CO_2 intensity and carbon factor	GDP per capita growth (annual %); Urban population (% of total population)	energy intensity of GDP at consumption; electricity consumption; electrification; share of renewables in electricity production; share of wind and solar in electricity production; coal and lignite domestic consumption; oil products consumption; natural gas consumption	average CO_2 emission factor

We considered that oil products production has weaker and not direct impact on CO_2 emissions generated internally by a country, while oil products consumption has direct and heavy impact on it. Since the energy can be produced for internal as well as external consumption and our current study focuses on decarbonisation at national level, hence external consumption and production have been excluded.

The same logic has been applied for natural gas, electricity, coal and lignite, and NGL production and consumption. Additionally, total energy primary consumption was excluded from our dataset, in order to omit double counting, since we viewed main energy products consumptions, which are part of total energy consumption. We had some concerns regarding electricity consumption, since the Enerdata mentioned that "Electricity production corresponds to gross production. It includes public production (production of private and public electricity utilities) and industrial producers for their own uses, by any type of power plant (including cogeneration)" in the report [47].

Based on obtained data we could not identify the source of electricity generation by country. Generally, nuclear, gas turbine, hydropower or solar thermal plants do not significantly change CO_2 emissions, conversely, coal-fired and fossil fuel power stations substantially contribute CO_2 emissions. Hereby, electrification and electricity consumption pollute but at different degree. In order to build the comprehensive model of identification of the CO_2 emission target at national level, such influence factors should be included.

As for the indicators of coal and lignite trade, electricity balance of trade, natural gas balance of trade, oil products balance of trade, crude oil, NGL trade, total balance of trade (trade surplus or deficit of energy products). In our analysis we focused on main factors of pollution, which actually arose from consumption of energy products regardless of their nature of production. Therefore, taking into account above mentioned indicators would lead to double counting and they were excluded from the input dataset.

Third subset is GHG emissions data, that provides information about emissions from energy combustion ($>80\%$ of CO_2 emissions), in particular the carbon factor. Since CO_2 intensity and carbon factor are mutually exclusive factors, we have decided that carbon factor should be included in the subset, while CO_2 emissions shows only physical emissions of CO_2, it can be excluded.

In our study, number of analyzed countries is 39, since the selected databases provide full, comprehensive and updated information (for key energy and economic figures) for these countries with minimum data gaps. The normalization or min-max scaling as a technique is employed when the distribution of input data does not follow the Gaussian distribution, hence, we applied it to switch data to a common scale.

So, for the validated factors from Table 2, we have composed the conglomerate table (see Table 3), which consists of normalized values of 11 indicators in a range of 0 to 1 (where 0 corresponds to the smallest value of the corresponding indicator, and 1 to the largest).

4   Results

4.1   Results Representation and Clustering Analysis

The Deductor Studio Academic software package was used in this study to construct self-organizing maps (SOM). Clustering of the countries has been conducted based on validated 11 indicators of energy consumptions, CO_2 emissions and economic growth, collected for ten-year period.

Vectors of 11 values are applied to the inputs of the map regarding the annual CO_2 emission levels by each country per year from 2012 till 2021 according to the database

Table 3. Fragment of database on indicators of carbon dioxide emission levels.

Countries	Year	Indicators										
		Energy intensity of GDP at consumption	Oil products consumption	Natural gas consumption	Electricity consumption	Share of renewables in electricity production	Share of wind and solar in electricity production	Electrification	Coal and lignite domestic consumption	GDP per capita growth (annual %)	Urban population (% of total population)	Average CO_2 emission factor
Brazil	2012	0.2	0.2	0.0	0.1	0.8	0.0	0.4	0.0	0.4	0.8	0.4
Canada	2012	0.7	0.1	0.1	0.1	0.6	0.1	0.5	0.0	0.4	0.7	0.6
Chile	2012	0.2	0.0	0.0	0.0	0.4	0.0	0.4	0.0	0.8	0.8	0.6
China	2012	0.8	0.6	0.2	1.0	0.2	0.1	0.4	1.0	1.0	0.3	0.9
Colombia	2012	0.0	0.0	0.0	0.0	0.8	0.0	0.4	0.0	0.6	0.7	0.6
Czech	2012	0.4	0.0	0.0	0.0	0.1	0.1	0.4	0.0	0.3	0.6	0.7
Egypt	2012	0.2	0.0	0.1	0.0	0.1	0.0	0.4	0.0	0.3	0.2	0.7
France	2012	0.2	0.1	0.1	0.1	0.2	0.2	0.5	0.0	0.3	0.7	0.3
Germany	2012	0.2	0.1	0.1	0.1	0.2	0.5	0.4	0.1	0.4	0.7	0.7
...	...	...	...	...	...	...	...	...	...	...	...	...
United Kingdom	2021	0.0	0.1	0.1	0.0	0.4	0.8	0.3	0.0	0.8	0.8	0.6
United States	2021	0.7	0.0	0.1	0.0	0.1	0.0	0.3	0.0	0.7	0.3	0.8
Uzbekistan	2021	0.3	0.9	1.0	0.5	0.2	0.4	0.3	0.0	0.8	0.7	0.6

from the Table 3. In the process of constructing a map, the task of finding its optimal dimension (number of neurons) arises, which is implemented experimentally on the basis of statistical data.

The dimension of the SOM has been chosen from various options according to the weighted average quantization error criterion, which reflects the average distance between the data vector supplied to the map inputs and neuron parameters [12]. The initialization of the map was carried out with small random values and the Gaussian function has been chosen for determining the neighborhood of neurons for the cooperation procedure.

After conducting several trial runs, we have decided that the 39-country SOM's most suitable structure is a hexagonal grid of 16 by 12 neurons, and the model of 8 clusters is visually more suitable for the further analysis compared to 4 or 16 cluster models (see Fig. 2). The optimal number of machine learning epochs was chosen to be 5,500, and 11 indicators have been additionally normalized by the Deductor Studio Academic software package to a range of -1 to 1, which increased the percentage of recognition from around 60% to 80%.

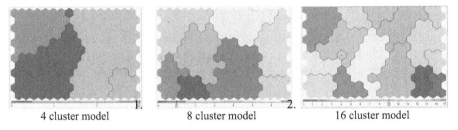

| 4 cluster model | 8 cluster model | 16 cluster model |

Fig. 2. Kohonen maps of 4, 8 and 16 clusters, respectively, for 39 countries based on 11 indicators for ten-year period.

As the result, 39 countries have been combined into eight clusters, where each cluster from 0 to 7 is distinguished by its size, color and has a certain number on the bottom scale of the Kohonen map in Fig. 3.

Note that in Fig. 3, not all countries and not for all years of observations are marked (otherwise the figure would be too cumbersome). The full result of clustering the analyzed countries is presented in the Table 4, where the year mark allows us to track the movements of countries between and within clusters over analyzed period of ten years. Some countries (United Kingdom, Chile, Ukraine, Turkey, Australia, etc.) changed their positions 2–3 times over 10 years. The Kohonen map helped us to track and analyze these movements.

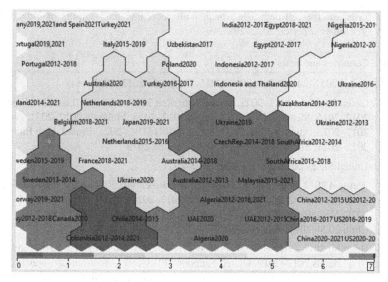

Fig. 3. Kohonen map of 8 clusters for 39 countries based on 11 indicators for ten years.

For example, United Kingdom, Turkey and Australia moved from cluster 1 to 4, then to cluster 3, and it is noticeable that these countries improved their positions in terms of decarbonisation. This conclusion is defined by the fact that the cluster 3 is located closer to the cluster 7, which composed by countries with the best energy, economic growth and CO_2 emission indicators values, hence can be considered as a cluster-leader in low-carbon economies (see Table 4 and Fig. 3).

Ukraine, for instance, in 2012–2018 was located in cluster 5 with Kazakhstan 2012–2021, Russia 2012–2021, Uzbekistan 2012–2016, 2018–2021, Nigeria 2012–2021 and South Africa 2012–2018 (see Table 4). At that period, Ukraine with all mentioned countries had very high energy intensity of GDP consumption and low level of domestic consumption of oil products, electricity and low shares of renewable, solar and wind usage in electricity generation (see Fig. 4).

In 2019 Ukraine moved to the cluster 5, then to the cluster 4 and stayed there from 2020 with such countries as Belgium 2012–2019 and 2021, France 2012–2021, Germany 2012–2014, Italy 2012, Netherlands 2012–2019, United Kingdom 2013–2016, Australia 2014–2019, Turkey 2016–2018, etc., so it improved its position in terms of decarbonisation policy.

Table 4. Clusters of the self-organizing map, built according to 3 subsets of indicators for 39 countries for ten-year period 2012–2021.

Clusters	Countries and years
Cluster 0	Brazil 2012–2016, Chile 2012–2015, Colombia 2012–2021
Cluster 1	Czech Republic 2012–2021, United Kingdom 2012, Turkey 2012–2015, Argentina 2012–2015, Mexico 2012–2017, Japan 2012–2015, Malaysia 2012–2021, Australia 2012–2013, Algeria 2012–2021, Saudi Arabia 2012–2021, United Arab Emirates 2012–2021, South Africa 2019–2021, Ukraine 2019
Cluster 2	United States 2012–2021, China 2012–2021
Cluster 3	Portugal 2012–2021, Spain 2012–2021, New Zealand 2012–2021, Italy 2013–2021, Germany 2015–2021, United Kingdom 2017–2021, Turkey 2019 & 2021, Belgium 2020, Netherlands 2020–2021, Romania 2017 & 2020–2021, Sweden 2020–2021, Chile 2020–2021, Australia 2021
Cluster 4	Belgium 2012–2019 & 2021, France 2012–2021, Germany 2012–2014, Italy 2012, Netherlands 2012–2019, United Kingdom 2013–2016, Australia 2014–2019, Turkey 2016–2018, Chile 2016–2019, Japan 2016–2021, Mexico 2018–2021, Argentina 2019–2021, Ukraine 2020–2021
Cluster 5	Kazakhstan 2012–2021, Russia 2012–2021, Ukraine 2012–2018, Uzbekistan 2012–2016 & 2018–2021, Nigeria 2012–2021, South Africa 2012–2018
Cluster 6	Poland 2012–2021, Romania 2012–2016 & 2018, India 2012–2021, Indonesia 2012–2021, Thailand 2012–2021, Egypt 2012–2021, Uzbekistan 2017
Cluster 7	Sweden 2012–2019, Norway 2012–2021, Canada 2012–2021, Brazil 2017–2021

Contrary, there are several countries such as Algeria, Saudi Arabia, United Arab Emirates, United States, China, Kazakhstan, Norway, France, Portugal, Spain, New Zealand, Canada, etc., which did not move between clusters, however some of them changed their positions within a certain cluster from 2012 till 2021. Hence, these movements may identify certain improvements in the process of their decarbonisation, or vice versa.

The clustering results (see Table 4 and Fig. 3 above) identified the leading countries – Norway, Canada and Sweden of Cluster 7, which had high values for electrification, urbanization, average growth rate in real GDP per capita, low levels of coal and lignite domestic consumption, and average CO_2 emissions (see Fig. 4) for ten-year period of 2012–2021.

For comparison purposes, Cluster 7 was proposed as the leader cluster with the best values for the 11 indicators, while other clusters were followers. This cluster is placed in the lower left corner of the map (see Fig. 3). The closest countries to this corner of the SOM can be identified as highly developed in term of its decarbonisation capabilities and renewable energy sources, and vice versa. Apparently, the clusters 5 and 6 are located opposite to the leader cluster on the map (see Fig. 3) and their countries have the worst values for all the indicators compared to the remaining clusters' countries. Up to 2021, Nigeria, Algeria, India, and Uzbekistan were quite slowly decarbonizing, hence were

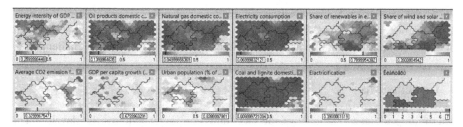

Fig. 4. Kohonen map for 39 countries based on 11 indicators for 2012–2021.

located far away from cluster 7 in the SOM's upper right corner (see Fig. 3 and Table 4 above).

We noticed that some countries, such as China and the United States in cluster 2, stayed together 10 years (2012–2021) without movement, which may indicate about absence of significant improvements in their decarbonization capabilities over analyzed period, while they have high CO_2 emission levels.

5 Further Discussion

This study highlights two methodological findings. First finding is that we explicitly demonstrated that the SOM developed can be used to determine each nation's best position on the map based on three subsets of validated indicators. Their normalized values are recommended as input for clustering to adequately group countries according to a set of influencing factors. Second finding − past several studies performed cluster analysis on single database and used a few clusters to explain the Carbone dioxide emissions profile of a country, while our analysis is based on merged and validated indicators of few databases with justifications, and clustering results analysis is dynamic, which demonstrates movement of countries between and within the clusters. These movements happen due to changes in nations' indicators such as consumption of energy products or/and altering decarbonisation regulations or policies.

For higher efficiency and effectiveness, it is important to find a similarities between countries in terms of their decarbonisation capabilities and design a low-carbon policies appropriately and mutually according to their positions in the SOM. In addition, the SOM analysis identified leaders and followers in low-carbon capabilities. Hence, the SOM can be used as a roadmap by followers, which want to improve their energy and business sectors, and identify their potential CO_2 emission level and keep track on changes. So, clustering as a tool can help analyst to identify country types by emissions (low/high) for further recognition of the targeted CO_2 emission level for particular country. Furthermore, the approach proposed by the authors, can be used for building a model of forecasting the CO_2 emission level or target for a country or group of countries with similar characteristics and development trends.

However, there might be variation in clusters due to different indicators compositions, and clustering as an instrument of artificial intelligence doesn't replace human expertise completely, nevertheless it can facilitate decision-makers reduce cost and increase efficiency. So that, the mathematical tool of the self-organizing map can play significant role in the success of decarbonisation assessing and planning. Using this information, the developed by authors SOM based on three subsets of indicators have high potential for successful implementation and allow countries to meet the upcoming challenges.

6 Conclusions

Determining the accurate level of the CO_2 emission target requires the development of appropriate effective mathematical models and the authors proposed a new scientific approach to solving this important and urgent problem. The first step, within the framework of this approach, is segmentation of analyzed countries according to the dynamics of the validated set of indicators by using of the toolkit of Kohonen self-organizing maps. The following step is to analyze the SOM in dynamic and identify which clusters are leaders in decarbonization and which are followers (passive participant in low-carbonization process). Thus, the closer the country is to leader cluster on the map, the more developed and efficient it is in terms of decarbonization activities. Based on the outcomes of analysis we can proceed with forming recommendations for countries to get the most effective transition to low-carbonization processes by avoiding mistakes of other countries in designing decarbonisation policies.

This paper demonstrates the application of a new scientific approach to assessing current and setting potential targeted level of CO_2 emissions towards efficient and effective decarbonisation at national and global levels. Additionally, it offers important implications for academics and policymakers, and also identifies potential ideas for future research.

References

1. Climate damage caused by Russia's war in Ukraine. https://climatefocus.com/publications/climate-damage-caused-by-russias-war-in-ukraine/. Accessed 17 May 2023
2. Decarbonisation during and after the war: Where Ukraine is headed. https://eu.boell.org/en/2023/03/15/decarbonisation-during-and-after-war-where-ukraine-headed. Accessed 17 May 2023
3. Devine-Wright, P.: Decarbonisation of industrial clusters: a place-based research agenda. Energy Res. Soc. Sci. **91**, 102725 (2022). https://doi.org/10.1016/j.erss.2022.102725
4. Gough, C., Mander, S.: CCS industrial clusters: Building a social license to operate. Int. J. Greenhouse Gas Control **119**, 103713 (2022). https://doi.org/10.1016/j.ijggc.2022.103713
5. Calvillo, C., Race, J., Chang, E., Turner, K., Katris, A.: Characterisation of UK industrial clusters and techno-economic cost assessment for carbon dioxide transport and storage implementation. Int. J. Greenhouse Gas Control **119**, 103695 (2022). https://doi.org/10.1016/j.ijggc.2022.103695
6. Geels, F.W., Sovacool, B.K., Iskandarova, M.: The socio-technical dynamics of net-zero industrial megaprojects: outside-in and inside-out analyses of the Humber industrial cluster. Energy Res. Soc. Sci. **98**, 103003 (2023). https://doi.org/10.1016/j.erss.2023.103003
7. Sun, X., Alcalde, J., Bakhtbidar, M., et al.: Hubs and clusters approach to unlock the development of carbon capture and storage – Case study in Spain. Appl. Energy **300**, 117418 (2021). https://doi.org/10.1016/j.apenergy.2021.117418

8. Bielinskyi, A.O., Matviychuk, A.V., Serdyuk, O.A., Semerikov, S.O., Solovieva, V.V., Soloviev, V.N.: Correlational and non-extensive nature of carbon dioxide pricing market. In: Ignatenko, O., Kharchenko, V., Kobets, V., et al. (eds.), ICTERI 2021 Workshops, Communications in Computer and Information Science, vol. 1635, pp. 183–199. Springer, Cham (2022). https://doi.org/10.1007/978-3-031-14841-5_12

9. Novo, R., Marocco, P., Giorgi, G., Lanzini, A., Santarelli, M., Mattiazzo, G.: Planning the decarbonisation of energy systems: the importance of applying time series clustering to long-term models. Energy Convers. Manag. X **15**, 100274 (2022). https://doi.org/10.1016/j.ecmx.2022.100274

10. Li, P.-H., Pye, S., Keppo, I.: Using clustering algorithms to characterise uncertain long-term decarbonisation pathways. Appl. Energy **268**, 114947 (2020). https://doi.org/10.1016/j.apenergy.2020.114947

11. Inekwe, J., Maharaj, E.A., Bhattacharya, M.: Drivers of carbon dioxide emissions: an empirical investigation using hierarchical and non-hierarchical clustering methods. Environ. Ecol. Stat. **27**, 1–40 (2020). https://doi.org/10.1007/s10651-019-00433-4

12. Zhytkevych, O., Brochado, A.: Modeling national decarbonization capabilities using Kohonen maps. Neuro-Fuzzy Model. Tech. Econ. **11**, 3–24 (2022). https://doi.org/10.33111/nfmte.2022.003

13. Ma, Z., Yan, R., Li, K., Nord, N.: Building energy performance assessment using volatility change based symbolic transformation and hierarchical clustering. Energy Build. **166**, 284–295 (2018). https://doi.org/10.1016/j.enbuild.2018.02.015

14. Tang, F., Kusiak, A., Wei, X.: Modeling and short-term prediction of HVAC system with a clustering algorithm. Energy Build. **82**, 310–321 (2014). https://doi.org/10.1016/j.enbuild.2014.07.037

15. Unternährer, J., Moret, S., Joost, S., Maréchal, F.: Spatial clustering for district heating integration in urban energy systems: application to geothermal energy. Appl. Energy **190**, 749–763 (2017). https://doi.org/10.1016/j.apenergy.2016.12.136

16. Yildiz, B., Bilbao, J.I., Dore, J., Sproul, A.B.: Recent advances in the analysis of residential electricity consumption and applications of smart meter data. Appl. Energy **208**, 402–427 (2017). https://doi.org/10.1016/j.apenergy.2017.10.014

17. Zhang, T., Zhang, G., Lu, J., Feng, X., Yang, W.: A new index and classification approach for load pattern analysis of large electricity customers. IEEE Trans. Power Syst. **27**(1), 153–160 (2012). https://doi.org/10.1109/TPWRS.2011.2167524

18. Yilmaz, S., Chambers, J., Patel, M.K.: Comparison of clustering approaches for domestic electricity load profile characterisation - Implications for demand side management. Energy **180**, 665–677 (2019). https://doi.org/10.1016/j.energy.2019.05.124

19. Hartigan, J.A., Wong, M.A.: A k-means clustering algorithm. J. R. Stat. Soc. Ser. C **28**(1), 100–108 (1979). https://doi.org/10.2307/2346830

20. Kaufman, L., Rousseeuw, P.J.: Partitioning around the medoids (Program PAM). In: Kaufman, L., Rousseeuw, P. J. (eds.) Finding Groups in Data: An Introduction to Cluster Analysis, Wiley Series in Probability and Statistics, pp. 68–125. John Wiley & Sons, Hoboken (1990). https://doi.org/10.1002/9780470316801.ch2

21. Jolliffe, I.T.: Principal Component Analysis. 2nd edn. Springer, New York (2002). https://doi.org/10.1007/978-1-4471-5571-3_12

22. Von Luxburg, U.: A tutorial on spectral clustering. Stat. Comput. **17**(4), 395–416 (2007). https://doi.org/10.1007/s11222-007-9033-z

23. Sokal, R., Rohlf, F.: The comparison of dendrograms by objective methods. Taxon **11**, 33–40 (1962). https://doi.org/10.2307/1217208

24. Caliński, T., Harabasz, J.: A dendrite method for cluster analysis. Commun. Stat. Theor. Methods **3**, 1–27 (1974). https://doi.org/10.1080/03610927408827101

25. Kohonen, T.: Self-organized formation of topologically correct feature maps. Biol. Cybern. **43**, 59–69 (1982). https://doi.org/10.1007/BF00337288
26. Kohonen, T.: Self-organizing maps, 3rd edn. Springer, Berlin (2001)
27. Schubert, E., Sander, J., Ester, M., Kriegel, H., Xu, X.: DBSCAN revisited, revisited: why and how you should (still) use DBSCAN. ACM Trans. Database Syst. **42**(3), 1–21 (2017). https://doi.org/10.1145/3068335
28. Campello, R., Moulavi, D., Sander, J.: Density-based clustering based on hierarchical density estimates. In: Pei, J., Tseng, V.S., Cao, L., Motoda, H., Xu, G. (eds.) Advances in Knowledge Discovery and Data Mining, Lecture Notes in Computer Science. vol. 7819, pp. 160–172. Springer, Heidelberg (2013). https://doi.org/10.1007/978-3-642-37456-2_14
29. Ankerst, M., Breunig, M., Kriegel, H.-P., Sander, J.: OPTICS: Ordering points to identify the clustering structure. ACM SIGMOD Rec. **28**(2), 49–60 (1999). https://doi.org/10.1145/304 182.304187
30. McInnes, L., Healy, J.: UMAP: Uniform Manifold Approximation and Projection for Dimension Reduction. arXiv, abs/1802.03426 (2018). https://doi.org/10.48550/arXiv.1802.03426
31. Zhang, T., Ramakrishnan, R., Livny, M.: BIRCH: an efficient data clustering method for very large databases. ACM SIGMOD Rec. **25**(2), 103–114 (1996). https://doi.org/10.1145/233 269.233324
32. Harkanth, S., Phulpagar, B.: A survey on clustering methods and algorithms. Int. J. Comput. Sci. Inf. Technol. **4**(5), 687–691 (2013). https://ijcsit.com/docs/Volume%204/Vol4Issue5/ijc sit2013040511.pdf
33. Kaminskyi, A., Miroshnychenko, I., Pysanets, K.: Risk and return for cryptocurrencies as alternative investment: kohonen maps clustering. Neuro-Fuzzy Model. Tech. Econ. **8**, 175–193 (2019). https://doi.org/10.33111/nfmte.2019.175
34. Kobets, V., Yatsenko, V.: Influence of the fourth industrial revolution on divergence and convergence of economic inequality for various countries. Neuro-Fuzzy Model. Tech. Econ. **8**, 124–146 (2019). https://doi.org/10.33111/nfmte.2019.124
35. Kobets, V., Novak, O.: EU countries clustering for the state of food security using machine learning techniques. Neuro-Fuzzy Model. Tech. Econ. **10**, 86–118 (2021). https://doi.org/10.33111/nfmte.2021.086
36. Lukianenko, D., Strelchenko, I.: Neuromodeling of features of crisis contagion on financial markets between countries with different levels of economic development. Neuro-Fuzzy Model. Tech. Econ. **10**, 136–163 (2021). https://doi.org/10.33111/nfmte.2021.136
37. Subasi, A.: Clustering examples. In: Subasi, A. (ed.) Practical Machine Learning for Data Analysis Using Python, pp. 465–511. Elsevier (2020). https://doi.org/10.1016/b978-0-12-821 379-7.00007-2
38. Velykoivanenko, H., Korchynskyi, V.: Application of clustering in the dimensionality reduction algorithms for separation of financial status of commercial banks in Ukraine. Univers. J. Acc. Finance **10**(1), 148–160 (2022). https://doi.org/10.13189/ujaf.2022.100116
39. Xu, R., Donald, W.: Survey of clustering algorithms. IEEE Trans. Neural Netw. **16**(3), 645–678 (2005). https://doi.org/10.1109/TNN.2005.845141
40. Lukianenko, D., Matviychuk, A., Lukianenko, L., Dvornyk, I.: Modelling the design of university competitiveness. In: Semerikov, S., et al. (eds.) Proceedings of 10th International Conference on Monitoring, Modeling & Management of Emergent Economy, pp. 204–214. SciTePress, Setúbal (2023)
41. Matviychuk, A., Lukianenko, O., Miroshnychenko, I.: Neuro-fuzzy model of country's investment potential assessment. Fuzzy Econ. Rev. **24**(2), 65–88 (2019). https://doi.org/10.25102/fer.2019.02.04
42. World Development Indicators. https://databank.worldbank.org/source/world-development-indicators. Accessed 17 May 2023

43. UNdata. http://data.un.org/Explorer.aspx. Accessed 17 May 2023
44. Greenhouse Gas Inventory Data. https://di.unfccc.int/time_series. Accessed 17 May 2023
45. IRENA. https://www.irena.org/Data. Accessed 17 May 2023
46. Database – Eurostat. https://ec.europa.eu/eurostat/en/web/main/data/database. Accessed 17 May 2023
47. World Energy & Climate Statistics – Yearbook 2022. https://yearbook.enerdata.net/total-energy/world-consumption-statistics.html. Accessed 17 May 2023
48. State Statistics Service of Ukraine. https://ukrstat.gov.ua/. Accessed 17 May 2023

Scene Classification in Enhanced Remote Sensing Images Using Pre-trained RESNET50 Architecture

M. Pranesh, A. Josephine Atchaya, J. Anitha, and D. Jude Hemanth[(✉)]

Department of ECE, Karunya Institute of Technology and Sciences, Coimbatore, India
judehemanth@karunya.edu

Abstract. Scene classification in enhanced remote sensing images is an important task for a variety of applications, including land cover mapping, disaster management, urban planning, agricultural monitoring, and forest monitoring. In recent years, deep learning techniques, especially convolutional neural networks (CNNs), have shown great promise in scene classification tasks. In this paper, we propose a scene classification method based on a pretrained RESNET50 architecture for enhanced remote sensing images. Our method involves fine-tuning the RESNET50 architecture on a large-scale remote sensing dataset, and using it to classify scene images into different classes. The proposed method can be used for various remote sensing applications that require accurate and efficient scene classification.

Keywords: Scene classification · Deep learning · Convolutional neural network · ResNet50

1 Introduction

Enhanced satellite images can provide valuable information for monitoring changes in land use, water resources, and vegetation cover. This information can be used to identify areas at risk of natural disasters and track the impacts of climate change. To determine the effectiveness of both filters, the peak signal to noise ratio (PSNR) has been determined. In general, noise reduction using the filter is improved when the PSNR value is higher [1]. The margins of the image are overly blurred by the standard methods of denoising since they are unable to maintain the quality of the image. To eliminate noise and preserve edge details while employing a bilateral filter to denoise the image, control parameters must be chosen. [2]. In some image applications, it is frequently desirable to remove noise that might be impulsive non-impulsive, with minimum distortion of the original image information. To overcome this, various techniques have been used [3] The recorded image processing technique named pre-handling care of was executed for improving the standard of the pictures. Two dimensional pictures are addressed with mechanized picture containing limited arrangement of picture normally contains to be pixels [4].

© The Author(s), under exclusive license to Springer Nature Switzerland AG 2023
F. Ortiz-Rodríguez et al. (Eds.): EGETC 2023, CCIS 1888, pp. 78–88, 2023.
https://doi.org/10.1007/978-3-031-43940-7_7

An appropriate method for noise reduction is one which enhances the signal to noise ratio while conserving the edges and lines in the image. Filtering techniques are used as preface action before segmentation and classification [5] During the processes of reception, transmission, acquisition, storage, and recovery, noise becomes accustomed. Hence, de-noising an image becomes a crucial duty for fixing flaws caused by these procedures [6, 7] A simple and efficient noise detection method is also used to detect noise candidates and dynamically assign zero or small weights to the noise candidates in the window [8]. After detecting the salt and pepper noise pixels, the self-adaptive median filter is use to find a suitable window containing more non-noise pixels. This proposed algorithm provides much better results than that of the standard median filter, weighed median filter and switching mean median filter [9]. The Saturn remote sensing image receives the same treatment, and the two are contrasted. Mean Square Errors (MSE) and Peak Signal to Noise Ratio (PSNR) are used to conduct the comparative investigation [10]. The existing filtering methods are capable of removing the noise in the image but is not much effective in preserving the image information such as edges, lines etc. [11].

In this paper, a novel pre-processing the visual quality of remote sensing photos can be enhanced by an algorithm that is proposed to simultaneously smooth noise and enhance edges [12, 13]. The majority of previously established techniques can be used to denoise photos that have been corrupted but have less noise density. Here, a brand-new decision-based method has been introduced that outperforms those currently in use [14]. Salt and Pepper Noise (impulse or spike noise), Poisson noise (shot noise), Gaussian or amplifier noise, and Speckle Noise are the sounds that were added to the ultrasound images [15].

The application of remote sensing images in land monitoring, geographical national census, urban greening monitoring and other aspects is increasing [16]. Noise can be defined as an unwanted entity that corrupts the significant information and disgraces the visual quality of digital image. Image de-noising process is used for removing the effect of noises, the goal of de-noising methods is to recover original image from the noisy measurements [17]. Noise is present because of a malfunctioning image sensor and transmission channel noise for image and video sequences. Due to the widespread use of webcams and smartphone cameras, the issue of image noise removal is still urgent and, in fact, becoming more crucial [18]. Using the MATLAB tool, the suggested methods are assessed. Performance indicators like the Peak Signal to Noise Ratio, Picture Enhancement Factor, and Structural Similarity Index have been used in both qualitative and quantitative statistical evaluations. Applying these performance criteria to picture denoising [19, 20]. It is common to practice to begin the process of implementing these sub-processes by first applying a noise filter to the digital image in the role of a pre-processing phase. Such filters, however, should properly maintain the image's borders and textures while reducing noise. Otherwise, even if the approach eliminates noises, it distorts or destroys certain important visual information [21]. Multiplicative noise is defined as a form of noise that relies on the density of the pixel, and speckle noise is at the forefront of this type of noise. Lastly, impulse noise is a sort of noise that modifies an image by setting certain pixels to a fixed or random value. Artificially intelligent algorithms are used because they have a large search space, which boosts their effectiveness. Meta-heuristic Cuckoo Search (CS) and Artificial Bee Colony (ABC) algorithms were selected for this task. For a variety of satellite photos, a number of tests are run to gauge how well the algorithm performs. The problem becomes more dimensional as low and high levels of segmentation are taken into consideration. The proposed method is contrasted with traditional colour picture thresholding approaches and cutting-edge satellite image thresholding methods using various criteria [22] (Fig. 1).

2   Proposed Methodology

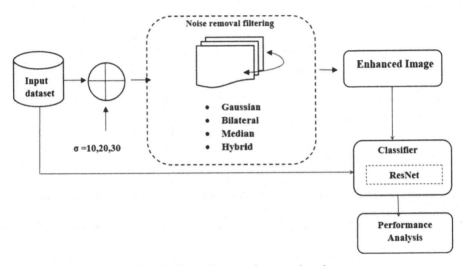

Fig. 1. Block diagram of proposed work

2.1 Input Dataset

The dataset consists of 21 categories of land-use classes, including airplanes, buildings, forests, and rivers, etc. There are a total of 2,100 images in the dataset, with 100 images for each class. Each image is a 256 x 256-pixel RGB image in JPEG format. In this Paper the data sets that are used are listed as follows (Fig. 2),

- **Agriculture**
- **Airplane**
- **Baseball diamond**
- **Freeway**
- **Golf course**
- **Overpass**
- **Parking lot**
- **Tennis court**

Sample Images:

Agriculture	**Airplane**	**Baseball diamond**	**Freeway**
Golf course	**Overpass**	**Parking lot**	**Tennis court**

Fig. 2. Remote Sensing (satellite) datasets.

2.2 Noise Removal and Filtering

Noise removal and filtering are important image processing techniques used to enhance the quality and clarity of digital images. Noise is a type of unwanted signal that can appear in images due to various factors such as electrical interference, sensor limitations, or environmental conditions. Filtering techniques are used as preface action before segmentation and classification.

2.3 Gaussian Filter

The Gaussian filter works by convolving the image with a Gaussian kernel, which is a matrix of values that define the weight and size of the filter. The filter is based on a Gaussian distribution, which is a mathematical function that describes the probability distribution of random variables. The output of gaussian filter can be calculated as,

$$g(\text{x,y}) = \frac{1}{2\pi\sigma^2} \cdot e^{\frac{-(x^2+y^2)}{2\sigma^2}} \tag{1}$$

where x is the distance from the origin in the horizontal axis, y is the distance from the origin in the vertical axis, and σ is the standard deviation of the Gaussian distribution.

The Gaussian filter can be applied to an image by convolving the image with a kernel that is generated from the Gaussian function. The size of the kernel and the value of σ determine the amount of smoothing that is applied to the image. Larger kernels and larger values of σ result in more smoothing, while smaller kernels and smaller values of σ result in less smoothing.

2.4 Bilateral Filter

The bilateral filter is a commonly used non-linear filter in image processing applications. It is used to smooth an image while preserving edges and details. Unlike the Gaussian filter, which applies a weighted average to all pixels in a window, the bilateral filter applies a weighted average only to nearby pixels that have similar intensity values.

The formula for the bilateral filter is as follows:

$$d(i, j, k, l) = -\frac{(i-k)^2 + (j-l)^2}{2\sigma_d^2}$$

$$r(i, j, k, l) = -\frac{\|f(i, j) - f(k, l)\|^2}{2\sigma_r^2}$$

When multiplied together these yield data dependent bilateral weight function,

$$w(i, j, k, l) = exp\left(-\frac{(i-k)^2 + (j-l)^2}{2\sigma_d^2} - \frac{\|f(i, j) - f(k, l)\|^2}{2\sigma_r^2}\right) \tag{2}$$

where $\|f(i, j) - f(k, l)\|^2$ refers to the squared magnitude of the difference between the two-pixel values.

2.5 Median Filter

A median filter is a non-linear filter commonly used in image processing to reduce noise and enhance edges. The filter works by replacing each pixel value in an image with the median value of its neighboring pixels within a defined window or kernel size.

2.6 RESNET50 Architecture

The term ResNet refers to residual networks. In addition to its core concept, ResNet has many variants with varying numbers of layers that are based on the same concept. ResNet50 consists of 50 layers, including convolutional layers, max pooling layers, and fully connected layers. It also uses skip connections, which allow the network to learn residual functions that bypass some layers, making it easier for the network to learn and reducing the risk of vanishing gradients. This guarantees that the performance of the model's higher levels is not worse than that of its lower layers. In other words, the leftover blocks greatly facilitate the layers' ability to learn identity functions. ResNet hence decreases error % while increasing the effectiveness of deep neural networks with more neural layers (Fig. 3).

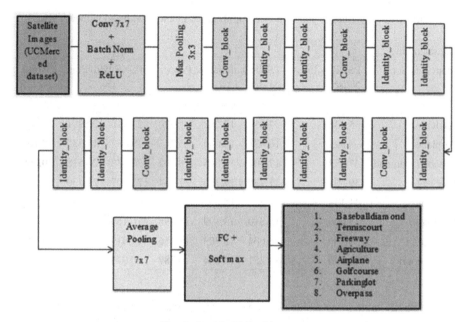

Fig. 3. ResNet50 Architecture

3 Results and Discussion

The image dataset considered is satellite images of size $256 \times 256 \times 3$. The proposed hybrid filter denoises the filter denoises the input image. The results are compared in terms of PSNR and MSE.

Peak Signal-to-Noise Ratio: PSNR (Peak Signal-to-Noise Ratio) is a measure of image quality used in image processing. It measures the difference between two images by comparing the peak signal level (the maximum possible value) to the level of noise (random variations) present in the images. The PSNR is calculated using the following formula:

$$PSNR = 10^* log_{10} \frac{R^2}{MSE} \tag{3}$$

The PSNR is expressed in decibels (dB). Higher values of PSNR indicate better image quality, while lower values indicate more noise or distortion in the image.

Mean Square Error: MSE is commonly used as a quality metric for image compression algorithms, where it is used to measure the amount of information loss that occurs when an image is compressed. The lower the MSE, the better the quality of the compressed image. However, it should be noted that MSE does not necessarily correlate with perceived image quality, and other metrics such as PSNR (Peak Signal-to-Noise Ratio) and SSIM (Structural Similarity Index) may provide a more accurate measure of image quality (Table 1).

$$MSE = \frac{\sum_1^n [x - y]^2}{M^*N} \tag{4}$$

Table 1. PSNR values of gaussian filter for proposed methods with and without noise.

Gaussian Filter

Input data Set	PSNR without Noise	PSNR with Salt & Pepper Noise			PSNR with Poisson Noise		
		$\sigma=10$	$\sigma=20$	$\sigma=30$	$\sigma=10$	$\sigma=20$	$\sigma=30$
Agriculture	35.236	17.359	17.242	17.120	21.216	20.991	20.886
Airplane	38.393	16.431	16.034	15.742	19.462	18.685	18.167
Baseball diamond	37.252	17.401	17.016	16.792	21.433	20.518	20.065
Freeway	39.507	17.738	17.376	17.134	22.207	21.330	20.698
Golf course	41.139	16.215	15.591	15.512	19.111	18.046	17.801
Overpass	35.906	14.310	13.399	12.996	16.160	14.777	14.210
Parking lot	34.869	15.604	15.303	15.216	17.819	17.322	17.144
Tennis court	36.490	17.251	16.884	16.787	20.973	20.330	19.953

The PSNR value for gaussian filter on different standard deviation values shows that less standard deviation gives better PSNR. The higher the PSNR, the better the quality of the enhanced, or reconstructed image. The PSNR increases for less standard deviation for both salt and pepper noise and for poison noise (Tables 2, 3 and 4).

Table 2. PSNR values of Bilateral filter for proposed methods with and without noise.

Bilateral Filter

Input data Set	Bilateral without Noise	Bilateral with Salt & Pepper Noise			Bilateral with Poisson Noise		
		$\sigma=10$	$\sigma=20$	$\sigma=30$	$\sigma=10$	$\sigma=20$	$\sigma=30$
Agriculture	35.747	26.241	18.687	18.700	26.241	26.208	26.218
Airplane	39.733	18.030	17.956	17.795	24.319	23.652	23.251
Baseball diamond	35.115	18.408	18.429	18.383	25.251	25.060	25.083
Freeway	38.490	29.374	25.132	24.895	18.535	18.392	24.835
Golf course	36.190	17.852	17.647	17.525	23.763	22.944	22.554
Overpass	38.304	17.527	17.536	17.443	24.235	23.981	23.871
Parking lot	38.653	18.098	18.030	17.916	24.242	23.565	23.362
Tennis court	35.707	18.349	18.298	18.302	24.600	24.370	24.303

Table 3. PSNR values of Median filter for proposed methods with and without noise.

Median Filter				
Input data Set	Median with Salt & Pepper Noise			Median with Poisson Noise
	Noise Density = 0.1	Noise Density = 0.2	Noise Density = 0.3	
Image1	26.592	24.827	21.852	26.561
Image2	29.827	26.557	22.338	29.780
Image3	28.446	26.013	22.472	28.144
Image4	30.216	26.990	22.896	29.653
Image5	31.337	27.816	23.056	30.811
Image6	26.429	23.688	20.348	26.823
Image7	25.382	23.419	20.448	25.716
Image8	27.411	25.204	21.788	27.032

Table 4. Comparison of PSNR values with proposed methods

Input dataset	Gaussian	Bilateral	Median	Hybrid
Agriculture	35.236	35.747	26.540	27.050
Airplane	38.236	39.733	29.871	31.192
Baseball diamond	37.252	35.115	28.417	29.265
Freeway	39.501	38.490	30.137	31.299
Golf course	41.139	36.190	31.376	32.047
Overpass	35.906	38.304	26.604	27.923
Parking lot	34.869	38.653	25.448	26.020
Tennis court	34.490	35.707	27.267	28.146

As a result, compared to gaussian filter, bilateral filter, median filter and hybrid filter the bilateral filter performs better in terms of the PSNR. Numerous techniques fall short of eliminating the Salt and Pepper noise that exists in the original image. All algorithms' performance is evaluated using real-world photos. One of the proposed algorithms, the Bilateral Filter, outperformed the others, according to the computational results. The adaptive median filter's cost and complexity of computation are two of its main drawbacks (Tables 5 and 6).

Table 5. Comparison of MSE values with proposed methods

Image dataset	MSE	
	Gaussian filter	Bilateral filter
Agriculture	21.188	20.369
Airplane	9.412	14.741
Baseball diamond	12.241	30.372
Freeway	7.293	13.441
Golf course	5.001	27.664
Overpass	16.690	17.988
Parking lot	21.188	20.369
Tennis court	14.590	23.928

MSE value denotes the average difference of the pixels all over the image. When the value is low the perfection of the image is high (Fig. 4).

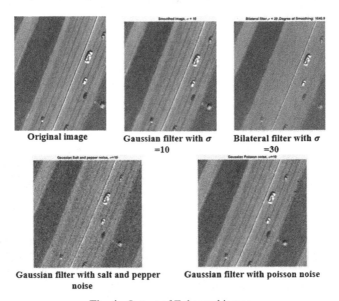

Original image   Gaussian filter with σ =10   Bilateral filter with σ =30

Gaussian filter with salt and pepper noise   Gaussian filter with poisson noise

Fig. 4. Output of Enhanced image

As part of the enhancement process, filtering technique was utilized. ResNet's performance is measured in terms of classification accuracy (AC), sensitivity (SE), specificity (SP), and positive predictive value (PPV). Compared with raw data, the enhanced classification method provides better outperformance. In order to reliably categorize satellite images, a deep learning approach based on an adaptive median filter can be used.

Table 6. Performance analysis of ResNet

Image	AC	SE	SP	PPV	NPV
Normal Image	89	86.9	87.1	77.3	94.7
RESNET50	AC	SE	SP	PPV	NPV
Median	88.7%	77.5%	97.7%	80%	87.9%
Gaussian with noise	87%	89.6%	85.8%	78%	96.9%
Gaussian without noise	89.5%	83.9%	92.6%	78.8%	96.1%
Bilateral	92.4%	91.1%	93.5%	89.7%	97.2%
Hybrid	91.3%	86.5%	93.4%	71.3%	93.8%

4 Conclusion

In this paper, gaussian, bilateral, median and hybrid filtering for denoising is presented. These methods are used to preserve the edge details in the image. In which the bilateral filter gives superior performance in terms of PSNR and MSE values. The pre-trained architecture of ResNet50 is used for classifying the enhanced images. The classification accuracy is enhanced with the filtered images rather than the raw image. Furthermore, the presentation discusses the use of supervised and unsupervised learning algorithms for scene classification, which involve the training of machine learning models to identify and classify different land cover types present in remote sensing imagery. As a future work modification can be done in the filtering approaches and other deep learning architectures.

References

1. Soni, H., Sankhe, D.: Image restoration using adaptive median filtering. In: International Research Journal of Engineering IT & Scientific Research, pp. 841–844 (2019). www.irj et.net
2. Asokan, A., Anitha, J.: Adaptive cuckoo search based optimal bilateral filtering for denoising of satellite images. In: ISA Transactions, Elsevier Ltd, pp. 308–321 (2020). https://doi.org/10.1016/j.isatra.2019.11.008
3. Hwang, H., Haddad, R.A.: Adaptive median filters: new algorithms and results. In: IEEE Transactions on Image Processing, pp. 499–502 (1995). https://doi.org/10.1109/83.370679
4. Sunitha, M.R., Asha, D.: Comparison of Gaussian and Median Filters to Remove Noise in Dental Images, pp. 25990–25994 (2020)
5. Sathesh, A., Rasitha, K.: A Nonlinear Adaptive Median Filtering Based Noise Removal Algorithm (2018)
6. Gupta, M., Taneja, H., Chand, L.: Performance enhancement and analysis of filters in ultrasound image denoising. In: Procedia Computer Science, Elsevier B.V., pp. 643–652 (2018). https://doi.org/10.1016/j.procs.2018.05.063
7. Gao, Z.: An Adaptive Median Filtering of Salt and Pepper Noise based on Local Pixel Distribution, pp. 473–483 (2018). https://doi.org/10.2991/tlicsc-18.2018.77

8. Vigneshwari, K., Kalaiselvi, K.: Adaptive Median Filter Based Noise Removal Algorithm for Big Image Data, pp. 154–159 (2018)

9. Khan, S., Lee, D.H.: An adaptive dynamically weighted median filter for impulse noise removal. In: Eurasip Journal on Advances in Signal Processing, EURASIP Journal on Advances in Signal Processing (2017).https://doi.org/10.1186/s13634-017-0502-z

10. Al-amri, S.S., Kalyankar, N.V., Khamitkar, S.D.: A Comparative Study of Removal Noise from Remote Sensing Image, pp. 32–36. http://arxiv.org/abs/1002.1148

11. Asokan, A., Anitha, J.: Edge preserved satellite image denoising using median and bilateral filtering. In: Santosh, K.C., Hegadi, R.S. (eds.) RTIP2R 2018. CCIS, vol. 1035, pp. 688–699. Springer, Singapore (2019). https://doi.org/10.1007/978-981-13-9181-1_59

12. Zheng, L., Xu, W.: An improved adaptive spatial preprocessing method for remote sensing images. In: Sensors, pp. 1–18 (2021). https://doi.org/10.3390/s21175684

13. Escudero, J.A.: The Pennsylvania State University School of Science Engineering & Technology Electrical Engineering Implementation of Weighted Median Filters in Images Prepared By : Juan Enrique Aguirre Prepared For : Dr. Morales Aldo Topics in Digital Signal Processing. (2019). https://doi.org/10.13140/RG.2.2.18606.66887

14. Shrestha, S.: Image denoising using new adaptive based median filter. In: Signal & Image Processing: An International Journal, pp. 1–13 (2014). https://doi.org/10.5121/sipij.2014. 5401

15. Cao, Y., et al.: Feature extraction of remote sensing images based on bat algorithm and normalized chromatic aberration. In: IFAC-PapersOnLine, Elsevier Ltd, pp. 318–323 (2019). https://doi.org/10.1016/j.ifacol.2019.12.429

16. Kuhad, H., Joshi, A., Gurpude, A., Chimankar, N., Maskey, R., Thakur, R.: Image Denoising by Hybrid Average Gaussian Filter for Different Noises, pp. 1–7 (2014)

17. Veerakumar, T., Esakkirajan, S., Vennila, I.: Salt and pepper noise removal in video using adaptive decision based median filter. In: 2011 International Conference on Multimedia, Signal Processing and Communication Technologies, IMPACT 2011, pp. 87–90 (2011). https:// doi.org/10.1109/MSPCT.2011.6150444

18. Rani, S., Chabbra, Y., Malik, K.: Adaptive window-based filter for high-density impulse noise suppression. Measur. Sens. **24**, 100455 (2022). https://doi.org/10.1016/j.measen.2022. 100455

19. Saleh, B.J., Saedi, A.Y.F., Al-Aqbi, A.T.Q., Salman, L.A.: Optimum median filter based on crow optimization algorithm. Baghdad Sci. J. **18**(3), 614–627 (2021). https://doi.org/10. 21123/BSJ.2021.18.3.0614

20. Rai, R., Das, A., Dhal, K.G.: Nature-inspired optimization algorithms and their significance in multi-thresholding image segmentation: an inclusive review. In: Evolving Systems, Springer Berlin Heidelberg, pp. 889–945 (2022). https://doi.org/10.1007/s12530-022-09425-5

21. Goel, S., Gaur, M., Jain, E.: Nature inspired algorithms in remote sensing image classification. In: Procedia Computer Science, Elsevier Masson SAS, pp. 377–384 (2015). https://doi.org/ 10.1016/j.procs.2015.07.352

22. Jia, H., Lang, C., Oliva, D., Song, W., Peng, X.: Hybrid grasshopper optimization algorithm and differential evolution for multilevel satellite image segmentation. Remote Sens. **11**(9), 1134 (2019). https://doi.org/10.3390/rs11091134

Do Trust and Quality Dimensions of Open Government Data (OGD) Impact Knowledge Sharing (KS)?: Gender Differences

Charalampos Alexopoulos[1]([⊠]) [iD], Stuti Saxena[2] [iD], and Nina Rizun[3] [iD]

[1] University of the Aegean, Samos, Greece
alexop@aegean.gr
[2] Graphic Era University, Dehradun, India
[3] Gdańsk University of Technology, Gdańsk, Poland
nina.rizun@pg.edu.pl

Abstract. Furthering Knowledge Sharing (KS) is important among the Open Government Data (OGD) adopters for providing the required impetus for value derivation and innovation endeavors. However, it is pertinent to ascertain if the OGD adopters consider trustworthy and reliable as well as the qualitatively robust OGD for engaging in KS. Thus, the present study seeks to derive inferences from an empirical investigation involving university students in Indian context (n ~ 397) via adapted modular framework with specific focus on the gender differentials. Research findings show that males are more concerned about OGD's information quality and system quality as far as knowledge sharing is concerned. The study closes with further research pointers and social and practical implications.

Keywords: Knowledge sharing · Open Government Data · India · gender · trust · system quality · data quality · information quality

1 Introduction

Electronic government (e-government) has attained its zenith with the infusion of Information and Communications Technologies (ICT) [1] for provisioning the structural and functional dimensions of the administration across dedicated web portals in machine-processable formats-a phenomenon called Open Government Data (OGD) initiative [2]. The edifice of OGD initiatives lies in furthering user engagement, citizen participation in administration apart from refurbishing the image of the government in terms of transparency and accountability [3, 4]. OGD initiatives have been spearheaded by the developed and developing countries alike in or der to further re-use of OGD by a range of stakeholders including academia, entrepreneurs, professionals, software app developers and the like for innovating and refurbishing the services and goods [5–7].

Value creation and innovation endeavours of the users is a function of knowledge sharing (KS) among them for furthering dialogue and deliberation regarding the provisioning or improvisation of services being rendered by the users. For instance, KS entails

F. Ortiz-Rodríguez et al. (Eds.): EGETC 2023, CCIS 1888, pp. 89–100, 2023.
https://doi.org/10.1007/978-3-031-43940-7_8

the user involvement for deliberating on the course of action and potential of OGD for value creation endeavours. However, it is pertinent to understand whether there is any impact of reliable and credible OGD apart from its quality, i.e. system quality, information quality and data quality, on KS. To address this research objective, the present study seeks to present an empirical analysis using an adapted modular framework such that the relationships between Trust, System Quality, Data Quality and Information Quality against Knowledge Sharing are being studied on the basis of the responses garnered from the university students (n ~ 397) in India. Also, it may be relevant to understand if there are any gender differences across the relationships identified here-this assumes importance given the fact that there are gender differences as far as KS is concerned [8–10]. Thus, by contributing to the extant body of literature on OGD and KS especially in terms of ICT4D (Information and Communications Technologies for Development) landscape, the study also furthers our understanding of KS mechanisms among the university students given the influence of KS on their learning performance [11, 12].

2   Related Research

2.1   Knowledge Sharing (KS) and Human-Computer Interaction

KS and knowledge acquisition have been considered pertinent in the context of IT (Information Technology) adoption among the university students-case in point being the e-learning technologies [13, 14]. Furthermore, KS is determined by the extent of individual involvement in terms of motivation [15] or self-efficacy [16, 17] apart from the conducive conditions like organization culture and the supportive leadership to steer KS activities [18–20]-case in point being the KS activities via the social media [21]. Such influence is being perceived differently across individual and group/team levels in addition to the determinants like the nature of technology, task/purpose and the degree of interaction with the relevant individuals [22, 23].

2.2   OGD and Value Derivation and Innovation

Given the user-centric focus of OGD initiatives wherein the value derivation and innovation pursuits are being emphasized upon for the improvization of products and services, it is pertinent to understand the potential impact of OGD for the same [6]. As such, OGD may be harnessed for value derivation and innovation by a range of amateur and professional stakeholders across diverse disciplines like economy, law, polity, and the like [24]. Value derivation and innovation via OGD re-use would result in economic value generation of a country as well [25]. Given the propensity of the users to engage in OGD re-use individually as well as in collaboration [26] via interoperability protocols [7]-case in point being the application of geographical data [27] or the public-private partnership for running the Smart City public services [28, 29], extant literature has underscored the need for providing training and development to the existing and potential stakeholders for facilitating value derivation and innovation [30]. Also, OGD literature has underscored the bottlenecks in the OGD-hinged value derivation processes and they may be linked with the individual/organizational, contextual/environmental, technical/systemic issues [31, 32].

2.3 Gender and Technology Adoption

Gender differences exist in terms of the propensity of technology adoption and usage [33]. For instance, ICT usage among the university students has been found to be determined by gender, socio-economic status and the availability of requisite ICT platforms [34–36]. Likewise, it has been attested that males-in comparison with the females- are more comfortable with the ICT [35, 37, 38, 39]. For instance, in the typical higher education setting, it was attested that e-learning format was adopted and used differently among the male and female students [40, 41]. In another context, it was found that females were more adept and comfortable in adopting smark locking systems [42]. In another instance, females-in contrast with the males- were comfortable in adopting and using the m-Health technologies [43]. Even in the context of e-government adoption, females -in comparison with the males- were particular about the adoption of such technologies [44]. Apart from these cases, there were instances where the gender differences across technology adoption and usage were not registered-case in point being the computers [45] or mobile commerce platforms [46].

As far as the specific case of OGD adoption is concerned, only two studies have attested their results: in the Indian case, males were found to be more inclined towards OGD adoption and usage [47] and in the other study involving the stakeholders, there was no gender difference at all [48].

2.4 Research Objectives

It is clear from the aforesaid that an understanding of the role of KS in the specific case of OGD technology adoption and usage is pertinent. Therefore, the research objective of the present study is to understand the influence of trust and quality dimensions for KS behaviors.

3 Research Methodology

3.1 Research Model and Hypotheses

The research model for the study is presented in Fig. 1 and Table 1 presents a summary of the hypotheses being tested. It is clear that as far as the four constructs of Trust, Information Quality, Data Quality and System Quality are concerned, OGD-focused research has attested differential findings. Trust has been attested as important for OGD adoption [49–52] but opposite results were obtained in terms of trust on data and system in another case [53]. Users' demand of Data Quality is a function of their methods of data acquisition along with the 'help' functions (i.e. user guide webpage, FAQ webpage, etc.) [54]. Furthermore, System Quality and Information Quality are considered to be significant determinantss of OGD adoption [55]. However, in another case, System Quality but not Information Quality had direct significant connotations for OGD adoption [50, 51].

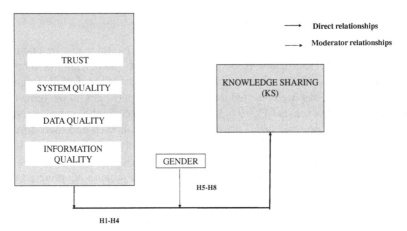

Fig. 1. Research model

Table 1. Hypotheses for the study

Construct	Definition	Reference	Hypothesis
Trust (T)	The extent to which OGD is considered to be trustworthy, credible and reliable by the users	[51]	H1: Trust has a positive effect on KS
Information quality (IQ)	The extent to which the characteristics of the output offered by the information system are accurate, timely and complete	[55, 56] IS-Success model	H2: Information Quality has a positive effect on KS
Data quality (DQ)	The extent to which OGD are free from errors, complete, accurate, appropriately formatted as per standards and ready for reuse	[57] IS-Success model	H3: Data Quality has a positive effect on KS
System quality (SQ)	The extent to which the performance of the information system are reliable, convenient, easy to use and equipped with the requisite functionality and other system metrics	[55, 56, 57] IS-Success model	H4: System Quality has a positive effect on KS

(continued)

Table 1. (*continued*)

Construct	Definition	Reference	Hypothesis
Moderating variable	Definition	Hypothesis	
Gender (Gender)	The extent to which the gender of the user impacts the KS behaviors vis-a-vis OGD	H5-H8: Gender has a moderating impact on the Trust, Information Quality, Data Quality, System Quality constructs-KS relationships such that they are positively strengthened for the males in comparison with the females	

3.2 Data Collection

Data collection phase ran from December, 2022 and March, 2023. Graduate and post-graduate students of a prominent Indian university were solicited to share their responses (n ~ 397). Table 2 provides a gist of the demographic profiles of the respondents. After ascertaining the respondents' actual OGD adoption, Google Form was shared with them via email or WhatsApp. Responses were registered across a Likert Scale (1-Strongly Agree and 5-Strongly Disagree). Statistical analysis was conducted via Warp PLS 8.0 software [58] wherein Partial Least Squares-Structural Equation Modelling (PLS-SEM) method [59] was adopted to assess the empirical relationships.

Table 2. Summary of demographic characteristics

Characteristic	Frequency	%	Characteristic	Frequency	%
Gender					
Male	197	49.62	Female	200	50.37
Age					
16–20 years	265	66.75	21–25 years	122	30.73
26–30 years	3	0.007	Above 30 years	7	0.017
Education					
Bachelor's	368	92.69	Master's/PhD's/PostDoc's	27	0.073
Field of Study					
Engineering	146	36.77	Humanities and Social Sciences	149	37.53
Law	12	3.02	Management/Commerce	35	8.81
Nursing/Medical	10	2.51	Hospitality/Hotel Management	24	6.62

(*continued*)

Table 2. (*continued*)

Characteristic	Frequency	%	Characteristic	Frequency	%
Other	41	10.57			
Year of Study					
1st year	121	30.47	2nd year	108	27.20
3rd year	135	34.00	4th year	24	0.060
5th year	1	0.002	Other	8	0.020
Perceived Importance of OGD					
Very Important	80	20.15	Important	189	47.60
Neutral	122	30.73	Unimportant	3	0.007
Very unimportant	3	0.007			
Usage Experience					
Daily or multiple times a day	46	11.58	Weekly or a few times in a week	134	33.75
Monthly or a few times in a month	99	24.93	Yearly or a few times in a year	43	10.83
Do not know	75	18.89			

4   Results

4.1   Measurement Model

The research model's ($R^2 = 0.469\%$) reliability was checked via Cronbach's alpha (α) and Composite reliability (CR) [60] (Hair et al., 2021). Also, Average Variance Extracted (AVE) was estimated for determining the convergent validity [60]. Across the three cases, the threshold criteria was fulfilled, i.e. $0.9 > \alpha > 0.778$; $0.955 > CR > 0.711$ and AVE > 0.50 (Table 3). Furthermore, multicollinearity diagnostics was run to ascertain the collinearity-free constructs and this condition was fulfilled given that the VIF values were less than 5 [60].

Table 3. Reliability validation for latent constructs.

Construct	Cronbach's alpha (α) [a]	Composite Reliability (CR) [b]	Average Variance Extracted (AVE) [c]	Variance Inflation Factor (VIF)	Construct	Cronbach's alpha (α) [a]	Composite Reliability (CR) [b]	Average Variance Extracted (AVE) [c]	Variance Inflation Factor (VIF)
Trust	0.899	0.899	0.833	2.570	Information Quality	0.826	0.896	0.742	2.936
Data Quality	0.861	0.861	0.706	3.532	System Quality	0.873	0.908	0.666	2.692

(*continued*)

Table 3. (*continued*)

Construct	Cronbach's alpha (α) [a]	Composite Reliability (CR) [b]	Average Variance Extracted (AVE) [c]	Variance Inflation Factor (VIF)	Construct	Cronbach's alpha (α) [a]	Composite Reliability (CR) [b]	Average Variance Extracted (AVE) [c]	Variance Inflation Factor (VIF)
Knowledge Sharing	0.772	0.772	0.805	1.819					

a. Cronbach's alpha should exceed 0.60.
b. Composite Reliabilities should exceed 0.60 but below 0.90.
c. Average Variance Extracted values should exceed 0.50.

Table 4. Hypotheses'decision summary

Constructs/Hypotheses	Path coefficients	Effect Size	p-value	Decision
TR-KS (H1)	0.303	0.179	< 0.001	**Supported**
IQ-KS (H2)	0.195	0.112	< 0.001	**Supported**
DQ-KS (H3)	0.010	0.005	0.424	Not supported
SQ-KS (H4)	0.260	0.153	< 0.001	**Supported**
GEN*TR-KS (H5)	0.065	0.017	0.098	Not supported
GEN*IQ-KS (H6)	0.072	0.019	0.075	Not supported
GEN*DQ-KS (H7)	-0.121	0.031	0.007*	**Supported**
GEN*SQ-KS (H8)	-0.115	0.025	0.010*	**Supported**

a. Sig. $*p < 0.05$.

4.2 Structural Model

Table 4 presents a summary of the path coefficients, effect sizes, T-statistics and the p-values vis-à-vis the hypothesized relationships. Among the direct relationships, it is clinched that Trust-KS, IQ-KS and SQ-KS relationships are supported and this is suggestive of the OGD adopters to perceive the affirmative stance of credible and reliable OGD and users' information quality seeking and system quality seeking propensities to have impact on knowledge sharing behaviors. Regarding the moderating impact, it is clear that males have a greater propensity of considering OGD's data quality and system quality to be pertinent for engaging in knowledge sharing behaviors.

5 Discussion

Findings from the study are in line with the previous research wherein OGD users seek trustworthy, credible and reliable OGD as the condition for furthering their OGD adoption and usage [49–52]. This is suggestive of the extended hypothesis tested in the present study wherein credible and reliable OGD furthers the knowledge sharing propensities among the users. As far as the impetus upon information quality is concerned, users' are found to be engaging in knowledge sharing behaviors as per our research findings and this is supportive of the previous research as well wherein information quality has been attested as important for furthering OGD adoption and usage [55]. Likewise, users' considering robust Data Quality has been attested to have significant bearing on OGD adoption and usage inclination [54] and this has been supported in the extended findings from our study wherein the males-in comparison with females- are considerate about OGD's Data Quality for furthering their knowledge sharing propensities. Finally, for the case of users' seeking system quality for furthering knowledge sharing with particular reference to the males, it has been shown that users consider the importance of seeking system quality for OGD adoption and usage too [55].

6   Conclusion

The present research sought to further our understanding of the manner in which trustworthy and quality parameters of OGD are influential for knowledge sharing behaviors among the OGD adopters. Contextualized in a developing country, i.e. India, wherein the university graduates and postgraduates (n ~ 397) were solicited to share their perspectives regarding their OGD interaction in line with the research aims, the study is the first one to plunge into the significance of knowledge sharing behaviors among the OGD adopters. Drawing inferences from an empirical assessment of the research model featuring hypotheses across Trust-KS, Information Quality-KS, Data Quality-KS, System Quality-KS apart from the moderating effect of gender on these relationships, it was attested that users consider the significance of trustworthy and credible OGD as also information quality and system quality for engaging in knowledge sharing behaviors. There was also attested difference across males and females regarding their engagement in knowledge sharing contingent upon their information quality and system quality seeking propensities.

Besides contributing to the extant OGD and KS literature in general, the study furthers our understanding of OGD engagement from the perspective of the users of a developing country. The study's limitations are in terms of the sample design wherein it has been attested that university students are not representative of the population [61], however, given the fact that academic community is considered as potential stakeholders in the OGD ecosystem, the representativeness of the sample stands clinched. For ensuring the generalibility of the findings, it is important that a more comparative stance be taken such that the replicability of the research model be attempted in other contexts across different stakeholders. Furthermore, it is pertinent to attempt a triangulation of the research findings wherein the experts' opinion be solicited regarding the other dimensions of knowledge sharing that may be empirically investigated in further research.

The study has social and practical implications too. Knowledge sharing across the OGD users would result in the furtherance of societal relationships and intellectual capitalism. Therefore, a knowledge economy might result on account of the intellectual exchange among the OGD adopters and users for furthering value derivation and innovation pursuits. Similarly, policy-makers stand to understand how the knowledge sharing behaviors might be furthered via the discussion forum and community engagement and dialogue during hackathons and fairs, etc. which calls for the institutionalization of OGD initiatives with state-of-the-art user-friendly OGD portals in place.

References

1. Gupta, B., Dasgupta, S., Gupta, A.: Adoption of ICT in a government organization in a developing country: an empirical study. J. Strateg. Inf. Syst. **17**(2), 140–154 (2008). https://doi.org/10.1016/j.jsis.2007.12.004
2. Safarov, I., Meijer, A., Grimmelikhuijsen, S.: Utilization of open government data: a systematic literature review of types, conditions, effects and users. Inf. Polity **22**(1), 1–24 (2017). https://doi.org/10.3233/IP-160012
3. Chen, T.Y.: The developmental state and its discontent: the evolution of the open government data policy in Taiwan. Third World Q. **43**(5), 1056–1073 (2022). https://doi.org/10.1080/01436597.2022.2042801
4. Nam, T.: Citizens' attitudes toward open government and government 2.0. Int. Rev. Adm. Sci. **78**(2), 346–368 (2012). https://doi.org/10.1177/0020852312438783
5. Chan, C.M.L.: From open data to open innovation strategies: creating e-services using open government data. In: 46th Hawaii International Conference on System Sciences, Wailea, HI, USA, pp. 1890–1899 (2013). https://doi.org/10.1109/HICSS.2013.236
6. Charalabidis, Y., Alexopoulos, C., Loukis, E.: A taxonomy of open government data research areas and topics. J. Organ. Comput. Electron. Commer. **26**(1–2), 41–63 (2016). https://doi.org/10.1080/10919392.2015.1124720
7. Jetzek, T., Avital, M., Bjorn-Andersem, N.: Data-driven innovation through open government data. J. Theor. Appl. Electron. Commer. Res. **9**(2), 100–120 (2012). https://doi.org/10.4067/S0718-18762014000200008
8. Chai, S., Das, S., Rao, H.R.: Factors affecting bloggers' knowledge sharing: an investigation across gender. J. Manag. Inf. Syst. **28**(3), 309–342 (2011). https://doi.org/10.2753/MIS0742-1222280309
9. Miller, D.L., Karakowsky, L.: Gender influences as an impediment to knowledge sharing: when men and women fail to seek peer feedback. J. Psychol. **139**(2), 101–118 (2005). https://doi.org/10.3200/JRLP.139.2.101-118
10. Moreno, E.F., Avila, M.M., Garcia-Conteras, R.: Can gender be a determinant of organizational performance and knowledge sharing in public sector organizations? AD-minister **32**, 137–160 (2018). https://doi.org/10.17230/ad-minister.32.6
11. Eid, M.I.M., Al-Jabri, I.M.: Social networking, knowledge sharing, and student learning: the case of university students. Comput. Educ. **99**, 14–27 (2016). https://doi.org/10.1016/j.compedu.2016.04.007
12. Kleine, D., Unwin, T.: Technological revolution, evolution and new dependencies: what's new about ICT4D? Third World Quarterly **30**(5), 1045–1067 (2009). https://doi.org/10.1080/01436590902959339
13. Al-Emran, M., Teo, T.: Do knowledge acquisition and knowledge sharing really affect e-learning adoption? An empirical study. Educ. Inf. Technol. **25**, 1983–1998 (2020). https://doi.org/10.1007/s10639-019-10062-w
14. Eid, M., Nuhu, N.A.: Impact of learning culture and information technology use on knowledge sharing of Saudi students. Knowl. Manag. Res. Pract. **9**(1), 48–57 (2011). https://doi.org/10.1057/kmrp.2010.25
15. Singh, J.B., Chandwani, R. Kumar, M.: Factors affecting Web 2.0 adoption: exploring the knowledge sharing and knowledge seeking aspects in health care professionals. J. Knowl. Manag. **22**(1), 21–43 (2018). https://doi.org/10.1108/JKM-08-2016-0320
16. Chen, I.Y.L., Chen, N.S., Kinshuk.: Examining the factors influencing participants' knowledge sharing behavior in virtual learning communities. Educ. Technol. Soc. **12**(1), 134–148 (2009). https://www.jstor.org/stable/jeductechsoci.12.1.134

17. Lee, M.K.O., Cheung, C.M.K., Lim, K.H., Ling Sia, C.: Understanding customer knowledge sharing in web-based discussion boards: an exploratory study. Internet Res. **16**(3), 289–303 (2006). https://doi.org/10.1108/10662240610673709

18. Paroutis, S., Al Saleh, A.: Determinants of knowledge sharing using Web 2.0 technologies. J. Knowl. Manag. **13**(4), 52–63 (2009). https://doi.org/10.1108/13673270910971824

19. Shim, J.P., Yang, J.: Why is wikipedia not more widely accepted in Korea and China? Factors affecting knowledge-sharing adoption. Decision Line, 12–15 (2009). https://citeseerx.ist.psu.edu/document?repid=rep1&type=pdf&doi=856c4330154b7a3a0b330fe4579fce300feaae2e

20. Tseng, S.M.: Investigating the moderating effects of organizational culture and leadership style on IT-adoption and knowledge-sharing intention. J. Enterp. Inf. Manag. **30**(4), 583–604 (2017). https://doi.org/10.1108/JEIM-04-2016-0081

21. Asghar, M.Z., Barbera, E., Rasool, S.F., Seitamaa-Hakkarainen, P., Mohelska, H.: Adoption of social media-based knowledge-sharing behaviour and authentic leadership development: evidence from the educational sector of Pakistan during COVID-19. J. Knowl. Manag. **27**(1), 59–83 (2023). https://doi.org/10.1108/JKM-11-2021-0892

22. Mc Evoy, P.J., Ragab, M.A.F., Arisha, A.: The effectiveness of knowledge management in the public sector. Knowl. Manag. Res. Pract. **17**(1), 39–51 (2019). https://doi.org/10.1080/14778238.2018.1538670

23. Pinjani, P., Palvia, P.: Trust and knowledge sharing in diverse global virtual teams. Inf. Manag. **50**(4), 144–153 (2013). https://doi.org/10.1016/j.im.2012.10.002

24. Ubaldi, B.: Open government data: Towards empirical analysis of open government data initiatives. OECD Working Papers on Public Governance, 22, OECD Publishing Press (2013). https://doi.org/10.1787/5k46bj4f03s7-en

25. Zeleti, F.A., Ojo, A., Curry, E.: Exploring the economic value of open government data. Gov. Inf. Q. **33**(3), 535–551 (2016). https://doi.org/10.1016/j.giq.2016.01.008

26. Harrison, T.M., et al.: Open government and e-government: democratic challenges from a public value perspective. In: 12th Annual International Digital Open Government Research Conference: Digital Government Innovation in Challenging Times, pp. 245–253 (2011). https://doi.org/10.1145/2037556.2037597

27. Geiger, C.P., von Lucke, J.: Open government and (linked) (open) (government) (data). J. eDemocracy **4**(2), 265–278 (2012). https://doi.org/10.29379/jedem.v4i2.143

28. Lodato, T., French, E., Clark, J.: Open government data in the smart city: interoperability, urban knowledge and linking legacy systems. J. Urban Aff. **43**(4), 586–600 (2021). https://doi.org/10.1080/07352166.2018.1511798

29. Pereira, G.V., Macadar, M.A., Luciano, E.M., Testa, M.G.: Delivering public value through open government data initiatives in a smart city context. Inf. Syst. Front. **19**, 213–229 (2017). https://doi.org/10.1007/s10796-016-9673-7

30. Gasco-Hernandez, M., Martin, E.G., Reggi, L., Pyo, S., Luna-Reyes, L.: Promoting the use of open government data: cases of training and engagement. Gov. Inf. Q. **35**(2), 233–242 (2018). https://doi.org/10.1016/j.giq.2018.01.003

31. Martin, C.: Barriers to the open government data agenda: taking a multi-level perspective. Policy Internet **6**(3), 217–240 (2014). https://doi.org/10.1002/1944-2866.POI367

32. Zuiderwijk, A., Shinde, R., Janssen, M.: Investigating the attainment of open government data objectives: is there a mismatch between objectives and results? Int. Rev. Adm. Sci. **85**(4), 645–672 (2019). https://doi.org/10.1177/0020852317739115

33. Venkatesh, V., Morris, M.G., Ackerman, P.L.: A longitudinal field investigation of gender differences in individual technology adoption decision-making processes. Organ. Behav. Hum. Decis. Process. **83**(1), 33–60 (2000). https://doi.org/10.1006/obhd.2000.2896

34. Lee, Y.H., Wu, J.Y.: The effect of individual differences in the inner and outer states of ICT on engagement in online reading activities and PISA 2009 reading literacy: exploring the

relationship between the old and new reading literacy. Learn. Individ. Differ. **22**(3), 336–342 (2012). https://doi.org/10.1016/j.lindif.2012.01.007

35. Livingstone, S.: Critical reflections on the benefits of ICT in education. Oxf. Rev. Educ. **38**(1), 9–24 (2012). https://doi.org/10.1080/03054985.2011.577938

36. Tomte, C., Hatlevik, O.E.: Gender-differences in self-efficacy ICT related to various ICT-user profiles in Finland and Norway. how do self-efficacy, gender and ICT-user profiles relate to findings from PISA 2006. Comput. Educ. **57**(1), 1416–1424 (2006). https://doi.org/10.1016/j.compedu.2010.12.011

37. Notten, N., Kraaykamp, G.: Parents and the media: a study of social differentiation in parental media socialization. Poetics **37**(3), 185–200 (2009). https://doi.org/10.1016/j.poetic.2009.03.001

38. Peter, J., Valkenburg, P.M.: Research note: individual differences in perceptions of Internet communication. Eur. J. Commun. **21**(2), 213–226 (2006). https://doi.org/10.1177/0267323105064046

39. Xiao, F., Sun, L.: Profiles of student ICT use and their relations to background, motivational factors, and academic achievement. J. Res. Technol. Educ. **54**(3), 456–472 (2022). https://doi.org/10.1080/15391523.2021.1876577

40. Park, C.W., Kim, D.G., Cho, S., Han, H.J.: Adoption of multimedia technology for learning and gender difference. Comput. Hum. Behav. **92**, 288–296 (2019). https://doi.org/10.1016/j.chb.2018.11.029

41. Wongwatkit, C., Panjaburee, P., Srisawasdi, N., Seprum, P.: Moderating effects of gender differences on the relationships between perceived learning support, intention to use, and learning performance in a personalized e-learning. J. Comput. Educ. **7**(2), 229–255 (2020). https://doi.org/10.1007/s40692-020-00154-9

42. Stanislav, M., Raquel, B.F.: Unlocking the smart home: exploring key factors affecting the smart lock adoption intention. Inf. Technol. People **34**(2), 835–861 (2021). https://doi.org/10.1108/ITP-07-2019-0357

43. Hoque, M.R.: An empirical study of mHealth adoption in a developing country: the moderating effect of gender concern. BMC Med. Inf. Decis. Mak. **16**, 1–10 (2016). https://doi.org/10.1186/s12911-016-0289-0

44. Al-Zaharani, L., Al-Karaghouli, W., Weerakkody, V.: Investigating the impact of citizens' trust toward the successful adoption of e-government: A multigroup analysis of gender, age, and internet experience. Inf. Syst. Manag. **35**(2), 124–146 (2018). https://doi.org/10.1080/10580494.2018.1440730

45. Al-Share, K., Grandon, E., Miller, D.: Antecedents of computer technology usage: considerations of the technology acceptance model in the academic environment. J. Comput. Sci. Coll. **19**(4), 164–180 (2004). https://doi.org/10.5555/1050231.1050254

46. Li, S., Glass, R., Records, H.: The influence of gender on new technology adoption and use-mobile commerce. J. Internet Commer. **7**(2), 270–289 (2008). https://doi.org/10.1080/15332860802067748

47. Saxena, S., Janssen, M.: Examining open government data (OGD) usage in India through UTAUT framework. Foresight **19**(4), 421–436 (2017). https://doi.org/10.1108/FS-02-2017-0003

48. Zuiderwijk, A., Janssen, M., Dwivedi, Y.K.: Acceptance and use predictors of open data technologies: drawing upon the unified theory of acceptance and use of technology. Gov. Inf. Q. **32**(4), 429–440 (2015). https://doi.org/10.1016/j.giq.2015.09.005

49. Fitriani, W.R., Hidayanto, A.N., Sandhyaduhita, P.I., Purwandari, B.: Determinants of intention to use open data website: An insight from Indonesia. In: PACIS 2017 Proceedings, p. 234 (2017). https://aisel.aisnet.org/pacis2017/234

50. Krismawati, D., Hidayanto, A.N.: The user engagement of open data portal. In: International Conference on Advanced Computer Science and Information Systems (ICACSIS), pp. 1–6 (2021). https://doi.org/10.1109/ICACSIS53237.2021.9631357

51. Lnenicka, M., Nikiforova, A., Saxena, S., Singh, P.: Investigation into the adoption of open government data among students: the behavioural intention-based comparative analysis of three countries. Aslib J. Inf. Manag. **74**(3), 549–567 (2022). https://doi.org/10.1108/AJIM-08-2021-0249

52. Zuiderwijk, A., Cligge, M.: The acceptance and use of open data infrastructures- Drawing upon UTAUT and ECT. In: Scholl, H.J., et al. (eds.) Electronic Government and Electronic Participation, pp. 91–98 (2016). https://doi.org/10.3233/978-1-61499-670-5-91

53. Subedi, R., Nyamasvisva, T.E., Pokharel, M.: An integrated-based framework for open government data adoption in Kathmandu. Webology **19**(2), 7936–7961 (2022). http://www.web ology.org/

54. Wang, D., Richards, D., Chen, C.: An analysis of interaction between users and open government data portals in data acquisition process. In: Yoshida, K., Lee, M., (eds.), Knowledge Management and Acquisition for Intelligent Systems: 15th Pacific Rim Knowledge Acquisition Workshop, 184-200. Springer Nature (2018). https://doi.org/10.1007/978-3-319-97289-3_14

55. Talukder, M.S., Shen, L., Talukder, M.F.H., Bao, Y.: Determinants of user acceptance and use of open government data (OGD): an empirical investigation in Bangladesh. Technol. Soc. **56**, 147–156 (2019). https://doi.org/10.1016/j.techsoc.2018.09.013

56. DeLone, W.H., McLean, E.R.: The DeLone and McLean model of information systems success: a ten-year update. J. Manag. Inf. Syst. **19**(4), 9–30 (2003). https://doi.org/10.1080/074 21222.2003.11045748

57. Purwanto, A., Zuiderwijk-van Eijk, A., Janssen, M.: Citizens' motivations for engaging in open data hackathons. In: Panagiotopoulos, P., et al. (eds.) Electronic Participation - 11th IFIP WG 8.5 International Conference, ePart 2019, Proceedings, pp. 130–141. Lecture Notes in Computer Science (including subseries Lecture Notes in Artificial Intelligence and Lecture Notes in Bioinformatics, 11686 LNCS, Springer (2019). https://doi.org/10.1007/978-3-030-27397-2_11

58. Kock, N.: WarpPLS User Manual: Version 7.0. Laredo, TX: ScriptWarp Systems (2021)

59. Wold, H.: Partial least squares. Encyclopedia of Statistical Sciences. https://doi.org/10.1002/0471667196.ess1914

60. Hair, J.F., Hult, G.T.M., Ringle, C.M., Sarstedt, M.: A primer on partial least squares structural equation modeling (PLS-SEM) (2016). http://hdl.handle.net/11420/4083

61. Landers, R.N., Behrend, T.S.: An inconvenient truth: arbitrary distinctions between organizational, mechanical Turk, and other convenience samples. Ind. Organ. Psychol. **8**(2), 142–164 (2015). https://doi.org/10.1017/iop.2015.13

Usability Evaluation of an Intelligent Mobile Chatbot for Crop Farmers

Patience U. Usip[1,2](✉) ⓘ, Otobong R. James[3], Daniel E. Asuquo[1,2] ⓘ,
Edward N. Udo[1,2] ⓘ, and Francis B. Osang[3]

[1] Department of Computer Science, Faculty of Science, University of Uyo, Uyo, Nigeria
patienceusip@uniuyo.edu.ng
[2] TETFund Center of Excellence in Computational Intelligence Research, University of Uyo, Uyo, Nigeria
[3] Computer Science Department, National Open University of Nigeria, Abuja, Nigeria

Abstract. The need for a mobile chatbot for crop farmers has been established by many as one major contributor to the sustainable development goals. Most of these chatbots adopt machine learning (ML) approaches. We previously developed a chabot with the ontology-based representation of domain knowledge along with word shuffling and ML-based Jacquard Similarity algorithm. However, its usability evaluation was not considered. This paper aims at evaluating the effectiveness of the developed mobile chatbot through a usability testing method called the Think-aloud Protocol. Using this approach, participants in testing express their thoughts on the application with ontology-based representation while executing set tasks. The users who had the chatbot already running, query the chatbot with randomly selected thirty (30) questions asked in different ways. The result of the experiment shows that twenty-five (25) questions were answered correctly. The user's intent was also considered. The percentage of accuracy of the chatbot is calculated to be 83.3%. The usability evaluation of the developed chatbot gives an acceptable satisfactory average score of 78.5%, being a clear indication that the chatbot is perceived positively and liked by the users as it is efficient, effective, user-friendly, flexible and easy to use. The chatbot usability evaluation results can guide decision makers on the right policies that will affect farmers positively through quality agricultural services for improved agricultural productivity and food security.

Keywords: Usability testing · Mobile chatbot · Crop farming · Food security · ML algorithm

1 Introduction

This paper is an extension of our work in [1] which was originally presented in Electronic Governance with Emerging Technology Conference in 2021. An intelligent mobile chatbot application was developed with the aim to assist farmers to answer farming related questions. Agricultural sector is one of the primary sectors that contribute to the economic development of developing countries and most countries depend on agriculture

F. Ortiz-Rodríguez et al. (Eds.): EGETC 2023, CCIS 1888, pp. 101–111, 2023.
https://doi.org/10.1007/978-3-031-43940-7_9

for their Gross Domestic Product (GDP) growth [2]. There are a lot of factors that can hinder the growth of agriculture in developing countries thus by extension impede the achievement of its major goal. One of such factors is the inaccessibility to effective question answering system as experienced by most farmers in Nigeria; a problem that called for the development of mobile chatbot for crop farmers [1].

Prior to the usability test of the chatbot developed in Usip et al. [1], the farmers were told to install the chatbot in their smart phones and use it to ask any form of question regarding cassava farming. The usability evaluation of the chatbot was done using chatbot Usability Scale developed by Brooke in 1996 [3] and modified to fit the proposed system. This system usability scale (SUS) computes the score for even and odd numbered questionnaire items differently. In summary, it computes the SUS score for each participant, averaging the score over all participants in order to obtain the final SUS score out of 100.

Usability has been defined as a measurement of systems' or products' effectiveness, efficiency, and satisfaction [4]. It refers to an assessment to measure the quality level and the overall views of a system by the users of the systems [5]. Furthermore, usability is defined by ISO 9241–11 as "the extent to which a product can be used by specified users to achieve specified goals with effectiveness, efficiency and satisfaction in a specified context of use" [6]. Usability is a quality attribute that looks at software product usage. A product has no intrinsic usability; it has a capability to be used in a particular context.[7]. Usability has five quality components, namely, learnability, efficiency, memorability, errors and satisfaction.

The term chatbot indicates a robot that can talk and allow interactions between humans and machines [8]. With natural language processing, human language can be communicated and represented in computer understandable language. In the context of the proposed system, the farmers interact with the chatbot through his natural language (English). The interaction can be any kind of queries, clarification, and suggestions required for increasing crop production.

Inaccessibility to effective question answering system is one major problem experienced by most farmers in Nigeria. This limited access to agricultural information was observed as a major factor that has adversely affected agricultural development in Nigeria [9]. Hence, the need for an efficient question answering system that works as a smart search engine generating answers for user's queries and serving as an information retrieval assistant for the user. The efficiency of the mobile chatbot developed by [1] has not been determined using any standard metric. This paper is aimed at determining the usability evaluation of the chatbot by various farmers who had the chatbot running on their mobile phones. Usability testing or evaluation is an assessment method adopted to measure the degree an interactive system is easy to use with a view to identifying usability problems and/or the collection of usability metrics [10].

This paper is organized as follows. The next section gives related literatures on the set task. Section 3 gives the ontological representation of the chatbot that aids in semantic retrieval by crop farmers. Section 4 describes the usability evaluation of the chatbot. Section 5 shows the results and discussion of the usability evaluation and the conclusion of the paper is as given in Sect. 6.

2 Related Literature

Many authors have developed chatbots to assist farmers in one way or the other. Usability and satisfaction testing was carried out on some while such testing was not done on others. There are four classes of usability evaluation methods namely usability evaluation through evaluation software, usability testing by evaluating the user interface by real system users, usability evaluation using models and formulas and usability evaluation based on rules of thumb and the general skill, knowledge and experience of the evaluators.

Santoso et al. [11] conducted usability testing for crop and farmer activity information system which was developed to record activities for farm fields in Indonesia in 2017.

Yashaswini et al. [12] developed a system to perform machine learning analysis on the parameters (weather, season, rainfall, type of soil) needed to increase farmers' yield. The system was trained using historic data to suggest which crops to grow and the crop mix that can grow together (what was the result?).

Ekanayake and Saputhanthri [13] developed a chatroom and chatbot to discuss the prevailing issues related to farming with intents which the user might want to know and examples to explain specific intents and entities. Artificial Intelligence Markup Language (AIML) was used to train the model.

Kaviya et al. [14] developed automatic talkbot to answer questions without human assistance. The talkbot was trained using Naïve Bayes algorithm (what was the result?).

Herrera et al. [15] designed a chatbot model called Milchbot used to provide information about the planning, feeding and care processes of dairy cows, as well as to provide news, and to display frequently asked questions. To evaluate the usability and satisfaction of the Milchbot, an instrument of 10 questions was used: five questions about usability, three about satisfaction and two others, based on the User Experience Questionnaire (UEQ) and applied through Google Forms to the participants. The results of the usability and satisfaction surveys show a high rating for both livestock producers and zootechnicians.

Adesina [18] developed a web-based virtual assistant chatbot to provide human-like responses to academic and general questions about the National Open University of Nigeria for text and voice input. A user-experience survey was administered using Think Aloud Usability Testing.

Ren et al. [19] conducted a systematic mapping study to identify the research questions, characteristics, and metrics used to evaluate the usability of chatbots in experiments. Effectiveness, efficiency, and satisfaction were usability characteristics used to identify how well users can learn and use chatbots to achieve their goals and how satisfied users were during the interaction.

Safitri et al. [20] conducted a study to see how useful Chatbot technology media is as a pedagogical support. This was done by quantitative method of data collection using a questionnaire containing questions about the usability system (SUS).

The usability of chatbots deployed in other areas like education, healthcare and business have been evaluated. This work is intended to evaluate the usability of the mobile chatbot for crop farmers shown in Fig. 1.

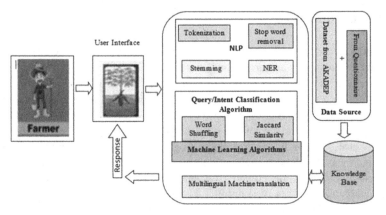

Fig. 1. A mobile chatbot for crop farmers [1]

3   Mobile Chatbot Ontology

The domain knowledge stored in the mobile ontology is as shown in Fig. 2 with the corresponding class hierarchy with ontograf from protégé in Fig. 3. The ontology includes concepts, sub-concepts and relations including farmer, query, answer, mobile-phone, biodata, crops, etc.

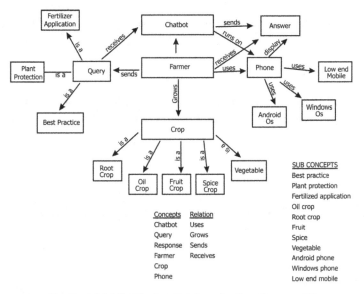

Fig. 2. A Mobile Chatbot Ontology for Crop Farmers [1]

From the mobile chatbot ontology, individuals for the sample farmers were viewed based on the type of crop they specialize in. Their usability evaluation result is also tied to their location, and the type of mobile phones they have. Age is another factor that

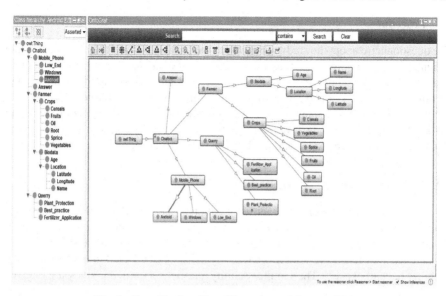

Fig. 3. Crop Chatbot Class Hierarchy and Ontograf [1]

is likely to affect their usability and all these were captured in the domain knowledge represented in the ontology. Instances used in the ontology are sample domain knowledge for demonstration purpose, as populating the ontology is ongoing.

4   System Usability Evaluation Method

Usability testing methods aim to evaluate the ease of use of a software product by its users. Existing methods are subjective and open to interpretation. Different studies attempt to determine the efficacy of each method and their adequacy to different subjects, comparing which one may be the most appropriate in fields like e-learning, e-commerce, or mobile applications. This study adopts the Think-aloud protocol because it is suitable at testing or release stage of the mobile application. It also takes into consideration usability issues of user satisfaction, efficiency, results accuracy and closeness to users' natural environment. Further, other advantages are that it is less expensive and results are close to what is experienced by users. A random selection of thirty (30) farmers from the selected villages/farming communities was made. This was made possible using the compiled name of farmers as obtained from Akwa Ibom State Agricultural Development Programmme (AKADEP). Time and cost were the basis for the sample size. However, assumptions about the population probability distribution were made using the central limit theorem, which states that, given a sufficiently large sample size ($n \geq 30$) from a population with a finite level of variance, the mean of all sampled variables from the same population will be approximately equal to the mean of the whole population [16]. The 30 participants were 10 female and 20 male and all participants were full time farmers.

4.1 Procedure

The questionnaire about the study was given to the participants and all participants were assigned identity numbers such as F1 for farmer number one, F2 for farmer number two, etc., for easy identification. The usability test of the chatbot lasted no longer than 30 min per session. Prior to the usability test of the chatbot, the farmers were told to install the chatbot in their smart phone and used it to ask any form of question regarding cassava farming. The usability evaluation of the chatbot was done using chatbot Usability Scale developed by Brooke[3] and modified to fit the proposed system.

4.2 System Usability Scale (SUS)

To evaluate the usability of the proposed chatbot, System Usability Scale (SUS) was used. The justification for the choice of this mechanism for evaluating the usability of the chatbot is because of its ease of use and capable of effectively distinguishing between a usable and non-usable system. More recently, it has been adapted in evaluation of the usability of chatbots [17]. The sample usability questions used in this study are as given in Fig. 4.

To be completed by farmer during and/or after using the chatbot

FARMER ID		Date:	

Instructions: For each of the following statements, mark one box that best describes your reactions to the chatbot on a scale of 1 to 5, with 1 being "**Strongly Disagree**" 2 "**Disagree**", 3 "**Neutral**", 4 "**Agree**" and 5 "**Strongly Agree**".

	1	2	3	4	5
1. I thought the Chatbot was easy to use	1	2	3	4	5
2. I think that I would like to use this Chatbot frequently	1	2	3	4	5
3. I found the Chatbot unnecessarily complex	1	2	3	4	5
4. I need the support of a technical person to be able to use this Chatbot	1	2	3	4	5
5. I found the various functions in this Chatbot were well integrated	1	2	3	4	5
6. I thought there was too much inconsistency in response from the Chatbot.	1	2	3	4	5
7. I would imagine that most people would learn to use this chatbot very quickly	1	2	3	4	5
8. I found the Chatbot very cumbersome to use	1	2	3	4	5
9. I felt very confident using the Chatbot	1	2	3	4	5
10. I needed to learn a lot of things before I could get going with this Chatbot	1	2	3	4	5

Fig. 4. Chatbot Usability Scale

(This questionnaire is based on the System Usability Scale (SUS), which was developed by John Brooke at Digital Equipment Corporation in 1996).

The questionnaire consists of ten (10) items with responses ranged from strongly agree to strongly disagree. Each response is assigned a value for the SUS score calculation. The breakdown of the points for each of the responses is as follows:

Strongly Agree: 5points

Agree: 4points

Neutral: 3points

Disagree: 2points

Strongly Disagree:1point

To calculate the SUS of the chatbot, the guidelines given by Brooke (1996) were adopted as follows:

Step 1: Add up the total score for all odd-numbered questions to get (X), then subtract 5 from the total to get A, i.e. [A $= \sum$X-5], where $x \in X$ are odd-numbered questions like Questions 1, 3, 5, 7, and 9.

Step 2: Add up the total score for all even-numbered questions to get (Y), and then subtract that total from 25 to get B, i.e. [B $= 25 - (\sum$Y)], where $y \in Y$ are even-numbered questions like Questions 2, 4, 6, 8, and 10.

Step 3: Add up the odd score and even score (A+B) and multiply the result by 2.5 to obtain the SUS score for each of the farmers i.e. [SUS $=$ (A+B)*2.5].

Step 4: Calculate the average of the SUS score to obtain the final SUS score out of 100.

5   Results and Discussion

From the experiment and scoring tabulation methodology deployed, the average SUS score of the proposed Chatbot was 78.5 out of 100 as shown in Table 1.

Information from usability.gov shows that an SUS score greater than or equals to 68 is considered average. Figure 5 gives an overview of the user perception of the proposed chatbot.

The user's evaluation of the proposed chatbot gives an acceptable and reasonable average of 78.5 score, this value is a clear indication of how the chatbot was perceived by the users in terms of how much a user likes or dislikes using it, and how simple it is to use.

5.1   Accuracy of Response Generation

To evaluate the effectiveness of the responses generated by the chatbot, a manual testing of the chatbot was conducted. Using this approach, the users randomly queried the chatbot with randomly selected thirty (30) questions asked in different ways. The result of the experiment shows that twenty-five (25) questions were answered correctly. If the user's intent is not found, the message: "I don't understand your question" "Please rephrase it" is triggered.

Table 1. System Usability Score of the chatbot

FARMERID	SUMX	SUMY	A = SUMX-5	B = 25-SUMY	(A + B)*2.5
F1	21	13	16	12	70
F2	22	10	17	15	80
F3	22	11	17	14	77.5
F4	25	10	20	15	87.5
F5	24	11	19	14	82.5
F6	19	10	14	15	72.5
F7	20	12	15	13	70
F8	20	10	15	15	75
F9	21	13	16	12	70
F10	21	10	16	15	77.5
F11	23	12	18	13	77.5
F12	24	14	19	11	75
F13	22	10	17	15	80
F14	24	11	19	14	82.5
F15	21	10	16	15	77.5
F16	24	12	19	13	80
F17	24	14	19	11	75
F18	21	13	16	12	70
F19	25	11	20	14	85
F20	25	13	20	12	80
F21	22	11	17	14	77.5
F22	25	11	20	14	85
F23	25	10	20	15	87.5
F24	25	10	20	15	87.5
F25	25	13	20	12	80
				AVERAGE SUS	**78.5**

The percentage of accuracy of the chatbot is calculation as follows:

$$Accuracy = \frac{Total\ number\ of\ questions\ tested}{Total\ number\ of\ correct\ responses\ generated} \times 100 \quad (1)$$

$$= \frac{30}{25} \times 100 = 83.3 \quad (2)$$

Therefore, the accuracy of the proposed chatbot = 83.3%.

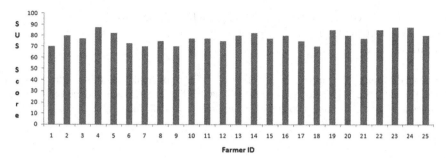

Fig. 5. Chatbot usability score by farmers

5.2 Discussions

This work develops an intelligent mobile based chatbot application aimed at assisting farmers to answer farming related questions. Chatbots have great potential to act as an extension officer while providing the user with a pleasant experience due to its efficiency, effectiveness and usability. The results of the above experiment indicate that most of the participants interacted with a chatbot for the first time, but they found the chatbot as usable source of obtaining useful answers to related farming questions. It was also observed that farmers showed trust in the information given by Chatbot as most of the participants (users) expressed willingness to frequently use the chatbot as means to enhance their information needs as indicated by the SUS score of 78.5. Besides, the chatbot also simplifies decision-making process and automates means of obtaining useful answers to questions on specific farming problems as indicated by the value of the SUS score.

Finally, the proposed chatbot achieved the aim that was set for the project, as it provides a solution to automate the process of the conversation and provides a real time question answering system for crop farmer in the study area. From the testing result, the chatbot answered correctly 25 of the 30 questions representing 83.3% accuracy. The SUS of the chatbot gives an acceptable and reasonable average of 78.5 score, which clearly indicates the user perception of the chatbot. Further analysis shows that the percentage accuracy of the chatbot increased with increased in the size of the training data used in training the chatbot. It was also observed that for most of the input questions given, the system generates good and accurate responses.

6 Conclusion

The usability of the mobile chatbot for crop farmers is evaluated in this paper. The results of the testing experiments conducted using Think-aloud protocol show that most of the participants interacted with a chatbot for the first time, but they found the chatbot as usable source of obtaining useful answers to related farming questions. During testing, the participants were able to express their thoughts on the application while executing set tasks. The chatbot answered correctly 25 of the 30 questions representing 83.3% accuracy. The SUS of the chatbot gives an acceptable and reasonable average of 78.5 score, which clearly indicates the user perception of the chatbot. It was also observed that farmers showed trust in the information given by Chatbot as most of the participants (users) expressed willingness to frequently use the chatbot as means to enhance their information needs.

Acknowledgement. The authors are grateful to TETFund for supporting this research through the TETFund Centre of Excellence in Computational Intelligence Research and the University of Uyo Management for creating a conducive environment for conducting the research.

References

1. Usip, P. U., Udo, E. N., Asuquo, D. E., James, O.R.: A machine learning-based mobile Chatbot for crop farmers. In: Ortiz-Rodríguez, F., et al. (Eds.): Electronic Governance with Emerging Technologies (EGETC 2022), CCIS 1666, pp. 1–20 (2022). https://doi.org/10.1007/978-3-031-22950-3_15
2. Vijayalakshmi, J., PandiMeena, K.: Agriculture TalkBot using AI. In: International Journal of Recent Technology and Engineering (IJRTE) ISSN: 2277 – 3878, Volume-8, Issue-2S5. Published By: Blue Eyes Intelligence Engineering & Sciences Publication, pp. 1–2 (2019)
3. Brooke, D., Taylor, C., Gunn, J., Maden, A.: Point prevalence of mental disorder in unconvicted male prisoners in England and Wales. BMJ **313**(7071), 1524–1527 (1996)
4. Chiew, T., Salim, S.: WEBUSE: website usability evaluation tool. Malays. J. Comput. Sci. **16**(1), 47–57 (2003)
5. Mvungi, J., Tossy, T.: Usability evaluation method and principle for the web. Int. J. Comput. Sci. Softw. Eng. **4**(7), 165–171 (2015)
6. World Bank. Strengthening Agricultural Extension and Advisory Systems: Procedures for Assessing, Transferring and Evaluating Extension Systems. A discussion paper. P3 (2016)
7. Bevan, N.: International standards for HCI and usability. Int. J. Hum. Comput. Stud. **55**(4), 533–552 (2001)
8. Nwachukwu. I.: Agricultural Communication: Principles and Practice. Lambhouse Publishers, Nigeria (2005)
9. Herrera. K., Miranda, J., Mauricio: DMilchbot: app to support the process of feeding and caring for dairy cows in Peru. AGRIS On-line Papers Econ. Inform. **14**(4), 27–37 (2022). https://doi.org/10.7160/aol.2022.140403
10. EL-firjani, N., Elberkawi, E., Maatuk, A.: A method for website usability evaluation: a comparative analysis. Int. J. Web Seman. Technol. **8**(3), 1–11 (2017)
11. Santoso, H., Wilbowo, A., Delima, R., Listyaningsih, E.: Usability testing for crop and farmer activity information system. Int. J. Adv. Comput. Sci. Appl. **9**(11), 147–158 (2018)
12. Yashaswini, D., Hemalatha, R., Niveditha, G.: Smart chatbot for agriculture. Int. J. Eng. Sci. Comput. **9**(5), 22203–22205 (2019)
13. Ekanayake, J., Saputhanthri, L.: E-AGRO: intelligent Chat-Bot IoT and artificial intelligence to enhance farming industry. AGRIS on-line Papers Econ. Inform. **12**(1), 15–21 (2020). https://doi.org/10.7160/aol.2020.120102
14. Kaviya, P., Bhavyashree, M., Krishnan, M., Sugacini, M.: Artificial intelligence based farmer assistant chatbot. Int. J. Res. Eng. Sci. Manage. **4**(4), 26–29 (2021)
15. Islam, M.: Sample size and its role in Central Limit Theorem (CLT). Comput. Appl. Math. J **4**(1), 1–7 (2018)
16. Cockton, G.: Usability Evaluation. The Encyclopedia of Human-Computer Interaction, 2nd Ed.15. (2014). https://www.interaction-design.org/literature/book/theencyclopedia-of-human-computer-interaction-2nd-ed/usability-evaluation

17. Coperich, K., Cudney, E., Nembhard, H.: Continuous improvement study of chatbot technologies using a human factors methodology. In: Proceedings of the 2017 Industrial and Systems Engineering Conference (2017)

18. Adesina, A.: iNOUN: architecture and usability of a chatbot for academic enquiries. West Afr J. Open Flexible Learn **10**(1), 1–21 (2021)

19. Ren, R., Zapata, M., Catro, J.W., Dieste, O., Acuna, S.T.: Experimentation for chatbot usability evaluation: a secondary study. IEEE Access **10**, 12430–12464 (2022). https://doi.org/10.1109/ACCESS.2022.3145323

20. Safitri, F., Hardini, T. I., Setiadi, R., and Mutiarsih, Y.: Usability measurement: chatbot as a pedagogical support for learning French grammar. In Proceedings of the Fifth International Conference on Language, Literature, Culture, and Education (ICOLLITE 2021), Advances in Social Science, Education and Humanities Research, vol. 595, pp. 272–276 (2021)

Comparative Analysis of E-Government Website Performances of European Countries Using Dynamic Grey Relational Analysis

Bilal Ervural$^{(\boxtimes)}$

Necmettin Erbakan University, 42090 Konya, Turkey
bervural@erbakan.edu.tr

Abstract. In the contemporary digital era, the pivotal role of information and communication technologies (ICT) in societal transformation and the revolutionization of public services cannot be underestimated. E-government, a manifestation of ICT, has profoundly influenced the efficiency and accessibility of governmental services, rendering them more user-friendly and convenient for citizens. Recognizing the crucial significance of realizing public services through ICT, governments worldwide are persistently engaged in enhancing their e-government initiatives. This study aims to evaluate the present state of countries in the digital society and provide insights into the performance of their e-government websites. A novel approach combining dynamic grey relational analysis (DGRA) and CRITIC methods is employed to establish a robust framework for evaluating and comparing the performance of e-government websites. Using the DGRA method, this study meticulously analyzes countries' e-government website performance, providing a detailed evaluation of their interrelationships and relative strengths and weaknesses in the digital domain. The research aims to offer valuable insights to policymakers, government officials, and public sector stakeholders. The findings have the potential to inform decision-making processes, enabling countries to identify areas for improvement, replicate successful strategies, and enhance their overall e-government capabilities.

Keywords: E-Government Websites · Grey Relational Analysis · Performance Analysis

1 Introduction

Information and communication technologies (ICT) are crucial in transforming societies and revolutionizing public services in today's digital era [1]. The advent of e-government has significantly impacted the efficiency and accessibility of governmental services, making them more convenient and user-friendly for citizens [2]. Recognizing the importance of realizing public benefits through ICT, governments continually strive to enhance their e-government initiatives.

While accessibility is an essential factor determining the quality of an e-government website, previous studies have reported accessibility problems in e-government websites

© The Author(s), under exclusive license to Springer Nature Switzerland AG 2023
F. Ortiz-Rodríguez et al. (Eds.): EGETC 2023, CCIS 1888, pp. 112–124, 2023.
https://doi.org/10.1007/978-3-031-43940-7_10

[3]. Accessibility and usability analyses for different countries exist in the literature. For example, Paul [3] presents the accessibility evaluation of Indian e-government websites using a sample of 65 websites of various ministries based on the Web Content Accessibility Guidelines (WCAG) standard. Similarly, Paul and Das [4] investigate the accessibility and usability of e-government websites in India. Another study [5] presents an Algerian and UK comparison for e-government usability evaluation. When the studies were analyzed, no study compared the e-government website performance of various countries.

This study attempts to address the existing gaps in the literature by comparing the performance of e-government websites in the context of European Countries. This study has been conducted to assess the current state of countries in the digital society and shed light on their e-government website performance. The study employs a novel approach that combines dynamic grey relational analysis (DGRA) and CRITIC methods, providing a robust framework to evaluate and compare the performance of e-government websites. The proposed approach utilizes data from Eurostat, the statistical office of the European Union, which serves as a reliable benchmark for measuring the performance of countries' e-government websites. Specifically, seven key indicators have been selected from the "Digital Economy and Society" database, a valuable resource periodically published under the ICT heading. These indicators serve as essential metrics to gauge the effectiveness and efficiency of e-government implementation.

With the application of the DGRA method, the study examines and analyzes the performance of countries in terms of their e-government websites. This method enables a detailed evaluation of the relationships and similarities among countries, shedding light on their relative strengths and weaknesses in the digital realm. By delving into the intricacies of countries' e-government website performance, this study aims to provide valuable insights for policymakers, government officials, and stakeholders in the public sector. The findings from this research endeavor have the potential to inform decision-making processes, allowing countries to identify areas for improvement, replicate successful strategies, and enhance their overall e-government capabilities.

The significance of robust e-government initiatives cannot be overstated as the world becomes increasingly interconnected and digitalized. This study is a valuable contribution to the ongoing discourse on leveraging ICT for public service delivery, emphasizing the need for continuous evaluation and enhancement of e-government websites. By harnessing the power of information and communication technologies, countries can propel themselves toward a more inclusive, efficient, and citizen-centric digital society.

The structure of this paper is as follows: Sect. 2 gives fundamental information on indicators. Section 3 provides a concise overview of the DGRA method. In Sect. 4, the application is presented to measure the performances of countries; also, results are discussed. Lastly, Sect. 5 concludes the study.

2   Indicators for Measuring E-Government Website Performance

In the proposed approach, the data provided by Eurostat, the statistical office of the European Union, was used to measure the performance of the e-government sites of the countries. Seven indicators were selected from the "Digital Economy and Society" database, published periodically under the title of E-government [6]. Explanations and examples of the indicators are presented in Table 1.

Table 1. Indicators used in the proposed methodology

	Indicator	Type	Explanations	
C1	Inaccessibility	–	Not able to access the service on a smartphone or tablet	non-compatible device version or non-available applications
C2	Perfection	+	no issue when using a website or app of public authorities	
C3	Technical problems	–	Technical problems experienced when using a website	long loading, the website crashed
C4	Other problems	–	Other issues	
C5	Unidentification	–	Problems in using the electronic signature or electronic identification	
C6	Complexity	–	The website or app was difficult to use	not user-friendly, the wording was not clear, the procedure was not well explained
C7	Payment problems	–	Not able to pay via the website or app	due to a lack of access to the payment methods required

Inaccessibility, perfection, technical problems, other problems, unidentification, complexity and payment problems were used as key indicators in this study. Perfection is a benefit criterion while the others are cost-based criteria.

3 Dynamic Grey Relational Analysis

Grey Relational Analysis (GRA) is an essential component of the grey system theory knowledge base. Grey system theory was initially proposed by Deng [7]. Subsequently, GRA models have been widely applied to various fields, such as selecting suppliers [8], optimization of process parameters [9], analysis of performance [10], etc.

Deng's GRA model is a technique used for absolute measurement evaluation. The primary process of GRA involves translating the performance of various alternatives into a comparability sequence, referred to as grey relational generating. Based on these sequences, a reference sequence often called the ideal target sequence, is established. Subsequently, the grey relational coefficient is computed between each comparability sequence and the reference sequence. Finally, the grey relational grade is calculated between the reference and comparability sequences using these grey relational coefficients. If a comparability sequence derived from an alternative exhibits the highest grey relational grade with the reference sequence, then that particular alternative is deemed the optimal choice [11].

To enhance the precision and accuracy of Deng's GRA model, Javed et al. [12] proposed the Dynamic Grey Relational Analysis (DGRA) model. This model aims to deal with the limitations of the static nature of the Distinguishing Coefficient in Deng's GRA model. We assume that the alternatives are demonstrated as $x_1, x_2, ..., x_i, ..., x_m$ and are evaluated by n criteria. The importance level of criterion j is denoted by $w(j)$; $x_i(j)$ is the performance value for alternative x_i concerning criterion j. If $X_0 = (x_0(1), x_0(2), ..., x_0(n))$ is an ideal (reference) data set, then the Grey Relational Grade (GRG) ensures an estimate of the correlation between the corresponding points of the ideal data and current data. This grey correlation is a function of four factors, three of which are constant. These are the following factors:

- $|x_0(j) - x_i(j)|$ - *Absolute Difference* between ideal and current data.
- $max_i\ max_j\ |x_0(j) - x_i(j)|$ - the highest of all *Absolute Difference* values.
- $min_i\ min_j\ |x_0(j) - x_i(j)|$ - the lowest of all *Absolute Difference* values.
- ξ – the *Distinguishing Coefficient*.

The basic steps of the Dynamic Grey Relational Analysis method are as follows:

Step 1: Collect the data. The data collection step involves obtaining alternative scores, $x_i(j)$, and criteria weights, $w(j)$, for each criterion.

Alternatives	Criteria				
	c_1	...	c_j	...	c_n
	w_1	...	w_j	...	w_n
x_1	$x_1(1)$	...	$x_1(j)$	...	$x_1(n)$
$\vdots$	$\vdots$		$\vdots$		$\vdots$
x_i	$x_i(1)$	...	$x_i(j)$	...	$x_i(n)$
$\vdots$	$\vdots$		$\vdots$		$\vdots$
x_m	$x_m(1)$	...	$x_m(j)$	...	$x_m(n)$

Step 2: Normalize the data. In the event that the data is measured on different scales, it is essential to normalize the data using a technique. The data are normalized to [0, 1] interval according to minimum and maximum performance values and type of criteria using the following equations:

$$r_i(j) = (x_i(j) - Min_j)/(Max_j - Min_j) \text{ for benefit indicators} \qquad (1)$$

$$r_i(j) = (Max_j - x_i(j))/(Max_j - Min_j) \text{ for cost indicators} \qquad (2)$$

where, Max_j and Min_j are maximum and minimum values of criteria j, respectively.

Step 3: Calculate the Absolute Difference Matrix $|\Delta(j)|$ using following equation:

$$|\Delta_{0i}(j)| = |x_0(j) - x_i(j)| \qquad (3)$$

Step 4: Estimate the vector of Δ_{avg} (j), which represents the average value of each criterion-specific vector within the matrix (refer to Eq. (4)). Subsequently, the ψ vector is estimated (refer to Eq. (5)).

$$\Delta_{avg}(j) = \frac{1}{m}\sum_{i=1}^{m}|x_0(j) - x_i(j)| \tag{4}$$

$$\Psi(j) = \frac{\Delta_{avg}(j)}{max_i max_j |x_0(j) - x_i(j)|} \tag{5}$$

Step 5: Estimate the $\xi(j)$ vector. After determining the optimal value of the multiplier h through the employment of the ψ vector, the $\xi(j)$ vector is then estimated.

$$\xi(j) = h\psi(j) \tag{6}$$

where unique continuous multiplier $h \in [1, 2]$ defines the relative position of each coefficient in the set of $\xi(j)$ and ensures that $\psi(j) \leq \xi(j) \leq 2\psi(j)$. The multiplier h is calculated using the following linear programming model.

$$\text{Maximize } \xi(j) = h(\psi(1) + \psi(2) + ...\psi(n)) \tag{7}$$

$$\text{s.t.} \quad \Psi(j) = \frac{\frac{1}{m}\sum_{i=1}^{m}|x_0(j) - x_i(j)|}{max_i max_j |x_0(j) - x_i(j)|}$$

$$h\psi(j) \leq 1$$

$$h \in [1, 2]$$

Step 6: Calculate the Dynamic Grey Relational Coefficients (GRCs) matrix using Eq. (8).

$$\gamma_{0i}(j) = \frac{\Delta_{min} + \xi(j)_{0i}\Delta_{max}}{|\Delta_{0i}(j)| + \xi(j)_{0i}\Delta_{max}}, \xi(j) \in (0, 1], i = 1, 2, \ldots, m \tag{8}$$

where,

$$\Delta_{min} = min_i\, min_j |x_0(j) - x_i(j)| \tag{9}$$

$$\Delta_{max} = max_i\, max_j |x_0(j) - x_i(j)| \tag{10}$$

Step 7: Calculate the Dynamic Grey Relational Grades (GRGs) using Eq. (11), and subsequently, the alternatives are ranked accordingly. GRG serves as a benefit-type metric, where higher values indicate superior performance.

$$\Gamma_{0i} = \sum_{j=1}^{n} w(j) \times \gamma_{0i}(j) \tag{11}$$

Step 8: Calculate the Grey Relational Standard Deviation (GRSD) using Eq. (12), which enables the ranking of alternatives based on this metric. In our case, GRSD is a benefit-type measure.

$$\sigma_{\Gamma_{0i}} = \sqrt{\frac{\sum_{j=1}^{n}(\Gamma_{0i} - \gamma_{0i}(j))^2}{n-1}} \tag{12}$$

Step 9: Compute the Rank Product Score (R) using Eq. (13), representing a cost-type metric where lower values indicate better performance. Finally, the R scores are arranged in ascending order to select the best alternative.

$$R_{0i} = rank(\Gamma_{0i}) * rank(\sigma_{\Gamma_{0i}}) \tag{13}$$

4   Measuring the E-Government Website Performance of Countries

In this section, while measuring the e-government website performance of countries using the DGRA approach, the data required for the assessment are initially collected and normalized. Then, the performance measurement is performed using the proposed approach, and the results are discussed.

After the specification of the indicators for measuring e-government website performance, the required data, mentioned in Sect. 2, obtained using the Eurostat database are collected and presented in Table 2. In the statistics, 33 geopolitical locations, including 31 countries and two aggregated regions (the Euro area and the European Union), are analyzed under seven indicators. Except for C2, all indicators are cost-type. The percentage of individuals was used as the unit of measurement. The most recent data for 2022 was selected, but there is incomplete information due to data not being available in the relevant database. Out of the total 231 data, 17 are not available. The missing data were first estimated using the multiple imputation method using SPSS software to cope with the missing data. The values in bold in Table 2 are the data imputed instead of the missing data.

The process of assigning weights to indicators is crucial for making decisions that involve multiple factors. The CRITIC method, a completely objective weighting method without needing expert opinion, is employed in this study (steps of the CRITIC method are given in [13]). Through the CRITIC method, the following weighting vector is obtained:

$$w(j) = \{0.095, 0.323, 0.111, 0.160, 0.113, 0.102, 0.097\}$$

After the construction of the normalized data, the absolute difference matrix is estimated (Table 3), and then the discriminant coefficient vector, $\xi(j)$, is found. As stated above, a linear programming method (see Eq. 7) is used to calculate the optimal vector of the dynamic discriminant coefficient. First, the linear programming method obtains the unique continuous multiplier $h = 2$. Then, using the computed value of h, the $\xi(j)$ vector is obtained based on Eq. 5 and Eq. 6.

Table 2. Data related to each indicator

| Indicator type | - | + | - | - | - | - | - |
Indicators / Countries	C1	C2	C3	C4	C5	C6	C7
European Union	6.45	37.71	15.35	4.14	6.82	12.84	2.49
Euro area	7.37	37.10	17.06	4.62	8.45	14.55	2.94
Belgium	5.37	44.62	14.56	3.56	16.61	13.76	3.61
Bulgaria	1.17	17.05	5.95	1.25	1.79	3.74	1.05
Czechia	8.24	54.80	10.56	10.04	**6.92**	15.40	**4.04**
Denmark	7.11	59.24	20.01	4.22	19.37	11.94	5.16
Germany	1.25	20.67	3.04	0.56	1.06	4.29	0.69
Estonia	4.27	15.97	11.89	0.46	5.37	8.10	3.16
Ireland	6.91	52.00	17.11	5.65	**7.54**	21.59	**4.59**
Greece	0.83	53.49	8.60	1.46	0.99	4.77	0.35
Spain	17.90	31.19	34.34	12.73	19.18	31.21	**4.23**
France	8.29	45.25	24.74	3.66	**8.81**	19.84	4.12
Croatia	**5.53**	41.03	10.59	**3.69**	3.21	6.75	0.21
Italy	7.28	40.76	13.49	5.15	**7.12**	10.10	**1.98**
Cyprus	4.53	64.33	8.18	13.40	3.87	8.86	4.04
Latvia	2.13	52.12	11.10	1.03	1.25	9.21	0.93
Lithuania	3.62	48.28	15.73	0.17	2.55	13.80	1.75
Luxembourg	9.31	50.54	18.56	4.76	7.43	18.38	5.72
Hungary	3.08	53.69	9.13	2.61	1.38	10.12	2.19
Malta	7.88	43.06	21.20	5.05	9.77	17.55	8.86
Netherlands	11.61	53.24	25.16	5.92	15.18	15.43	6.38
Austria	4.41	53.47	7.81	4.32	8.59	9.22	3.70
Poland	1.32	41.89	8.88	1.18	1.94	4.29	1.17
Portugal	9.92	32.88	25.13	3.41	10.56	23.21	7.09
Romania	0.69	14.83	3.79	0.58	0.56	1.54	0.36
Slovenia	2.69	47.41	10.07	3.30	9.40	8.90	2.18
Slovakia	3.58	43.50	18.98	4.60	4.81	12.27	2.84
Finland	11.98	49.46	28.32	9.77	7.66	22.19	6.94
Sweden	11.15	53.05	21.86	3.75	6.76	19.49	**3.90**
Norway	14.50	44.48	29.99	8.77	26.11	32.93	14.68
Montenegro	3.97	27.80	5.73	4.82	**7.28**	5.83	**4.13**
Serbia	1.72	40.95	6.89	4.51	**5.99**	1.45	**2.87**
Türkiye	5.35	51.80	11.32	0.27	**8.69**	6.58	**3.89**

The grey relational coefficients of the dynamic GRA model are calculated using Eq. 8 and provided in Table 4. These are used to assess the Grey Relational Grades (GRGs) and the digital performance of countries, as shown in Table 5. GRG values are calculated using Eq. 9. Accordingly, Greece, Latvia, and Romania are found to be the most reliable choices in terms of information and communication technologies, while Spain, Portugal, and Norway are found to be the lowest-performing countries, respectively.

After assessing and ranking country performances, the next step is to classify countries as low performance, medium performance, and high performance. Thus, appropriate actions can be defined for each class. For this purpose, the RPS value will be used. The RPS is calculated according to Eq. 13; the results are shown in Table 5. This table shows the GRG, GRSD, and RPS values and rankings.

Table 3. Absolute Difference Matrix

	C1	C2	C3	C4	C5	C6	C7
European Union	0.335	0.538	0.393	0.300	0.245	0.362	0.158
Euro area	0.388	0.550	0.448	0.336	0.309	0.416	0.189
Belgium	0.272	0.398	0.368	0.256	0.628	0.391	0.235
Bulgaria	0.028	0.955	0.093	0.082	0.048	0.073	0.058
Czechia	0.439	0.193	0.240	0.746	0.249	0.443	0.265
Denmark	0.373	0.103	0.542	0.306	0.736	0.333	0.342
Germany	0.033	0.882	0.000	0.029	0.020	0.090	0.033
Estonia	0.208	0.977	0.283	0.022	0.188	0.211	0.204
Ireland	0.361	0.249	0.450	0.414	0.273	0.640	0.303
Greece	0.008	0.219	0.178	0.098	0.017	0.105	0.010
Spain	1.000	0.669	1.000	0.949	0.729	0.945	0.278
France	0.442	0.385	0.693	0.264	0.323	0.584	0.270
Croatia	0.281	0.471	0.241	0.266	0.104	0.168	0.000
Italy	0.383	0.476	0.334	0.376	0.257	0.275	0.122
Cyprus	0.223	0.000	0.164	1.000	0.130	0.235	0.265
Latvia	0.084	0.247	0.258	0.065	0.027	0.247	0.050
Lithuania	0.170	0.324	0.405	0.000	0.078	0.392	0.106
Luxembourg	0.501	0.279	0.496	0.347	0.269	0.538	0.381
Hungary	0.139	0.215	0.195	0.184	0.032	0.275	0.137
Malta	0.418	0.430	0.580	0.369	0.360	0.511	0.598
Netherlands	0.635	0.224	0.707	0.435	0.572	0.444	0.426
Austria	0.216	0.219	0.152	0.314	0.314	0.247	0.241
Poland	0.037	0.453	0.187	0.076	0.054	0.090	0.066
Portugal	0.536	0.635	0.706	0.245	0.391	0.691	0.475
Romania	0.000	1.000	0.024	0.031	0.000	0.003	0.010
Slovenia	0.116	0.342	0.225	0.237	0.346	0.237	0.136
Slovakia	0.168	0.421	0.509	0.335	0.166	0.344	0.182
Finland	0.656	0.300	0.808	0.726	0.278	0.659	0.465
Sweden	0.608	0.228	0.601	0.271	0.243	0.573	0.255
Norway	0.802	0.401	0.861	0.650	1.000	1.000	1.000
Montenegro	0.191	0.738	0.086	0.351	0.263	0.139	0.271
Serbia	0.060	0.472	0.123	0.328	0.213	0.000	0.184
Türkiye	0.271	0.253	0.265	0.008	0.318	0.163	0.254
$\Delta_{avg}(j)$	0.315	0.432	0.382	0.316	0.278	0.358	0.241
$\psi(j)$	0.315	0.432	0.382	0.316	0.278	0.358	0.241
$\xi(j)$	0.629	0.863	0.764	0.631	0.556	0.717	0.483

The GRG and GRSD are also plotted in Fig. 1 to show the interval over which the GRG can vary. If RPSs are ranked and graphed in ascending order, a plot can be obtained to visualize countries. This classification is shown in three different categories in Fig. 2.

Table 4. Grey relational coefficients matrix and the criteria weights

	0.095	0.323	0.111	0.160	0.113	0.102	0.097
	C1	C2	C3	C4	C5	C6	C7
European Union	0.653	0.616	0.660	0.678	0.694	0.665	0.754
Euro area	0.618	0.611	0.631	0.652	0.643	0.633	0.719
Belgium	0.698	0.684	0.675	0.711	0.470	0.647	0.673
Bulgaria	0.958	0.475	0.892	0.885	0.920	0.908	0.893
Czechia	0.589	0.818	0.761	0.458	0.691	0.618	0.646
Denmark	0.628	0.894	0.585	0.673	0.430	0.683	0.585
Germany	0.951	0.495	1.000	0.955	0.966	0.888	0.936
Estonia	0.752	0.469	0.730	0.966	0.747	0.772	0.703
Ireland	0.635	0.776	0.630	0.604	0.671	0.528	0.615
Greece	0.987	0.798	0.811	0.866	0.971	0.872	0.980
Spain	0.386	0.563	0.433	0.399	0.433	0.431	0.635
France	0.588	0.691	0.524	0.705	0.633	0.551	0.641
Croatia	0.691	0.647	0.760	0.703	0.843	0.810	1.000
Italy	0.622	0.645	0.696	0.626	0.684	0.723	0.798
Cyprus	0.738	1.000	0.823	0.387	0.811	0.753	0.646
Latvia	0.883	0.778	0.748	0.907	0.954	0.744	0.907
Lithuania	0.787	0.727	0.653	1.000	0.877	0.646	0.819
Luxembourg	0.557	0.756	0.607	0.645	0.674	0.571	0.559
Hungary	0.819	0.801	0.797	0.774	0.945	0.722	0.779
Malta	0.601	0.668	0.569	0.631	0.607	0.584	0.447
Netherlands	0.498	0.794	0.520	0.592	0.493	0.617	0.531
Austria	0.744	0.797	0.834	0.668	0.639	0.744	0.667
Poland	0.945	0.656	0.804	0.892	0.912	0.888	0.879
Portugal	0.540	0.576	0.520	0.720	0.587	0.509	0.504
Romania	1.000	0.463	0.970	0.953	1.000	0.996	0.979
Slovenia	0.844	0.716	0.773	0.727	0.617	0.752	0.780
Slovakia	0.789	0.672	0.600	0.653	0.770	0.676	0.727
Finland	0.490	0.742	0.486	0.465	0.667	0.521	0.509
Sweden	0.509	0.791	0.560	0.700	0.696	0.556	0.654

(*continued*)

Table 4. (*continued*)

	0.095	0.323	0.111	0.160	0.113	0.102	0.097
	C1	C2	C3	C4	C5	C6	C7
Norway	0.439	0.683	0.470	0.493	0.357	0.417	0.326
Montenegro	0.767	0.539	0.899	0.642	0.679	0.837	0.641
Serbia	0.913	0.646	0.861	0.658	0.724	1.000	0.724
Türkiye	0.699	0.773	0.743	0.988	0.636	0.815	0.655

Table 5. Dynamic grey relational grades

	GRG (Γ)	Rank	GRSD (σ)	Rank	$\Gamma - \sigma$	$\Gamma + \sigma$	RPS	Rank
European Union	0.661	23	0.045	32	0.617	0.706	736	30
Euro area	0.637	27	0.037	33	0.600	0.674	891	33
Belgium	0.660	24	0.083	21	0.577	0.743	504	24
Bulgaria	0.767	10	0.187	4	0.580	0.954	40	6
Czechia	0.681	18	0.121	12	0.560	0.802	216	16
Denmark	0.695	15	0.152	6	0.543	0.848	90	11
Germany	0.804	6	0.196	2	0.608	0.999	12	2
Estonia	0.689	16	0.153	5	0.536	0.843	80	10
Ireland	0.666	22	0.082	22	0.585	0.748	484	23
Greece	0.873	1	0.085	20	0.788	0.958	20	3
Spain	0.485	33	0.095	18	0.390	0.579	594	27
France	0.639	26	0.072	27	0.568	0.711	702	29
Croatia	0.746	12	0.124	11	0.621	0.870	132	13
Italy	0.672	21	0.064	31	0.609	0.736	651	28
Cyprus	0.777	8	0.193	3	0.583	0.970	24	4
Latvia	0.834	2	0.087	19	0.746	0.921	38	5
Lithuania	0.786	7	0.126	10	0.659	0.912	70	8
Luxembourg	0.656	25	0.081	23	0.575	0.737	575	26
Hungary	0.804	5	0.069	29	0.735	0.873	145	14
Malta	0.608	29	0.073	26	0.534	0.681	754	32
Netherlands	0.626	28	0.118	14	0.508	0.744	392	20

(*continued*)

Table 5. (*continued*)

	GRG (Γ)	Rank	GRSD (σ)	Rank	Γ- σ	Γ + σ	RPS	Rank
Austria	0.740	13	0.074	25	0.666	0.814	325	19
Poland	0.812	4	0.107	17	0.704	0.919	68	7
Portugal	0.577	31	0.077	24	0.500	0.654	744	31
Romania	0.813	3	0.222	1	0.591	1.036	3	1
Slovenia	0.735	14	0.071	28	0.664	0.806	392	20
Slovakia	0.689	17	0.068	30	0.621	0.757	510	25
Finland	0.592	30	0.114	15	0.478	0.706	450	22
Sweden	0.676	19	0.109	16	0.568	0.785	304	18
Norway	0.507	32	0.130	9	0.378	0.637	288	17
Montenegro	0.673	20	0.133	8	0.540	0.807	160	15
Serbia	0.750	11	0.143	7	0.607	0.893	77	9
Türkiye	0.775	9	0.121	13	0.654	0.895	117	12

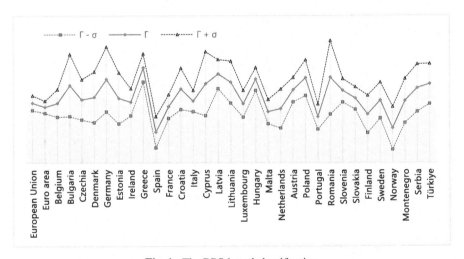

Fig. 1. The RPS-based classification

The RPS provides analysts with an insightful way to classify countries according to their relative performance measured objectively. From the information provided in Fig. 2, it can be easily seen that three categories can be formed. The first group, shown in green, is the category of the most favorable/prosperous countries; the third cluster, shown in red, is the category of the most unfavorable/unprosperous countries; the second group, shown in orange, lies between the green and red categories and generally indicates that there is still room for improvement.

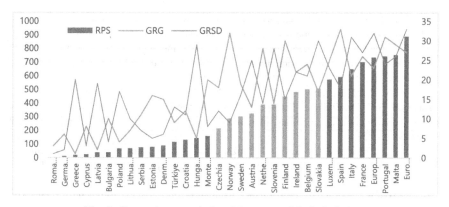

Fig. 2. Dynamic grey relational degrees and their deviations

5   Conclusion

This study aims to assess the current state of countries in the digital society and provide insights into the performance of their e-government websites. To achieve this, an approach combining DGRA and CRITIC methods is employed, offering a robust framework for evaluating and comparing e-government website performance. The study utilizes data from Eurostat, the statistical office of the European Union, as a reliable benchmark for measuring countries' e-government website performance. By applying the DGRA method, the study analyzes countries' e-government website performance, enabling a detailed evaluation of relationships and similarities among nations. The findings aim to provide valuable insights for policymakers, government officials, and stakeholders in the public sector, facilitating informed decision-making and the identification of areas for improvement.

In an increasingly interconnected and digitalized world, the importance of robust e-government initiatives cannot be overstated. This study contributes significantly to the ongoing discourse on harnessing ICT for public service delivery, emphasizing the need to evaluate and enhance e-government websites continuously. By harnessing the potential of information and communication technologies, countries can propel themselves toward a more inclusive, efficient, and citizen-centric digital society. In addition, the framework based on MCDM proposed in this study is used for the first time in this field.

References

1. Liu, S.M., Yuan, Q.: The evolution of information and communication technology in public administration. Public Adm. Dev. **35**, 140–151 (2015)
2. Manoharan, A.P., Ingrams, A., Kang, D., Zhao, H.: Globalization and worldwide best practices in E-Government **44**, 465–476 (2020). https://doi.org/10.1080/01900692.2020.1729182
3. Paul, S.: Accessibility analysis using WCAG 2.1: evidence from Indian e-government websites. Univers. Access Inf. Soc. **22**, 663–669 (2023)
4. Paul, S., Das, S.: Accessibility and usability analysis of Indian e-government websites. Univers. Access Inf. Soc. **19**, 949–957 (2020)

124   B. Ervural

5. Benaida, M.: e-Government usability evaluation: a comparison between Algeria and the UK. (IJACSA) Int. J. Adv. Comput. Sci. Appl. **14,** 680–690 (2023)
6. Eurostat: Statistics | Problems experienced when using e-government websites (2022). https://ec.europa.eu/eurostat/databrowser/view/ISOC_CIEGI_PB22/default/table?lang=en. Accessed 15 Jun 2023
7. Deng, J.: Control problems of grey systems. Syst. Control Lett. **1,** 288–294 (1982)
8. Hashemi, S.H., Karimi, A., Tavana, M.: An integrated green supplier selection approach with analytic network process and improved Grey relational analysis. Int. J. Prod. Econ. **159,** 178–191 (2015)
9. Aslantas, K., Ekici, E., Çiçek, A.: Optimization of process parameters for micro milling of Ti-6Al-4V alloy using Taguchi-based gray relational analysis. Measurement **128,** 419–427 (2018)
10. Vatansever, K., Akgül, Y.: Performance evaluation of websites using entropy and grey relational analysis methods: the case of airline companies. Decis. Sci. Lett. **7,** 119–130 (2018)
11. Kuo, Y., Yang, T., Huang, G.W.: The use of grey relational analysis in solving multiple attribute decision-making problems. Comput. Ind. Eng. **55,** 80–93 (2008)
12. Javed, S.A., Gunasekaran, A., Mahmoudi, A.: DGRA: Multi-sourcing and supplier classification through dynamic grey relational analysis method. Comput. Ind. Eng. **173,** 108674 (2022)
13. Diakoulaki, D., Mavrotas, G., Papayannakis, L.: Determining objective weights in multiple criteria problems: The critic method. Comput. Oper. Res. **22,** 763–770 (1995)

FSOL: Financial Document Recommendation Using Hybridized Semantics Oriented Learning

Maddikera Vijay[1], Gerard Deepak[2(✉)], and A. Santhanavijayan[3]

[1] School of Minerals, Metallurgical and Materials Engineering, Indian Institute of Technology Bhubaneswar, Bhubaneswar, India
[2] Department of Computer Science Engineering, Manipal Insititute of Technology Bengaluru, Manipal Academy of Higher Education, Manipal, India
`gerard.deepak.christuni@gmail.com`
[3] Department of Computer Science Engineering, National Institute of Technology, Tiruchirappalli, India

Abstract. Extracting financial documents from the structured World Wide Web is a complex and tedious task due to their scientific and socio-technical relevance. This Paper proposes FSOL, a semantically-driven framework for recommending financial documents that utilize dense auxiliary knowledge for epistemic and semantic reasoning. The financial document dataset undergoes classification using a logistic regression classifier, employing features extracted from context trees, built with knowledge derived from financial news, API stacks, and glossary/index terms from relevant financial e-books in the required finance domain. TF-IDF and category extraction techniques are applied to obtain informative terms, which are further utilized in conjunction with the user's chosen topic to drive the recommendation process. NPMI and Ahmed-Bealle Index metrics are employed to facilitate the final recommendation, along with strategically determined thresholds and step deviance measures. The suggested FSOL framework achieves an impressive Precision Percentage of 96.77% with an extremely small False Discovery Rate (FDR) of 0.04.

Keywords: TF-IDF · NPMI · glossary terms · Semantics Index · Ahmed-Bealle Index · Recommendation System

1 Introduction

The growing significance of finance in the contemporary digital era has sparked a heightened interest in financial events and knowledge. However, with the increasing volume of financial content and news, people are confronted with the information overload. To effectively tackle this matter, we propose an innovative methodology for recommending financial documents, drawing inspiration from the FSOL framework. Financial documents play a crucial role in tracking and assessing financial transactions and activities. Providing recommendations regarding these documents is vital for ensuring regulatory compliance, facilitating astute decision-making, optimizing financial planning endeavours, effectively managing risks, and facilitating thorough auditing processes. Through

F. Ortiz-Rodríguez et al. (Eds.): EGETC 2023, CCIS 1888, pp. 125–139, 2023.
https://doi.org/10.1007/978-3-031-43940-7_11

the implementation of streamlined operations, enhanced precision, and improved over-all efficiency, these recommendations aim to facilitate strict adherence to regulatory frameworks, provide valuable insights, and promote seamless collaboration. Financial management tools are vital in enabling individuals and organizations to effectively man-age and oversee their financial matters. The transition from Web 1.0 to Web 3.0 signifies a substantial evolution in the characteristics and functionalities of the Internet. The lim-itations of conventional algorithms and search engines become apparent in this context. Therefore, a semantically-driven model that possesses a comprehensive understanding of document semantics and adheres to the principles of Web 3.0 is required to recommend financial documents. FSOL's semantic focus, utilization of relevance computation mech-anisms, incorporation of auxiliary knowledge, and robust regression classifier contribute to its exceptional performance and efficiency in financial document recommendation [1].

Motivation: Finding highly specialized financial documents with socio-technical rele-vance and scientific value using existing conventional models is quite a cumbersome task. The existing models struggle to identify highly specialized documents with some scientific scope of value that fall outside the regular categories. Therefore, there is a need for sophisticated semantics-oriented deep interpretation models that can strategi-cally learn and utilize epistemic referential knowledge from these technically critical financial documents. The method we proposed in this paper is semantically oriented, deep semantics-driven model that incorporates auxiliary knowledge of an epistemic nature to tackle this issue effectively.

Contribution: The paper proposes FSOL, a semantically-driven model for recommend-ing financial documents that encompasses auxiliary knowledge. FSOL leverages auxil-iary knowledge to extract categories and informative terms from a financial document dataset using TF-IDF. Additionally, it incorporates financial news, API stacks, and e-books to gather indexes and glossary terms, which are used to build context trees and classify the dataset based on features. The user's preferred topic is then processed, and highly semantically relevant models such as NPMI and Ahmed-Bealle Index are employed to compute relevance within the model. FSOL improves Precision, Recall, Accuracy, and F-Measure Percentages, compared to baseline models, while reducing False Discovery Rate (FDR).

Organisation: The remaining sections of the paper are as follows. In Sect. 2, we discuss Related Work. The Proposed System Architecture is detailed in Sect. 3. The Performance Evaluation and Implementation are presented in Sect. 4. Dataset and Implementation are explained in Sect. 5. Conclusions are explained in Sect. 6.

2 Related Works

Rui Ren et al. [2] proposed a personalized financial news recommendation algorithm based on ontology to help users find interesting articles and deal with information over-load. The algorithm builds user profiles based on their behaviours and applies relevance feedback to predict current interests in real-time. José Luis Sánchez-Cervantes et al. [3] proposed a tool called FINALGRANT that analyses and visualizes digital financial data by retrieving XBRL-based financial data and transforming them into RDF triples through a process inspired by linked data principles. The tool addresses limitations of financial statements and can search for financial ratios to support fund investment decisions. Jiangtao Ren et al. [4] proposed a method for financial news recommendation to specific users by building a heterogeneous graph consisting of users, news, companies, concepts, and industry categories. The graph embeddings of the nodes are generated using node2vec and user-news relatedness can be computed based on them, which can provide decision support for companies choosing news to be recommended to target users and allow users to obtain personalized real-time news recommendations. Tiwari S et al. [5] proposed the cutting-edge combination of semantic technology and artificial intelligence (AI) to build intelligent systems that deliver more precise results. It focuses on the forefront of this development, Semantic AI in Knowledge Graphs, utilizing graph mapping and corpus-based ontology learning to extend knowledge graphs with the power of machine learning. Gupta S et al. [6] proposed a knowledge graph called KG4ASTRA for Indian missiles, consisting of 177 entities linked using 400 relationships. This graph was used to answer natural language queries about Indian missiles. This model utilizes Cypher queries to execute queries and generate tabular or graph representations for the natural language question. The knowledge graph was evaluated based on precision, recall, and macro-F1-measure. Ortiz F et al. [7] have put forth facets of E-Governance via semantic models and technologies. E-Governance is quite essential, and when ontological elements along with knowledge graphs are intersected with governance-based data entities, the success rate for E-Governance is massive.

In their study, Luis et al. [8] presented a novel framework aimed at establishing a financial knowledge base within the Linked Open Data (LOD) cloud. Their work emphasized the underutilization of Linked Data in financial information management and introduced a deep learning-powered hybrid recommendation system for enhancing knowledge base access. An operational prototype of a financial news knowledge base was developed and subjected to validation, providing empirical evidence for the efficacy of the proposed approach. The automated news recommender system, Discovery News, was proposed by C. Wang et al. [9] as a tool for financial analysis. Its primary purpose is to streamline the monitoring process involved in financial analysis. The automation of news ingestion, relevancy assessment, clustering, and ranking processes has been developed to enhance efficiency and minimize errors. The flexibility of the framework allows for the accommodation of various news data inputs, enabling seamless integration with financial data for a comprehensive analysis.

The back propagation (BP) neural network sorting method and deep learning was introduced by C Jingyu, C Qing, et al. [10] as a means of analysing news pertaining to finance network communication. The study aims to enhance page ranking by extracting associations between page content and user preferences by analysing user browsing and search history. The research highlights the significance of understanding the distinctive characteristics of financial news broadcasting within the context of new media. It also emphasises the need to leverage user behaviours in order to create innovative communication channels. The recommendation method proposed by Sajad Ahmadian et al. [11] aims to improve collaborative filtering by integrating tag information and trust relationships. The extraction of latent properties from sparse data is achieved through the utilisation of deep neural systems, more specifically an autoencoder that may be considered inadequate for the task at hand. The retrieved features are utilised in the construction of similarity values, resulting in enhanced recommendation accuracy and decreased computational complexity.

In their study, Cerchiello et al. [12] introduced a Deep Learning System that specifically targets the enhancement of a bank distress classifier through the utilisation of financial news. This research strategy explores the utilisation of doc2vec representation as a means to effectively map textual data onto a compact implicit semantic space. The categorization of troubled and healthy banks can be achieved through the utilisation of a supervised neural system. The significance of incorporating news data into the classifier's predictive capabilities is evident. In the field of computational finance, Ching-Yun Chang et al. [13] introduced a novel approach by proposing a deep neural network for evaluating the informational significance of news text. The utilisation of a tree-structured LSTM allows for the derivation of target-specific syntax-based representations of news content. The empirical findings presented in this study highlight the effectiveness of Natural Language Processing (NLP) advancements in the field of finance. Specifically, the research showcases how neural systems outperform sentiment-based techniques in terms of efficiency.

In a study conducted by Shubham Chhipa1 et al. [14], a novel smartphone application named Recipe Recommendation System was introduced. By utilising this system, users can conveniently explore a wide range of recipes that align with their existing supplies. The research employs content-based recommendation techniques, specifically utilising TF-IDF and Cosine Similarity algorithms, on a dataset consisting of Indian cuisine recipes. In their study, Gilles Jacobs et al. [15] introduced SENTiVENT, a meticulously documented corpora of fine-grained firm-specific occurrences in English economic news publications. This resource addresses the need for event extraction resources that specifically focus on economic events. It provides annotations that are compatible with benchmark datasets, ensuring compatibility and comparability with existing research in the field. The dataset consists of a wide range of factors that are associated with events, participant disputes, co-reference of incidents, and attributes of events. According to the research conducted by Lukas Brenner et al. [16], it has been suggested that the utilisation of automated advisors can potentially reduce the reliance on human financial guidance. This is particularly beneficial for individuals who harbour concerns regarding investment fraud and potential conflicts of interest. The research findings indicate that automated advisors offer a viable alternative for individuals who have concerns about potential conflicts of interest associated with traditional financial advice.

In their study, Xinshi Chen et al. [17] introduced a framework that utilises a model-based approach for recommendation models, specifically focusing on Feedback-based learning. The utilisation of a Generative Adversarial Network (GAN) enables the modelling and replication of user behavioural patterns, while concurrently gaining an understanding of the user's reward system. The Cascading DQN algorithm, as proposed, demonstrates the capability to effectively manage a substantial volume of candidate items.This leads to enhanced long-term user rewards and increased click rates within the system. Arodh Lal Karn et al. [18] proposed a recommendation system based on Hybrid Recommendation Model (HRM) and hybrid sentiment analysis (SA) to overcome cold-start and limited data issues in recommender systems (RS).The proposed method combines HRM with SA to generate a preliminary recommendation list and refine it for improved accuracy and correctness. Experimental results demonstrate that the HRM with SA outperforms traditional models across various evaluation criteria, enhancing recommendation accuracy in RS.

This research proposed by Gerard Deepak et al. [19] a dynamic ontology alignment technique for recommending relevant webpages, addressing the challenge of information diversity and dynamically changing web content. The strategy involves constructing a knowledge tree by computing semantic similarity between query terms and ontological entities. The proposed approach achieves an overall accuracy of 87.73%. Deepak G et al. [20] proposed an OntoBestFit strategy for faceted semantic search using RDF. It aims to minimize ambiguity in search results and increase result diversity by incorporating dynamic query expansion and best-fit occurrence estimation algorithm. The approach focuses on deriving an RDF prioritization vector from a Term-Frequency Matrix and a Term co-occurrence Matrix formulated from the reduced dyadic RDF entities over a corpus of web pages to yield Query Indicator terms. Pushpa C et al. [21] proposed an ontology modelling strategy called Onto Collab for the efficient and organized construction of knowledge bases. The research introduces a review-based approach within a secure messaging system for authoring ontologies and provides a platform to trace domain ontologies for individuals and teams.

The existing literature gaps identified are that most document recommendation frameworks do not focus on highly specialized domains of social and economic importance like Finance as a prospective domain. In a technical perspective, most of the existing frameworks, even for Finance as a domain are not semantically driven. They either use statistical models or depend on learning alone. Semantics oriented learning and reasoning is either absent or conventional semantic models are encompassed. There is a need to improve these models by hybridizing statistical models improving the strength of semantic relevance computation models, and integrating knowledge from the existing structure of the Web 3.0.

3 Proposed System Architecture

The Financial Document Recommendation Framework employs a hybrid approach that is both data-driven and knowledge-centric. This framework utilizes a categorical financial document dataset, which is processed through category extraction and a TF-IDF model. The TF-IDF model is used to identify the most frequent and rare terms across the document copies, resulting in the extraction of the most informative term pool. This hybrid approach facilitates the identification of important entities and categories within the financial documents. The Fig. 1 presents the architecture of the Financial Document Recommendation Framework using hybrid schematics.

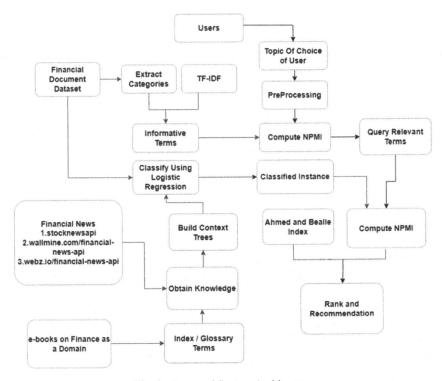

Fig. 1. Proposed System Architecture

In information extraction and data retrieval, TF (Term Frequency) and IDF (Inverse Document Frequency) are important ways to measure the importance of words in a document or group of documents. TF quantifies the recurrence of a term in a document by dividing the number of occurrences by the total number of words in a document. Equation (1) depicts TF equation

$$\text{tf}(t, d) = \frac{f_{t,d}}{\sum_{t' \in d} f_{t;,d}} \tag{1}$$

The document d's total term t occurrences are denoted by $f_{t,d}$. TF's denominator is document d's total terms, taking into account each instance of the same term. IDF quantifies the distinctiveness of a term within the collection of documents. IDF quantifies how distinctive a term is among a collection of documents. Calculating it involves taking the logarithm of quotient of the collection's total number of papers to the number of papers that contain the term. Equation (2) depicts IDF equation.

$$\text{idf}(t, D) = \log \frac{N}{|\{d \in D : t \in d\}|} \tag{2}$$

N: corpus document count $N = |D|$. $|\{d \in D: t \in d\}|$: the count of documents with term "t" (i.e., tf(t,d) $\neq$ 0). To avoid an undefined operation of dividing a number by zero, adjust the denominator to $1 + |\{d \in D: t \in d\}|$, When a term is not present in the corpora.

The e-book focuses on the domain of finance and incorporates auxiliary knowledge derived from various sources, specifically, from glossaries, index terms, and randomly generated keywords extracted using specialised tools and techniques. These extracted keywords and terms are then processed using customised algorithms and extractors. The resulting information is stored in a shared knowledge repository, which serves as a repository for auxiliary knowledge related to finance. In the subsequent steps, a comprehensive API stack comprising three distinct financial news APIs is established. These APIs include stocknewsapi, wallmine.com/financial-news-api, and webz.io/financial-news-api. These APIs are integrated together to form a cohesive system. Subsequently, the constructed API stack is utilised to extract domain-specific knowledge. To achieve this, the index and glossary terms from the e-books are provided as input to these APIs. As a result, a substantial amount of auxiliary knowledge is generated. This knowledge is then consolidated and presented in a common knowledge repository, serving as a centralised hub for the accumulated information. Furthermore, all the entities extracted from the common knowledge repository undergo the computation of Shannon Entropy. Shannon Entropy equation is depicted as Eq. (3)

$$H(X) = - \sum P(X)\log_2 P(X) \tag{3}$$

Here, the entropy of a random variable X is denoted by the symbol $H(X)$. The probability that an event x will take place is denoted by the variable $P(X)$. The equation calculates the entropy by summing over all possible events (X) and weighting them by their probability ($P(X)$). The logarithm is used with base 2 to measure the information in units of bits. Shannon's entropy is a measure of the uncertainty or information content of a random variable or a probability distribution. In technical terms, entropy measures information or bits needed for an event/outcome. It quantifies uncertainty, with lower values indicating predictability and higher values indicating unpredictability. This computation makes it possible to evaluate the level of uncertainty related to entities and informational content. The utilisation of Shannon's entropy via a state of an agent involves the computation of entropy and the behaviour of the agent in categorising similar terms and creating a unified link. This approach facilitates the construction of large context trees, enabling the avoidance of ambiguity. To maintain simplicity and optimise efficiency, these context trees are structured into seven distinct levels, starting from the roots.

The context trees serve as features and are employed as randomised features for the Feature-controlled Logistic Regression Classifier. The Logistic Regression Classifier is a common supervised learning technique that is extensively applied in diverse domains, including financial document recommendation. It is specifically designed for classification tasks, estimating the probability of an instance belonging to a specific class. Its versatility makes it well-suited for various applications, including predicting class membership based on input features. In the context of financial document recommendation, the Logistic Regression Classifier plays a crucial role in accurately categorizing and recommending relevant financial documents to users. It relies on a set of features derived from the document content, such as keywords, financial indicators, or sentiment analysis scores. These features are carefully selected and engineered to capture meaningful information for classification. As a part of training phase, the Logistic Regression model learns the relationships between the features and the labelled categories using a mathematical optimization algorithm.

It estimates the coefficients (weights) associated with each feature, which determine their contribution to the final classification decision. The model is trained through the minimization of a cost function, which quantifies the difference between predicted and actual class labels. Once trained, the regression model enables the classification of new financial documents into appropriate categories. Each category is assigned a probability or confidence score, representing the likelihood of the document belonging to that specific category. Based on these scores, the system can recommend the most relevant financial documents to users based on their specific queries or interests. Ultimately, the Logistic Regression Classifier is a powerful tool in financial document recommendation systems. It leverages the relationships between features and categories to make accurate predictions and provide personalized recommendations to users.

The classifier's performance is influenced by the standard and applicability of the features used, along with the accessibility of an adequate amount of labelled training data. The choice of Logistic Regression Classifier is deliberate, as it provides strong classification capabilities. Unlike Deep Learning Classifiers, which may introduce noise due to implicit feature selection that can deviate from the domain, the context trees themselves form the features in a controlled manner. Consequently, the classification process remains consistent and aligned with the document's content. Hence, the decision to opt for the Logistic Regression classifier is to maintain feature control and avoid potential deviations in classification. The results obtained from the Logistic Regression Classifier, which categorizes instances, are subsequently utilised to compute relevant terms related to the user's query. The user's chosen topic or query is initially subjected to pre-processing, which involves essential steps such as tokenization, lemmatization, and stop word removal.

Once these pre-processing steps are completed, the pre-processed terms undergo the calculation of Normalised Pointwise Mutual Information (NPMI). During the pre-processing phase, the user's input undergoes tokenization, breaking it down into individual terms or tokens. Lemmatization is then applied to reduce these terms to their base or canonical forms, ensuring consistency and reducing noise in the data. Additionally, stop word removal also gets rid of words that are overused and don't add anything to the overall meaning. After the pre-processing stage, the pre-processed terms are further analysed using the concept of NPMI. NPMI and Pointwise Mutual Information (PMI) are measures used to quantify the association between two terms in a corpus or dataset. They are commonly employed in natural language processing and information retrieval tasks, including financial document recommendation. NPMI is a normalized variant of PMI that scales the PMI values to a range of -1 to 1. Eq. (4) is used to compute it.

$$\text{NPMI}(x, y) = \frac{\text{PMI}(x, y)}{-\log_2(\text{P}(x, y))} \qquad (4)$$

In this equation, the joint probability of terms x, y occurring together is represented by $P(x, y)$, while $P(x)$ and $P(y)$ are, correspondingly, the probabilities of terms x and y.

The logarithm is applied for normalization. PMI equation is depicted as Eq. (5)

$$PMI(x, y) = \log_2\left(\frac{P(x, y)}{P(x) * P(y)}\right) \tag{5}$$

NPMI takes into account the rarity of term co-occurrence and adjusts the PMI score accordingly. In the context of financial document recommendation, NPMI measures the statistical significance of the co-occurrence of terms and provides insights into the strength of their association. NPMI is calculated between the pre-processed query terms and the informative terms obtained by merging the extracted categories and the TF-IDF dataset. The NPMI calculation considers only positive values between 0 and 1, using a median threshold of 0.5. The choice of the median threshold is based on empirical considerations to encompass a wide range of terms during the term aggregation phase. The resulting query relevant enriched terms represent the intersection of the query terms and the informative terms from the dataset. These enriched terms are further subjected to schematic similarity computation using two distinct models: the NPMI and the Ahmed-Bealle Index. This process involves aggregating a large number of instances with classified terms to enhance the understanding of the query context. The computation of NPMI involves considering positive values between 0 and 1. However, in this particular stage, the threshold is increased to 0.75 and the Ahmed-Bealle Index is set to 0.15, as this is the last phase of recommendation. This adjustment is made due to the presence of a substantial population of classified instances, necessitating the extraction of the most pertinent and relevant terms. Next, the entities that meet the predefined NPMI and Ahmed-Bealle Index thresholds, along with step deviance measures, are ranked in ascending order based on the NPMI measure. These entities are then recommended to the user as facets or topics of choice. If the user clicks on a particular topic, the system proceeds to recommend relevant financial documents from the dataset based on the categories of the dataset. If the user is happy with the recommendations, the user's search concludes at this point, and the search process stops. The user's recent clicks are tracked, nevertheless, if they are not satisfied. These recorded clicks are fed as a new topic of choice or query, and the entire process is repeated recursively, allowing for further refinement of the recommendations.   •

4   Implementation and Performance Evaluation

The evaluation of the FSOL framework for financial document recommendation involves assessing its semantic aspects and hybridized learning. For measuring performance, Precision, Recall, Accuracy, and F-measure percentages of each are utilised as standard metrics. Additionally, the False Discovery Rate (FDR) is considered as a novel evaluation criterion for quantifying False Positives. The choice of Precision, Recall, Accuracy, and F-measure percentages as standard metrics is justified by their ability to compute and quantify the relevance of the results obtained. To establish a baseline for comparison, the proposed FSOL framework is benchmarked against three distinct models: PFNR [2], FINALGRANT [3], and FNRGE [4] frameworks. These models are also recommendation systems designed specifically for the financial domain, encompassing both document and news recommendation. The PFNR, FINALGRANT, and FNRGE models, being recommendation models with similar characteristics, serve as effective benchmarks for evaluating the performance and effectiveness of the FSOL framework.

Table 1 compares the efficacy of the suggested FSOL framework to the three baseline models. The FSOL framework has an FDR of 0.04 and the highest mean precision percentage (96.77), highest mean recall percentage (98.37), highest mean accuracy percentage (97.55), and the highest mean F-measure percentage (97.54).The remarkable effectiveness of the suggested FSOL framework, with the highest precision, recall, accuracy, F-measure, and lowest False Discovery Rate (FDR), can be attributed to its semantics-oriented hybridized learning approach and several key factors. It leverages financial document categories and informative terms extracted through TF-IDF as central elements to effectively match and map them with user queries on desired topics. FSOL benefits from enriching its knowledge base through the integration of auxiliary information from e-books focused on the financial domain by considering the glossaries and index terms from multiple e-books, FSOL enhances the density of financial knowledge assimilated into the framework. Additionally, the utilization of standard APIs such as stocknewsapi, wallmine.com/financial-news-api, and webz.io/financial-news-api enables the acquisition of large volumes of real-world financial information. This helps bridge the semantic discrepancy between the knowledge present in the external environment and that utilized by the model.

Moreover, the inclusion of a logistic regression classifier, known for its robust performance in machine learning, ensures effective handling of domain-specific deviations. By controlling the model's features, FSOL minimizes domain deviance while preserving the richness and relevance of the financial domain. The incorporation of NPMI and Ahmed-Bealle Index, with varying thresholds at different stages of the model, further strengthens the relevance computation mechanisms within the framework. Another significant aspect is the construction of context trees, which involve integrating knowledge from external sources like e-books, glossaries, index terms, and financial news APIs. These context trees are utilized as features for the logistic regression classifier, enhancing the accuracy of dataset classification while maintaining domain consistency and avoiding deviations.

Collectively, these factors contribute to the enhanced efficacy of the suggested FSOL model compared to the baseline models. FSOL's emphasis on semantics, its utilization of relevance computation mechanisms such as NPMI and Ahmed-Bealle Index, the incorporation of auxiliary knowledge from e-books, glossaries, and financial news APIs, and the deployment of a robust regression classifier all play vital roles in achieving its high level of performance and efficiency.

In Table 1, PFNR demonstrates a mean precision of 90.22, a mean recall of 92.84, a mean accuracy of 91.53, and a mean F-measure of 91.51, with an FDR of 0.10. FINALGRANT achieves a mean precision of 91.74, a mean recall of 93.08, a mean accuracy of 92.41, and a mean F-measure of 92.40, with an FDR of 0.09. FNRGE yields a mean precision of 93.84, a mean recall of 94.89, a mean accuracy of 94.18, a mean F-measure of 94.17, and an FDR of 0.07.

The PFNR model's performance is limited due to its reliance on personalized financial user recommendation using an ontology and OF-IDF model. This approach heavily emphasizes user profiles for personalization, transforming unstructured text into concept

Table 1. Comparison of Performance of the proposed FSOL with other approaches

Model	Average Precision %	Average Recall %	Average Accuracy %	Average F-Measure %	FDR
PFNR [2]	90.22	92.84	91.53	91.51	0.10
FINALGRANT [3]	91.74	93.08	92.41	92.40	0.09
FNRGE [4]	93.48	94.89	94.18	94.17	0.07
Proposed FSOL	96.77	98.34	97.55	97.54	0.04

synonyms and syntax within a domain ontology. However, the use of domain ontology based on existing unstructured data requires significant computational resources. Additionally, the PFNR model lacks a learning component, relying solely on pre-existing ontology knowledge, which is lightweight but lacks sufficient knowledge density. Consequently, the model's performance is relatively shallow, particularly when dealing with large datasets that require incorporation of knowledge entities from data, a time-consuming task. Due to these limitations, the PFNR model falls behind the proposed FSOL model in terms of performance.

The underperformance of the FINALGRANT model compared to the proposed FSOL framework can be attributed to several factors such as linked data graph analysis and recommendation, necessitating the use of open linked data and XBRL-based financial data. This entails the generation of RDF ripples, which can be a complex task that requires eliciting semantic properties and maintaining a reserve of relevant data. While the model utilizes open-linked data from the World Wide Web to prepare knowledge, it lacks robust mechanisms for relevance computation. It heavily relies on pre-existing semantics aligned with the created RDF, which limits its ability to decipher semantics accurately. Furthermore, the FINALGRANT model lacks a learning component, making it suitable only for handling small amounts of data. In real-time deployments or with large datasets, the model is prone to lagging and poor performance. As a result of these limitations, the FINALGRANT model falls short in the evaluated dataset when compared to the proposed FSOL model, which demonstrates superior performance.

The underperformance of the FNRGE model can be attributed to its reliance solely on graph-based embeddings. While these embeddings are considered superior to other baseline models, they lack strong relevance computation mechanisms. Additionally, the density of auxiliary knowledge provided by the embeddings is shallow compared to the comprehensive knowledge incorporated into the proposed FSOL model. In order to achieve scientific inference in the financial domain, a significant amount of financial data is required. Graph embeddings alone are unable to generate or infer scientific value, and deep-level inferences become limited. As a result, the FNRGE model fails to meet expectations due to the shallow nature of graph embeddings, the absence of robust relevance computation mechanisms, and the limited density of auxiliary knowledge. In contrast, the proposed FSOL model outperforms the FNRGE model by incorporating a deep level of knowledge, strong relevance computation mechanisms, and a richer density of auxiliary knowledge.

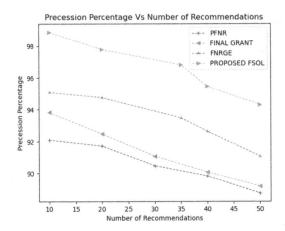

Fig. 2. Precession Percentage Vs Number of Recommendations

The superior efficacy of the proposed FSOL model over the baseline models can be attributed to its strong relevance computation mechanisms, namely the Ahmed-Bealle Index and NPMI. These mechanisms incorporate empirically determined thresholds to preserve domain deviance through the logistic regression classifier. Additionally, the FSOL model leverages context trees as features, synthesized from a diverse range of financial knowledge sources, including e-books, glossaries, index terms, and financial news APIs. This integration of heterogeneous auxiliary knowledge enriches the framework.

To conduct fair experiments, FSOL and the baseline models were evaluated under identical environmental conditions. A total of 1,143 queries were used, and ground truth data was collected over a 45-day period from a diverse group of 6,400 financial users. These users encompassed various backgrounds, including training participants, stock exchange professionals, financially literate students, BBA students, financial management students, MBA students, financial experts, investment bankers, and stock exchange brokers. The queries were randomly assigned to these individuals, and their corresponding ground truth responses were recorded. The relevance of the query results was determined by measuring the deviation from the top 10 ground truth responses. If the Pearson correlation coefficient indicated a deviation of more than 10%, the results were considered irrelevant. Based on these benchmarks, the experimentation and evaluation of the models were conducted, demonstrating the enhanced performance of the suggested FSOL model.

In Fig. 2, the distribution curve of precision vs. number of recommendations for the suggested FSOL model and the baseline models (PFNR, FINALGRANT, and FNRGE) is depicted. It is evident that FSOL has the top spot in the rank system while PFNR holds the bottom spot. FNRGE holds the second-highest position, and FINALGRANT holds the third-highest position. FSOL integrates a wide range of auxiliary knowledge from sources like e-books, glossaries, index terms, and financial news APIs, providing a comprehensive understanding of the financial domain and effectively preserves domain deviance through the use of a logistic regression classifier and context trees as features.

Moreover, the relevance of results is quantified by strong relevance computation mechanisms, such as the Ahmed-Bealle Index and NPMI, which are incorporated in FSOL model.

On the other hand, the PFNR model's limitation lies in its reliance on personalized financial user recommendation, which restricts its learning component. This means that the model cannot adapt and improve its recommendations based on user feedback or changing trends in the financial domain. The emphasis on user profiles may not accurately capture users' evolving preferences and needs. The FINALGRANT model has several limitations, including its dependence on specific data sources, lack of robust relevance computation mechanisms, and inadequate performance for real-time deployments and large datasets. These factors make it a wasteful investment in terms of computational resources and user satisfaction. Similarly, the FNRGE model's exclusive reliance on graph-based embeddings hampers its ability to achieve accurate and meaningful results in the financial domain. The shallow density of auxiliary knowledge provided by the embeddings further restricts the model's access to comprehensive and rich financial information, leading to underperformance. In summary, the FSOL model excels by incorporating a wide range of auxiliary knowledge, preserving domain deviations, and employing strong relevance computation mechanisms.

5 Dataset and Implementation

The experimentation utilized three separate datasets, which were subsequently merged into a unified dataset. This integrated dataset was created by merging the Financial Statement IDX Stocks dataset authored by Greeg Titan [22], the Ministry of Finance and Economic Planning Documents dataset sourced from the Resource Governance Index Source Library [23], and the Financial News dataset utilized for data mining by Turenne Nicolas et al. [24]. A tailored web crawler was utilized to retrieve financial documents from the organized World Wide Web, with a specific emphasis on entities referenced in the financial statement documents from the IDX Stock dataset. The Ministry of Finance and Economic Planning dataset and the Turenne Nicolas dataset were utilized in their original form, and custom metatag generators and annotators were employed for data annotation. The integration of these three datasets was achieved by identifying shared categories through annotation. Records that did not match were assigned a lower priority.Python 3.0 was used for the implementation, and Google Collaboratory was selected as the (IDE). For pre-processing and carrying out various Natural Language Processing (NLP) activities, the Python's Natural Language Toolkit (NLTK) framework was used. Context trees were designed using AgentSpeak, and a customized web crawler was employed to retrieve finance-related e-books from the structured World Wide Web.

6 Conclusions

This Paper proposes the FSOL framework, which combines deep-level semantics with lightweight machine learning classification for financial document recommendation. FSOL builds context trees from financial news, API stacks, and accumulates Index and Glossary terms from financial e-books and financial documents. A logistic regression classifier is used to classify financial document datasets based on these trees. Informative terms are extracted from the dataset and combined with the user's topic of choice to compute query-relevant terms using NPMI with a specific threshold. To enhance semantic relevance, NPMI, and Ahmed-Bealle Index with empirical step deviance measures are applied. The instances are then ranked and recommended based on NPMI, serving as financial domain indicators relevant to the user's chosen topic. The proposed FSOL achieves a Precision Percentage of 96.77, Recall Percentage of 98.37, Accuracy Percentage of 97.55, and F-Measure Percentage of 97.54, with the lowest False Discovery Rate (FDR) of 0.04.Although the proposed FSOL Framework has no explicit limitation, there is a scope for improvement by increasing the strength of semantic relevance computation mechanisms and using better reasoning mechanisms in the model.

References

1. Dominic, M., FrancisFrancis, S., Pilomenraj, A.: E-learning in web 3.0. Int. J. Mod. Educ. Comput. Sci. **6**(2), 8–14 (2014)
2. Ren, R., Zhang, L., Cui, L., Deng, B., Shi, Y.: Personalized financial news recommendation algorithm based on ontology. Procedia Comput. Sci. **55**(2015), 843–851 (2015)
3. Sánchez-Cervantes, J.L., Alor-Hernández, G., del Pilar, M., Salas-Zárate, J.L., García-Alcaraz, L.R.-M.: FINALGRANT: a financial linked data graph analysis and recommendation tool. In: Valencia-García, R., Paredes-Valverde, M.A., del Pilar, M., Salas-Zárate, G.A.-H. (eds.) Exploring Intelligent Decision Support Systems. SCI, vol. 764, pp. 3–26. Springer, Cham (2018). https://doi.org/10.1007/978-3-319-74002-7_1
4. Ren, J., Long, J., Zhikang, X.: Financial news recommendation based on graph embeddings. Decis. Support Syst. **125**, 113115 (2019)
5. Gupta, S., Tiwari, S., Ortiz-Rodriguez, F., Panchal, R.: KG4ASTRA: question answering over Indian missiles knowledge graph. Soft. Comput. **25**, 13841–13855 (2021)
6. Vakaj, E., Tiwari, S., Mihindukulasooriya, N., Ortiz-Rodríguez, F., Mcgranaghan, R.: NLP4KGC: Natural Language Processing for Knowledge Graph Construction. In: Companion Proceedings of the ACM Web Conference 2023, p. 1111 (2023)
7. Ortiz, F., Tiwari, S., Amara, F.Z., Sahagun, M.A.: E-Government success: an end-user perspective. In: Medina-Quintero, J.M., Sahagun, M.A., Alfaro, J., Ortiz-Rodriguez, F. (eds.) Global Perspectives on the Strategic Role of Marketing Information Systems:, pp. 168–186. IGI Global (2023). https://doi.org/10.4018/978-1-6684-6591-2.ch010
8. Colombo-Mendoza, L. O., García-Díaz, J. A., Gómez-Berbís, J. M., Valencia-García, R.: A deep learning-based recommendation system to enable end user access to financial linked knowledge. In: Hybrid Artificial Intelligent Systems: 13th International Conference, HAIS 2018, Oviedo, Spain, June 20–22, 2018, Proceedings 13, pp. 3–14. Springer International Publishing (2018). https://doi.org/10.1007/978-3-319-92639-1_1
9. Wang, C., et al.: Discovery news: a generic framework for financial news recommendation. Proc. AAAI Conf. Artif. Intell. **34**(08), 13390–13395 (2020)
10. Jingyu, C., Qing, C.: Application of deep learning and BP neural network sorting algorithm in financial news network communication. J. Intell. Fuzzy Syst. **38**(6), 7179–7190 (2020)
11. Ahmadian, S., Ahmadian, M., Jalili, M.: A deep learning based trust-and tag-aware recommender system. Neurocomputing **488**, 557–571 (2022)
12. Cerchiello, P., Nicola, G., Ronnqvist, S., Sarlin, P.: Deep learning bank distress from news and numerical financial data. arXiv preprint arXiv:1706.09627 (2017)

13. Chang, C.Y., Zhang, Y., Teng, Z., Bozanic, Z., Ke, B.: Measuring the information content of financial news. In: Proceedings of COLING 2016, the 26th International Conference on Computational Linguistics: Technical Papers, pp. 3216–3225 (2016)
14. Chhipa, S., Berwal, V., Hirapure, T., Banerjee, S.: Recipe recommendation system using TF-IDF. ITM Web of Conf. **44**, 02006 (2022)
15. Jacobs, G., Hoste, V.: SENTiVENT: enabling supervised information extraction of company-specific events in economic and financial news. Lang. Resour. Eval. **56**(1), 225–257 (2022)
16. Brenner, L., Meyll, T.: Robo-advisors: a substitute for human financial advice? J. Behav. Exp. Financ. **25**, 100275 (2020)
17. Chen, X., Li, S., Li, H., Jiang, S., Qi, Y., Song, L.: Generative adversarial user model for reinforcement learning based recommendation system. In: International Conference on Machine Learning, pp. 1052–1061. PMLR (2019)
18. Karn, A.L., et al.: Customer centric hybrid recommendation system for e-commerce applications by integrating hybrid sentiment analysis. Electron. Commer. Res. **23**(1), 279–314 (2023)
19. Deepak, G., Ahmed, A., Skanda, B.: An intelligent inventive system for personalised webpage recommendation based on ontology semantics. Int. J. Intell. Syst. Technol. Appl. **18**(1–2), 115–132 (2019)
20. Deepak, G., Santhanavijayan, A.: OntoBestFit: a best-fit occurrence estimation strategy for RDF driven faceted semantic search. Comput. Commun. **160**, 284–298 (2020)
21. Pushpa, C.N., Deepak, G., Thriveni, J., Venugopal, K.R.: Onto Collab: Strategic review oriented collaborative knowledge modeling using ontologies. In: 2015 Seventh International Conference on Advanced Computing (ICoAC), pp. 1–7. IEEE (2015)
22. Titan, G.: Financial Statement IDX Stocks (2022)
23. Resource Governance Index Source Library. Ministry of Finance and Economic Planning: Documents (2021)
24. Turenne Nicolas: Financial News dataset for text mining. Zenodo (2021)

Enhancing Productivity in Peru's Public Works Value Chain Through AI Monitoring: A Paradigm Shift

Oscar Miranda-Hospinal[1,2,3(✉)], David Valle-Cruz[1,2,3], Jorge Yrivarren-Lazo[1,2,3], Carlos Yula-Inca[1,2,3], and Kevin Ronceros-Ponce[1,2,3]

[1] Universidad Nacional de Ingeniería, Rimac, Peru
{oscar.miranda.h,cyu-lai,kevin.ronceros.p}@uni.pe,
davacr@uaemex.mx, jyrivarren@uni.edu.pe
[2] Unidad Académica Profesional Tianguistenco, Santiago Tianguistenco, Mexico
[3] Universidad Autónoma del Estado de México, Toluca, Mexico

Abstract. Public works generally have very low productivity, from the conception of the project. An example is the Billinghurst Bridge, also called the Continental Bridge, in Madre de Dios, which connects Peru with Brazil. It took more than half a century to materialize, from the conception of the project to its start-up [1]. In this regard, artificial intelligence (AI), as an emerging technology, can help reduce time and increase productivity. The adaptation of AI to different organizations is also considered feasible, and the corresponding monitoring and measurement of its performance is of interest, particularly concerning productivity in the value chain (project cycle) of public works. This research proposes to explore not only the challenges and opportunities of AI in the productivity of public works but also the perceptions and expectations of improvement through an exploratory survey based on the instrument designed by Criado et al. [2]. This survey was addressed to engineers, architects, logisticians, experts, and arbitrators who are related to public works. The paper ends with some lessons and recommendations for researchers and professionals interested in the study area.

Keywords: Artificial intelligence · machine learning · public works · development · productivity

1 Introduction

Historically, public works projects have been notorious for low productivity, delays, long schedules, and indecisive decision-making. As an example, the Billinghurst Bridge, also called the Continental Bridge, took more than half a century since the conception of the project until its commissioning [1]. However, with the advent of artificial intelligence (AI), there is a growing trend to bring this technology to the public sector. AI offers promising solutions for better management of public services, greater responsibility, and added value for the public sector.

F. Ortiz-Rodríguez et al. (Eds.): EGETC 2023, CCIS 1888, pp. 140–154, 2023.
https://doi.org/10.1007/978-3-031-43940-7_12

The use of AI in public works clearly has the potential to improve productivity. Fixing inefficiencies and decreasing delays affecting public projects can be mitigated through AI-driven processes. Advanced machine learning algorithms and models enable data-driven decision-making to streamline project planning, optimal resource allocation, and on-time execution. Automation and predictive analytics streamline workflows, improve coordination among stakeholders, and identify potential bottlenecks and risks to minimize project delays and cost overruns.

Moreover, the integration of AI in the public sector offers opportunities to improve the delivery of services to citizens. Intelligent systems enable personalized and efficient public interactions by providing timely information, automating routine tasks, and enabling self-service options. Chatbots and virtual assistants with AI technology can handle citizen queries timely. More applications should be sought in public works, taking advantage of the AI transformative potential in the governance of public services and public works.

Developed countries are already implementing some AI techniques to improve internal governance processes. Therefore, AI could be useful in the decision-making process, prevention and response to disasters, detection of changes in the environment, improvement of the interaction between government and citizens, and improvement of productivity in public works [3].

Technology is the product of human action and has been used to help modify the structure of government agencies [4]. In this case, it is intended to link AI technology and public organizations to improve productivity in public works [5].

The technology could intervene in the improvement of the productivity indices registered by Ghio [6] in the works of Peru. According to this study, the productive work (PW) in Peru on average was 28%, while in Chile the average PW was 47%. Consequently, adequate use of constructability and the implementation of "lean construction" philosophy in the projects could be facilitated. Also, other research indicates that by implementing AI in construction sites, productivity could be increased by up to 50% [7].

A very healthy practice is for countries to have a Bank of Projects or technical files, which must be prepared well in advance, long before the tenders or initiatives that can expedite public investment. It is even better if these organizations are computerized to support the decision-making of the authorities in all phases of public projects [8]. Hence, it seeks to replicate technological initiatives in the Peruvian context.

However, it is believed that the implementation of AI in the Peruvian public administration will not be simple, due to the low custom and the little capacity to share databases between the different executing units, as well as the lack of capacity and deficient technological infrastructure [9]. Considering that the development of a construction project arises from the existence of the need for public works, and the project cycle's development follows a sequence, shown in Fig. 1 [10], the activities that could be elaborated -given by different actors and at different stages or moments, and monitored by AI- would significantly increase productivity in public works. Consequently, it is necessary to measure the potential of AI through a survey aimed at engineers, architects, logisticians, experts, and arbitrators related to public works.

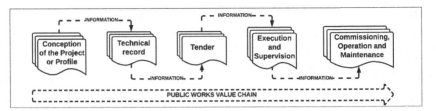

Fig. 1. Project cycle or value chain of public works

This paper is divided into six sections, including the introduction; the second section shows the literature review on the technology-organization interaction as a framework to understand the potential of AI in public works. The third section shows the methodological approach of the study. The fourth section presents the results. The fifth section discusses the findings. The document ends with some conclusions and recommendations for researchers and professionals interested in the subject of study.

2 Literature Review

The construction industry is severely constrained by the long list of complex challenges it faces. This is how technological initiatives arise in the context of construction. One of these initiatives is the advanced digital technology, Artificial Intelligence (AI), which is currently revolutionizing industries such as manufacturing, retail, telecommunications and other industries [9].

Likewise, applications are found in government policies in various countries around the world. Where there are several opportunities to improve in health and well-being, in education, in transport and energy consumption, in finances and in government management [11]. AI poses great challenges to government leaders, in this context, numerous national policies have recently emerged that incorporate the vision and objectives on how AI should be adopted at the public administration level and its adoption in public works [12].

For years, the benefits of AI for statecraft have been a concern for government policy researchers. However, with declining costs of computing and data storage, governments can now afford the widespread implementation of AI, attracting the attention of researchers [13]. Since AI can be of great help to governments in various areas, its application to improve productivity in public works is of interest.

Artificial intelligence can improve emergency response capacity and support proactive management of cyber-physical infrastructures in a smart city [14].

Some researchers address the applied rhetoric of governments to minimize the risks or exalt the opportunities of AI. They also define four prominent roles that governments seek to assume with respect to AI implementation: facilitator role, leader role, regulator role, and/or user role. This is how regulatory governments legislate various regulatory acts and provide a regulatory environment to reduce potential risks and dangers [15], pending regulation through AI, government-to-government contracts, the participation of foreign contractors, works for taxes, the participation of organizations such as the

United Nations Development Program (UNDP) in awarding contracts outside of national regulations.

Open and public data must be modeled, analyzed, used and exploited in a safe and ethical way by public organizations. With this, it is intended to obtain the maximum benefit from open data using AI techniques, achieving efficiency gains in processes and fostering collaboration between the public and private sectors to reduce costs. Thus, as in other areas, productivity in public works increases because of the synergy of these technologies. This model does not close the doors to private companies that can use open and public data with the aim of offering better results in public works, ensuring social welfare or public value. Therefore, the commitment of the Peruvian government is that public sector organizations must respect privacy and data protection regulations, in order to guarantee the benefit for citizens [2].

The role of the Facilitator and promoter of adoption of AI by governments, not only to the investment executing units, but also to public works contractors, allowing not only greater transparency, but also greater productivity in public works [16].

One of the leading emerging technologies, artificial intelligence (AI), has helped make significant contributions to improving business operations, service processes, and industry productivity in recent years [17]. Among the advantages of AI is the increase in productivity and the efficiency of easy access and interactions with strong domain knowledge required that makes inferences and reaches conclusions that are heuristic, flexible, and transparent, and provides the logic behind the advice given when needed [18].

The role of AI technology user is motivated by the internal optimization of state management, solving complicated political issues, improving participation or for public decision-making [19].

In Peru, public works are those that show the greatest inefficiency in the management of the public works value chain. A report from the comptroller general of the republic called "Report of paralyzed works 2019" indicates that at the national and regional level there are 867 paralyzed works for a contracted amount of $4,619,695,822. Of which 39% were paralyzed due to deficiencies in the technical file, 28% in arbitration and 15% due to budgetary limitations [20].

The little coordination between specialists from the conceptual stages of the project generates deficient technical files, which according to traditional logic will have to be solved during execution. Generating controversies in the contractual execution, during the operation and maintenance of the asset. In addition, additional costs are generated for additional requests, term extensions and even reformulation of the technical file. This generates that the efficiency in the investment management of public works is not what is expected by public governments. This is how a great window of challenges and opportunities opens for the adoption of AI in public works, specifically to efficiently manage the public works value chain. Since there is little evidence of academic literature on AI in public investment management in Peru.

3 Methodology

In this study, a questionnaire based on an improved version of the instrument developed by Criado et al. [2]. The purpose of this study is to evaluate the perspectives of various professionals involved in public works, such as engineers, architects, logisticians, experts, and arbitrators.

The research technique for collecting data involved a survey (see the Appendix to review the analytical strategy and survey questions). The questionnaire consisted of 19 questions addressed to professionals involved in public works. The period to receive responses to the survey opened from May 12 to June 11, 2023. The survey obtained a high level of commitment from high-level public professionals; the response rate was almost 75 percent of the ministries surveyed (150 of 201 nationally in Peru). The validation of this survey was supported by expert reviews of public works who examined the content in a pilot study to avoid inconsistencies. The surveys guarantee that the answers are treated anonymously, which guarantees the confidentiality of the participants.

This study aims to clarify the three dimensions covered by the questionnaire.

RQ1: What is the perception of the concept of AI in increasing productivity in public works?

RQ2: What are the expectations of AI in the productivity of public works?

RQ3: What are the main challenges and opportunities of AI in the productivity of public works?

This research is based on primary data on the perceptions of professionals related to Peruvian public works, an online survey by sending the Google Form web link, via email or WhatsApp.

4 Results

In the first instance, our study examines the perceptions of the personnel involved in public works on the concept of AI, and the increase in productivity in public works, who will help to recognize the scope and potential of AI. This part of the study sheds light on the related concepts and techniques most commonly associated with AI. In the second instance, our study evaluates the expected impact of AI in different areas of public sector works, particularly on the expectations of AI in the productivity of public works that help to recognize the scope and potential of AI.

Questions number 01, 02 and 03 were asked on a Likert scale, with 1 being totally disagree and 7 totally agreeing, rate each of the options and questions number 04, 05, 06 and 07 are multiple choice, with a minimum of three options.

4.1 Perceptions About the Concept of AI in Increasing Productivity in Public Works

Question 1:
To what extent do you agree that artificial intelligence can increase the productivity of the personnel involved in the public works value chain? The results were as follows: In the

tendering and supplier selection stage (5.01); In the stage of Commissioning, operation and maintenance (4.69), In the stage of elaboration of the Technical File (4.68); the same as shown in Table 1.

Table 1. Survey Results – Question N°1

N° of respondents: 150	Mean	Standard deviation	Asymmetry	kurtosis
In the Conception stage of the Project or Profile	4.17	2.00	−0.01	−1.27
In the stage of elaboration of the Technical File	4.68	1.71	−0.41	−0.89
In the stage of Tendering and selection of suppliers	5.01	1.78	−0.70	−0.46
In the Execution and Work Supervision stage	4.49	1.64	−0.12	−0.96
In the commissioning, operation and maintenance stage	4.69	1.75	−0.32	−0.95
Mean	4.61	1.78		

Question 2:

Which of the following involved in public works will improve their productivity with the adoption of artificial intelligence? The results, in order of substitution, were the following: Construction administrator (4.91); Work Monitor (4.77) and Work Supervisor (4.77); the same as shown in Table 2.

Table 2. Survey Results – Question N°2

N° of respondents: 150	Mean	Standard deviation	Asymmetry	kurtosis
Designer	4.52	1.86	−0.36	−0.99
Supervisor or work coordinator	4.77	1.72	−0.43	−0.83
Construction resident	4.59	1.77	−0.46	−0.72
Construction manager	4.91	1.76	−0.55	−0.85
Work supervisor	4.77	1.80	−0.63	−0.63
Mean	4.71	1.78		

Question 3:

To what extent do you agree that the implementation of AI will increase the productivity of public works? The results, in order of implementation, were the following: The new professions linked to Artificial Intelligence and the optimization of the production system of public works, must be addressed in depth (4.92); They naturally assume that on-site production monitoring would be more efficient with AI. (4.83) and during the execution of public works, the process of identifying and estimating risks will be more efficient and less expensive (4.81); the same as shown in Table 3.

Table 3. Survey Results – Question N°3

N° of respondents: 150	Mean	Standard deviation	Asymmetry	kurtosis
I am totally open to the adoption of AI in public works, and that it will increase productivity	4.55	1.91	−0.22	−1.99
I naturally assume that on-site production monitoring would be more efficient with AI	4.83	1.85	−0.53	−0.86
During the execution of public works, the process of identifying and estimating risks would be more efficient and less expensive	4.81	1.78	−0.47	−0.84
Other "intelligence" will be required to improve productivity in public works	4.67	1.75	−0.38	−0.77
The new professions linked to Artificial Intelligence and the optimization of the public works production system must be addressed in depth	4.92	1.86	−0.56	−0.84
Mean	4.76	1.83		

4.2 Expectations of AI in the Productivity of Public Works

Question 4

From your point of view, what activities would increase your productivity in public works, at an early stage of the implementation of AI? The results on the activities that will increase productivity at an early stage are: Share the database with the Peruvian State Procurement Supervisory Body (OSCE) and other executing units (66%), monitoring of transparency by AI (65%). On the contrary, the least affected would be the records of similar technical files (53%) and having updated records of consultants (51%). The same as shown in Fig. 2.

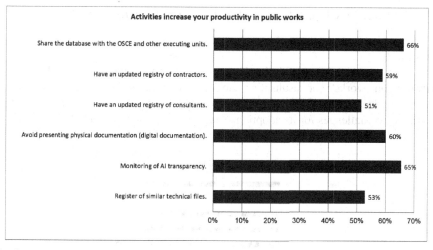

Fig. 2. Activities that increase their productivity due to the implementation of AI in public works.

Question 5

From your point of view, which of the following public works functions will be automated and optimized by artificial intelligence in the short term? The results on functions in the short term are: information management (67%) and transaction processing and financial operations (65%). On the contrary, the least affected would be regulations (33%) and construction operations (40%) The same as shown in Fig. 3.

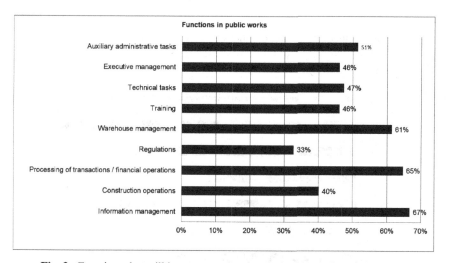

Fig. 3. Functions that will be automated and optimized by AI in public works.

4.3 Challenges and Opportunities of AI in the Productivity of Public Works

Question 6
What are the main inhibitors of the implementation of artificial intelligence in the productivity of public works? The results illustrate that, in both cases, there are 3 key inhibitors: low training (62%), technological infrastructure (61%) and resistance to change (52%). Are the main challenges for its adoption. The results are shown in Fig. 4.

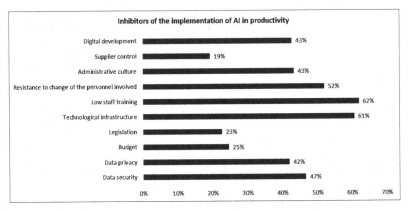

Fig. 4. Main inhibitors of the implementation of AI in public works.

Question 7
What are the main enablers of change that drive the implementation of artificial intelligence in the productivity of public works? The responses in the survey were to a

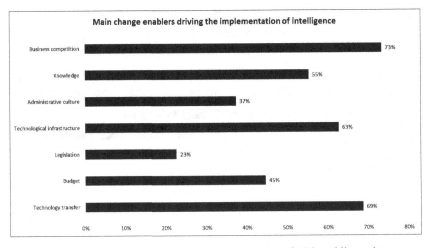

Fig. 5. Main enablers driving the implementation of AI in public works

multiple-choice question (with a minimum of three options, illustrating that, in both cases, there are 3 most important key enablers: business competence (73%); technology transfer (69%) %) and technological infrastructure (63%), the same as those shown in Fig. 5.

5 Discussion

The results of this study demonstrate a general consensus on the potential benefit of artificial intelligence (AI) in the productivity of public works. Its ability to improve various stages of the value chain, such as bidding, operation and maintenance, and preparation of technical files, is recognized. In addition, specific roles are identified, such as administrators, monitors and construction supervisors, which could improve their productivity with the partial adoption of AI. In terms of expectations, activities such as sharing the database with entities such as the OSCE and monitoring transparency through AI, as well as information management and financial transaction processing, are expected to benefit in the short term. Term with the implementation of AI. Although there are challenges such as staff training and insufficient technological infrastructure, change enablers are also identified, such as business competition and technology transfer, which can promote greater adoption of AI in public works. The research provides a vision of the scope and potential of AI in the public works sector, which allows other investigations to delve more deeply into the potential of each of the outstanding approaches in the three dimensions studied. in this article.

6 Final Comments, Limitations and Future Work

Regarding the perceptions of artificial intelligence (AI) and its impact on the productivity of public works, the results reveal that there is a certain degree of agreement among the study participants. In general, it is recognized that AI can increase productivity in different stages of the public works value chain, such as the stage of tendering and selection of suppliers, start-up, operation and maintenance, and preparation of technical files. In addition, it was possible to identify who would improve their productivity, with the adoption of AI, the administrator, the monitor and the construction supervisor, could improve their productivity with the partial replacement by AI. And finally, in the implementation of AI that can improve productivity, the results indicated that the new professions linked to Artificial Intelligence and the optimization of the production system of public works must be addressed in depth, naturally It assumes that the monitoring of on-site production would be more efficient with AI during the execution of public works, in addition, the risk identification and estimation process will be more efficient and less expensive. These insights provide a first glimpse of the scope and potential of AI in the public works sector.

Regarding the expectations related to the implementation of AI in public works, there are glimpses of certain activities and functions that are expected to benefit in the short term. At an early stage, the importance of sharing the database with entities such as the State Procurement Supervisory Agency (OSCE) and other executing units is highlighted, as well as monitoring transparency through AI. Likewise, information management and the processing of financial transactions and operations are expected to be areas that will be automated and optimized through AI. These expectations indicate the areas of public works that could undergo significant changes with the adoption of this technology.

In relation to the challenges and opportunities, some key inhibitors for the implementation of AI in the productivity of public works are identified. Among them are low training, technological infrastructure and resistance to change. These aspects represent important challenges that need to be addressed in order to achieve a successful adoption of AI in the sector. However, the enablers of change that drive the implementation of AI, such as business competition, technology transfer and technological infrastructure, are also identified. These factors can provide opportunities to overcome the aforementioned challenges and promote greater adoption of AI in public works.

The results of this study show that there is widespread recognition of the potential of artificial intelligence to increase productivity in public works. The implementation of AI is expected to benefit different stages and roles within the public works value chain. In addition, specific activities and functions are identified that AI is expected to improve in the short term. However, to achieve a successful implementation, it is necessary to face the challenges related to training, technological infrastructure and resistance to change. At the same time, it is important to take advantage of change enablers, such as business competition and technology transfer, to drive AI adoption in the public works sector. The study highlights the potential benefits of AI in public works, such as rapid systematization of government data, impartial decision-making in the selection of contractors, and increased productivity. The research suggests the possibility of replicating and comparing the study in different contexts and countries to improve understanding of the implementation of AI policies in public works.

APPENDICE 1: Questions asked to professionals

Sections of the analytical strategy and survey questions

Section	Questions	Items	Opinions of answers
Perceptions about the concept of AI and the increase in productivity in public works	To what extent do you agree that artificial intelligence can increase the productivity of the personnel involved in the value chain of a public project?[1]	- In the Conception stage of the Project or Profile - In the stage of elaboration of the Technical File - In the stage of Tendering and selection of suppliers - In the Execution and Work Supervision stage - In the commissioning, operation and maintenance stage	Being 1 totally disagree and 7 totally agree

(continued)

(continued)

Sections of the analytical strategy and survey questions

Section	Questions	Items	Opinions of answers
	Which of the following involved in public works will improve their productivity with the adoption of artificial intelligence?	- Designer - Work monitor - Construction resident - Construction manager - Work supervisor	Being 1 totally disagree and 7 totally agree
	To what extent do you agree that the implementation of artificial intelligence will increase the productivity of public works?	-I am totally open to the adoption of AI in public works, and that it will increase productivity -I naturally assume that on-site production monitoring would be more efficient with AI -During the execution of public works, the process of identifying and estimating risks would be more efficient and less expensive -Other "intelligence" will be required to improve productivity in public works -The new professions linked to Artificial Intelligence and the optimization of the public works production system must be addressed in depth	Being 1 totally disagree and 7 totally agree

(continued)

(*continued*)

Sections of the analytical strategy and survey questions

Section	Questions	Items	Opinions of answers
Expectations of AI in the productivity of public works	From your point of view, what activities increase your productivity in public works, at an early stage of the implementation of artificial intelligence?	-Share the database with the OSCE and other executing units -Have an updated registry of contractors -Have an updated registry of consultants -Avoid presenting physical documentation (digital documentation) -Monitoring of AI transparency -Register of similar technical files	Select at least 3 options
	From your point of view, which of the following public works functions will be automated and optimized by artificial intelligence in the short term?	-Auxiliary administrative tasks -Executive management -Technical tasks -Training -Warehouse management -Regulations -Processing of transactions / financial operations -Construction operations -Information management	Select at least 3 options

(*continued*)

(*continued*)

Sections of the analytical strategy and survey questions

Section	Questions	Items	Opinions of answers
Challenges and opportunities of AI in the productivity of public works	What are the main inhibitors of the implementation of artificial intelligence in the productivity of public works?	-Digital development -Supplier control -Administrative culture -Resistance to change of the personnel involved -Low staff training -Technological infrastructure -Legislation -Budget -Data privacy -Data security	Select at least 3 options
	What are the main enablers of change that drive the implementation of artificial intelligence in the productivity of public works?	-Business competition -Knowledge -Administrative culture -Technological infrastructure -Legislation -Budget -Technology transfer	Select at least 3 options

References

1. Tolentino, S.: El segundo puente más largo del Perú: dónde se ubica. La República (2023)
2. Criado, J.I., Sandoval-Almazán, R., Valle-Cruz, D., Ruvalcaba-Gómez, E.A.: Percepciones de los directores de información sobre inteligencia artificial: un estudio comparativo de implicaciones y desafíos para el sector público. Primer lunes **26**(1) (2020). https://doi.org/10.5210/fm.v26i1.10648
3. Criado, J., Gil, J.: Creando valor público a través de tecnologías y estrategias inteligentes: de los servicios digitales a la inteligencia artificial y más allá. Revista Internacional de Gestión del Sector Público **32**(5), 438–450 (2019)
4. Fuente, J.: La construcción del estado virtual: tecnologías de información y cambio instituto (2012)
5. Orlikowski, W.J., Scott, S.V.: Sociomaterialidad: desafiando la separación de tecnología, trabajo y organización. Academia de Anales de Gestión **2**(1), 433–474 (2008)
6. Ghio, V.: Productividad en Obras de Construcción. Repositorio de la Pontificia Universidad Católica del Perú (2001). https://repositorio.pucp.edu.pe/index/handle/123456789/181910
7. Instituto Global McKinsey (MGI): Reinventar la construcción: una ruta hacia una mayor productividad (2017). Recuperado de: https://www.mckinsey.com/capabilities/operations/our-insights/reinventing-construction-through-a-productivity-revolution

8. Frasco: Consultoras de Ingeniería en la cadena de valor de las obras públicas (2021). Recuperado de: https://revistavial.com/consultoras-de-ingenieria-en-la-cadena-de-valor-de-las-obras-publicas/
9. Abioye, S.O., et al.: Inteligencia artificial en la industria de la construcción: una revisión del estado actual, oportunidades y desafíos futuros. Revista de Ingeniería de la Construcción **44**, 103299 (2019). https://doi.org/10.1016/j.jobe.2021.103299
10. McCarthy, J.: ¿Qué es la Inteligencia Artificial? (2007). Obtenido de http://jmc.stanford.edu/articles/whatisai/whatisai.pdf
11. Kankanhalli, A., Charalabidis, Y., Mellouli, S.: IoT e IA para un gobierno inteligente: una agenda de investigación. Información Gubernamental Trimestral **36**(2), 304–309 (2019)
12. OCDE: Inteligencia Artificial en la Sociedad. Recuperado de (2019). https://doi.org/10.1787/eedfee77-es
13. Markus, M.L.: Datificación, estrategia organizacional e investigación SI: ¿Cuál es el puntaje? Revista de sistemas de información estratégica **26**(3), 233–241 (2017)
14. Ogie, R.I., Rho, J.C., Clarke, R.J.: Inteligencia artificial en la comunicación del riesgo de desastres: una revisión sistemática de la literatura. En Documento presentado en las Actas de la 5ª Conferencia Internacional sobre Tecnologías de la Información y la Comunicación para la Gestión de Desastres (ICT-DM), Sendai, Japón (2018)
15. Fátima, S., Desouza, K.C., Dawson, G.S.: Planes estratégicos nacionales de inteligencia artificial: un análisis multidimensional. Análisis económico y política **67**, 178–194 (2020). https://doi.org/10.1016/j.eap.2020.07.008
16. Susar, D.Y, Aquaro, V.: Inteligencia artificial: Oportunidades y desafíos para el sector público. En Documento presentado en las Actas de la 12ª Conferencia Internacional sobre Teoría y Práctica de la Gobernanza Electrónica, Melbourne, Australia (2019)
17. Chui, M. (2017). Artificial Intelligence the Next Digital Frontier. McKinsey and Company Global Institute, 47(3.6)
18. Kolodner, J.: Case-based reasoning. Morgan Kaufmann (2014)
19. Androutsopoulou, A., Karacapilidis, N., Loukis, E., Charalabidis, Y.: Transformando la comunicación entre los ciudadanos y el gobierno a través de chatbots guiados por IA. Información Gubernamental Trimestral **36**(2), 358–367 (2019)
20. Contraloría General de la República del Perú (2019). Informe de Obras Paralizadas 2019. https://doc.contraloria.gob.pe/estudiosespeciales/documento_trabajo/2019/Reporte_Obras_Paralizadas.pdf

OISHI: An Ontology Integration Framework for Domains of Socio-Humanitarian Importance Incorporating Hybrid Machine Intelligence

E. Bhaveeasheshwar[1] and Gerard Deepak[2]([✉])

[1] Concordia University, Montreal, Canada
[2] Department of Computer Science and Engineering, Manipal Institute of Technology Bengaluru, Manipal Academy of Higher Education, Manipal, India
gerard.deepak.christuni@gmail.com

Abstract. There is a need for strategic ontology integration as the integration of ontologies that are cognitive entities and by themselves are knowledge representation, and description models based on certain logic is essential as the integral structure of the ontology concerning the context and reason it was created must be preserved. So, owing to this, there is a strategic need for automating the strategy of ontology integration, at least up to a certain extent, for that Semantically Inclined Knowledge Centric models and strategies are required as ontologies have to be conceptualized based on human interpretation and cognition and also have to be integrated without any loss or significant modifications concerning the associations between the ontology. In this paper, an ontology integration model for domains such as Mass Communications, Liberal Arts, Media and Journalism, and Public Policy is made use of where the ontologies are specifically generated from distinct heterogeneous document datasets to which the Term Frequency-Inverse Document Frequency (TF-IDF) is applied to identify the rare and yet the most informative terms and for topic modeling, Latent Dirichlet Allocation (LDA) is employed. Furthermore, the classification of the ontologies is achieved using the XGBoost classifier. The strategy involves the extraction of indices from E-books and formalized Taxonomy using the Renyi Entropy with a specific standard deviance measure. The Knowledge Stack achieves entity aggregation formalized using the LOD Cloud, Wiki Data, and Google KG API from that the Semantic Network is formalized. The classified ontologies are the formalized Semantic Network, that is further used to compute the Semantic Similarity under the Tabu search Metaheuristic optimization to formalize, finalize, and integrate the ontologies. The SemantoSim measure, that incorporates differential thresholds, is used in the Tabu search framework to compute semantic similarity. The proposed OISHI framework has achieved an overall Precision of 94.39%, Recall of 96.44%, Accuracy of 95.41%, F-Measure of 95.40%, and the lowest FDR of 0.06.

Keywords: LDA · Tabu Search · TF-IDF · XGBoost · Socio Informatics

© The Author(s), under exclusive license to Springer Nature Switzerland AG 2023
F. Ortiz-Rodríguez et al. (Eds.): EGETC 2023, CCIS 1888, pp. 155–167, 2023.
https://doi.org/10.1007/978-3-031-43940-7_13

1   Introduction

Ontologies are the knowledge representation models used for reasoning and inferencing. So, ontologies are organized into concepts, sub-concepts, and individuals, and traditionally, ontologies were deemed as formal, explicit specifications of a shared conceptualization. Knowledge in the current base scenario is sparse and scarce online. However, data is extensive, scattered, and abundant, especially on any online platform like the World Wide Web. The information must be extracted from the data, and many schemes exist. But, deriving knowledge from information is a very tedious task, and only a few existing techniques are available because knowledge requires some amount of cognition, human cognitive verification, or cognitive reasoning using standard reasoners. So, understanding involves some level of human cognition, and ontologies are the most viable entities to represent knowledge. However, ontologies are only available on a small scale. Pockets of ontologies can be generated for particular concepts, but integrating these ontologies is a challenge because ontologies are developed from different perspectives. Ontology tools also involve domain experts and knowledge engineers to engineer ontologies, and ontology engineering is not a single-step process. Still, it is a multi-step process, out of that one mandatory step is the human verification or human contribution, human cognitive ability. So, there are many perspectives. So, integrating ontology is a challenge. However, the domains are highly constructive, restrictive, and similar, so incorporating the ontologies becomes challenging. Therefore, there is some level of learning and cognition that is required, especially in domains like sociology, socio-humanitarian importance, mass communication, media and techno media, journalism, and liberal arts are pretty independent as a domain but quite relative because some of the concepts like mass communication, media, and journalism can overlap, but they can also have different meanings. So, therefore indicating ontologies requires a high level of solid cognitive algorithms and reasoners.

Motivation: There is a need for an Ontology Integration framework because of the exponential growth of digital information, and organizations need help managing and integrating diverse and heterogeneous data sources. An urgent requirement arises for an ontology integration framework to address these challenges effectively. By incorporating ontologies, such frameworks can provide a unified and consistent representation of knowledge, enabling precise and valuable analysis and interpretation of data. Furthermore, aligning and integrating ontologies facilitates bridging semantic gaps, fostering a shared comprehension of concepts and relationships among individuals and organizations. This, in turn, promotes seamless communication and collaboration, making ontology integration an indispensable aspect of the current information landscape. Hence, the main impetus behind this lies in the absence of frameworks addressing Ontology Integration in a semantically driven manner, modeled to suit the architectural layout of Web 3.0.

Contribution: Following are some novel contributions delivered by the proposed OISHI. First, Mass Communication, Media and Journalism, Public Policy, and Liberal Arts ontologies are generated through TF-IDF and LDA. Furthermore, the classification of ontologies is performed using the XGBoost classifier. The approach involves extracting indices from e-books and establishing a taxonomy using the Renyi Entropy method with a specific standard deviation measure. Entity aggregation is accomplished by utilizing a formalized Knowledge Stack using resources such as the LOD Cloud, Wiki Data, and the Google KG API, creating a formalized Semantic Network. This formalized Semantic Network is then utilized to compute the Semantic Similarity using a Tabu search Metaheuristic optimization technique. The aim is to formalize, refine, and integrate the ontologies through this process. The Tabu search architecture calculates Semantic Similarity using the SemantoSim measure and integrating differential thresholds. As a result, the total FDR is reduced while Precision, Recall, Accuracy, and F-Measure are all increased.

Organization: The following is the structure of the paper: Sect. 2 provides a comprehensive review of related works. Section 3 presents an overview of the proposed system architecture. Section 4 outlines the acquired outcomes and evaluates the system's performance. Finally, the paper is concluded in Sect. 5.

2 Related Works

Babalou et al. [1] examine the impact of selecting an appropriate subsumer from all shared progenitors of two ideas on the accuracy of the word similarity assessment. Using the PSO algorithm, they framed this challenge as an optimization one. Paneque et al. [2] proposed an Ontology Integration model for the e-Learning domain to combine data from several e-learning knowledge sources. Semantic data querying, time series prediction, and the formulation of SWRL reasoning are all steps in the validation process. Fu et al. [3] propose an ontology for examining "double carbon" policies using exterior qualities and internal characteristics. It creates a knowledge graph using an adaptive policy knowledge extraction method for these policies. Employed methods include reserved dictionary utilization, expression format-based rule extraction, sentiment dictionary-based keyword matching, and improved compound topic LDA based on high-quality phrase standards. Maghawry et al. [4] introduce a method to create knowledge graphs by merging two medical ontologies. This methodology relies on a medical website and encyclopedia to automatically annotate and establish links between biomedical and medical text. It employs BERT and BI-LSTM models while leveraging UMLS concepts for the task. Hnatkowska et al. [5] introduced a semi-automated approach that utilizes WordNet to establish attribute meanings. Pérez-Pérez et al. [6] introduced a framework that employed various automated domain recognition methods to aid document curation, making the process more efficient for curators and minimizing the need for extensive manual annotation. The framework used six advanced NER taggers and a random forest model to annotate and filter relevant documents, supporting manual annotation efforts. Capuano et al. [7] presented a system designed to enhance the crawling process by applying semantic-based techniques. Their framework integrated cutting-edge technologies, including CNN and LOD, to improve the obtained results. In their work, Delgoshaei et al. [8] presented an approach that combined semantic knowledge of weather conditions with the K-means clustering algorithm to identify distinct seasons of electricity consumption. Bulygin [9] idealizes ontology and schema matching as crucial tasks for data integration. They propose a fusion of various matches utilizing machine learning techniques to enhance the matching process. Specifically, the training process involves the usage of basic Bayesian classifiers, logistic regression models, and gradient tree-boosting algorithms, utilizing the features extracted from lexical and semantic similarity functions. Chakraborty et al. [10] developed a framework that employs recursive neural networks for ontology alignment. Their approach focuses on extracting the structural information of classes between the ontologies.

Shrivatsava et al. [11] presented a method to integrate Internet of Things ontologies in the IoT domain. The process involves labeling the dataset with tags and then classifying the data with the AdaBoost classifier. This classifier uses metrics like Shannon's entropy, pointwise mutual information, and a differential step deviation measure. It is aligned with random core classes from existing variational Ontologies in the Internet of Things area. Deepak G et al. [12] present a knowledge-centric recommendation method for Infographics. It uses metadata from various sources, including crowd-sourced ontologies, to offer personalized infographic recommendations based on user interests and clicks. The system builds an ontology from research paper titles and keywords to model user interests effectively. It leverages Query Words, Current User-Clicks, and established Knowledge Stores like BibSonomy, DBpedia, Wikidata, LOD Cloud, and crowd-sourced Ontologies for semantic alignment, using measures such as Horn's index, EnAPMI, and information entropy. Manoj et al. [13] present a method for Automatic Ontology Integration tailored to the Internet of Things (IoT). Through integrating Hybrid Machine Learning Techniques, spectral clustering, and ANOVA–Jaccard similarity index, the researchers employ sunflower optimization to gauge the similarity for Ontology matching. Gupta et al. [14] constructed a model involving a Missile Knowledge Graph. By leveraging this carefully curated knowledge graph, a query-answering model generates tabular or graph representations in response to natural language questions. Cypher queries were used to execute the queries, and the Neo4j platform was chosen for knowledge graph creation. Panchal et al. [15] elucidate their work in designing an ontology dedicated to the realm of Public Higher Education. Notably, they demonstrate using SPARQL queries to enable advanced reasoning with the newly created ontology. The EGO model incorporates the e-Government Documentation Ontology, as outlined by Ortiz-Rodriguez et al. [16], to effectively manage and provide access to governmental documents, both official and non-official, streamlining administrative processes.

3 Proposed Architecture

Figures 1 and 2 depict the suggested system architecture for the integration framework of ontology in domains about socio-humanitarian significance. Figure 1 is a document-centric ontology generation for four different domains. It is a mirror architecture wherein documents about the Mass communication dataset, documents belonging to Liberal arts as a dataset, the dataset of documents belonging to the media and journalism, and the dataset of documents related to public policy are independently extracted. Independent datasets are used wherein the TF-IDF [17] is applied on these documents individually to identify the most informative terms. The terms frequently occurring within the document corpus and rarely occurring terms across the document corpus are yielded via the TF-IDF. The terms extracted through the TF-IDF model are subjected to Latent Dirichlet Allocation (LDA) [18] model for topic modeling. The main reason for topic modeling is to uncover the hidden and yet relevant terms that were not discovered through the TF-IDF, specifically from the external document of Web corpora. In this case, the document directly from the Web is used as an external corpus to generate the terms relevant to the terms discovered through the TF-IDF on applying the LDA strategy. The terms found through the LDA and TF-IDF are subjected to ontology generators like Stardog and OntoCollab separately, and a large ontology is generated with different perspectives using Stardog and Ontocollab, and the ontology for the Mass communication domain is generated. The developed ontology is further subjected to the Pellet reasoner for removing the inconsistencies.

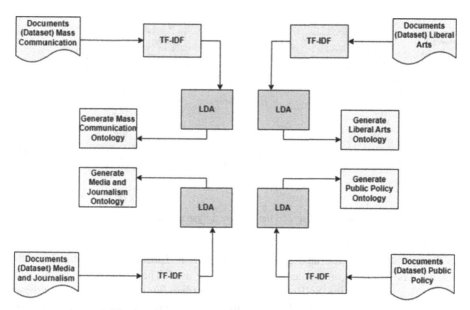

Fig. 1. Phase 1 of the Proposed System Architecture

For the Liberal Arts, the same strategy is followed, where the documents about Liberal Arts are subjected to TF-IDF and then LDA. Further, the terms discovered from the LDA and TF-IDF are subjected to the Stardog and OntCollab frameworks for Ontology generation, and finalized Liberal Arts Ontology is yielded. Similarly, for Media and Journalism, the documents on Media and Journalism are subjected to TF-IDF and then LDA. Further, the terms discovered from the LDA and TF-IDF are subjected to the Stardog and OntCollab frameworks for Ontology generation, and finalized Ontology for Media and Journalism is yielded. The documents on Public Policy are similarly subjected to TF-IDF and then LDA. The terms obtained from the LDA and TF-IDF are then subjected to the Stardog and OntCollab frameworks to generate ontologies. The result is a finalized ontology for Public Policy. Handling the documents about a domain individually is to demarcate domain-specific ontologies and develop domain-specific ontologies without any deviation. Instead of amalgamating and indicating all the documents, a single large-scale ontology will yield deviations and highly domain-specific ontologies will not be considered. Henceforth, the treatment of individual ontology generation is considered at first. Unique ontology generation is done step by step for respective domains, and the significant domains are Mass Communication, Liberal Arts, Public Policy, and Media, and Journalism is connected because the documents about Media and Journalism are correlative. So, correlative documents alone are used; subsequently, they are treated as one single domain.

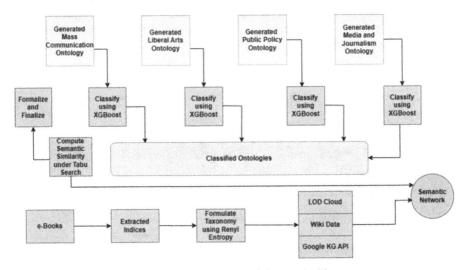

Fig. 2. Phase 2 of the Proposed System Architecture

Furthermore, the generated Mass Communication, Liberal Arts, Media, Journalism, and Public Policy ontologies from Phase 1 are used. The ontologies are subjected to classification using the XGBoost [19] Machine Learning model. Individually these ontologies are subjected to an individual sequential pipeline of the XGBoost algorithm. Separately the XGBoost algorithm is applied to each of these ontologies and classified. For classification, e-books related to all four domains are considered. Seventeen e-books, four related to Public Policy, six on Media and Journalism, four related to Liberal Arts, and three associated with Mass Communication, were considered. The extracted index from the e-books was subjected to parsing, and the indexes were extracted. Indexes and the contents of the e-books, along with the glossary terms if present in the e-books considered as an index and this index was extracted using customized NLP parsers to formulate a Taxonomy. This Taxonomy is developed by computing the Renyi Entropy, that quantifies the information content.

The indexes formulated as a Taxonomy were subjected to individual querying of the LOD cloud, or individually they were subjected to the Wiki Data API and the Google KG API. LOD Cloud was accessed based on SPARQL querying via agents. However, Wiki and Google KG APIs were accessed via their respective APIs. So the reason for using LOD Cloud, Wiki Data, and Google KG API is to obtain a large lateral rich set and ensure that existing Knowledge from the actual World Wide Web, is a community-contributed, verified, and accepted by a community, is used to enrich the Taxonomy and reduce the

Semantic gap or the cognitive gap between the external Knowledge as well as the Knowledge into the localized framework and all the entities from LOD Cloud, Wiki Data, and Google KG API is formulated into a large Semantic Network. The entities relevant to the Semantic Network are intricately linked to specific domains and are utilized to compute Semantic Similarity in conjunction with the classified ontologies. The classification of all ontologies is performed using XGBoost. For the XGBoost classifier, the Semantic Network themselves are used as a feature. The XGBoost classifier employed the Pearson correlation coefficient to select elements from the Semantic Network and subsequently performed classification. To ensure a sufficient number of features are included in the XGBoost classifier for generating classified ontologies, a threshold of 50 percent is set for the Pearson correlation coefficient. The entities from the classified ontologies and the Semantic Network are then employed to compute Semantic Similarity. This computation uses the SemantoSim [20] measure within the Tabu search algorithm [21]. To encompass a considerable number of pertinent entities within the framework, the SemantoSim measure is established with a threshold of 0.75. The adoption of the Tabu search predominantly stems from its classification as a Metaheuristic algorithm. It will convert the first generated feasible solution set into a considerably more optimal solution set by utilizing SemantoSim as the objective function for Tabu search and again setting a threshold of 0.85. So ultimately, relevant entities are formulated and formalized and are subjected to axiomatization to establish the relationship between the terms, and a single large integrated ontology highly relevant to these domains is yielded.

XGBoost stands for Extreme Boost Grading. Decision tree boosting is the fundamental component of XGBoost. Boosting is an ensemble learning technique that involves creating a series of models sequentially, with each model attempting to improve upon the deficiencies of its predecessor. Every additional model integrated into the ensemble is a decision tree in tree boosting. As each tree boosts, the prior tree is incorrectly labeled using the ensemble boosting approach. In the predictive modeling technique of decision tree learning, subsets of the training samples are split repeatedly to create a model. According to this method, decision trees are made in order. The use of weights is crucial in XGBoost. Weights for each independent variable are allocated to the decision tree, that forecasts results. The objective function of XGBoost is represented by Eq. (1), that is the outcome of adding the loss function computed overall predictions and the regularisation function for all predictors (k trees). The symbol f_k in the formula represents a forecast from the k_{th} tree.

$$obj(\theta) = \sum_{i}^{n} l(y_i - \hat{y}_i) + \sum_{k=1}^{k} \Omega(f_k) \tag{1}$$

LDA is a widely utilized technique for topic modeling. Each document uses various words, and each subject is related to a few words. Based on the words in the document, the LDA seeks to identify issues to that the document belongs. It is assumed that texts on related subjects will employ comparable terminology. Latent themes are probability distributions. Therefore, the documents can map the probabilities across them.

Pearson's correlation coefficient is used to determine a linear relationship's strength and existence (p-value) between two variables or sets of data. Between "−1" and "+1," the value of "r" can fall. There is no correlation between the two variables, as represented by the value "0". Examining the indicator value higher than zero for a positive relationship can determine whether two variables are associated. In this case, an increase in one variable will correspondingly raise the value of the other. Conversely, a value less than '0' signifies a negative correlation, indicating that when one variable increases, the further decreases. Pearson's correlation coefficient, symbolized as 'r' in Eq. (2), determines the degree to that two continuous variables are linearly connected.

$$r = \frac{\sum(a_i - \overline{a})(b_i - \overline{b})}{\sqrt{\sum(a_i - \overline{a})^2 \sum(b_i - \overline{b})^2}} \tag{2}$$

where r stands for the Pearson correlation coefficient, a_i represents a variable sample, b_i represents a variable sample, etc. The mean values in a variable are $\overline{a}$, and the mean in the b variable is $\overline{b}$.

The samples associated with a variable are denoted by a_i, while the samples associated with the b variable are denoted by b_i. The symbol "r" stands for the Pearson correlation coefficient. $\overline{a}$ represents the average of the values in a variable, and $\overline{b}$ represents the average values in the b variable.

Semantic similarity measurement employs the SemantoSim measure, rooted in the Point-wise Mutual Information Measure. Keywords are combined as (a,b), and SemantoSim (a,b) is used to quantify their semantic similarity. The calculation of SemantoSim utilizes Eq. (3) and relies on the relationship pmi(a,b), representing the probability of an event involving both keywords x and y. Furthermore, the presence of terms a and b are individually assessed through probabilities p(a) and p(b), respectively.

$$SemantoSim(a, b) = pmi(a, b) + p(a, b)log[p(a, b)]/[p(a).p(b)] + log(p(b, a)) \tag{3}$$

The Rényi entropy of order β is defined by the Eq. (4) if a discrete random variable Y has m potential values and the j_{th} occurrence has probability p_j.

The Eq. (4) defines the Rényi entropy of order β if a discrete random variable Y has m potential values and the p_j occurrence has probability p_j.

$$H_\beta(Y) = \frac{1}{1-\beta} log_2 \left(\sum_{i=1}^{m} p_i^\beta \right) \tag{4}$$

TF, denoted as tf(x,dt) in Eq. (5), is the frequency with which the term x appears in document d_t.

$$tf(x, d_t) = \frac{f_{x,d_t}}{\sum_{x\prime d_t} f_{x\prime d_t}} \tag{5}$$

where f_{x,d_t} is how often a word appears in all a document's text.

Equation depicts IDF (6) computes the prevalence or rarity of a term throughout the whole document data. A phrase occurs more often when it is near 0 than far from it.

$$idf(x, D) = log \frac{M}{Df(t) + 1} \tag{6}$$

Document frequency, or Df(t), is a metric for how frequently a word appears in documents, and (M) is expressed as a proportion of the collection's total number of documents. Equation (7) illustrates the TF-IDF.

$$tfidf(x, d_t, D) = tf(x, d_t).idf(x, D) \tag{7}$$

4   Performance Evaluation and Result

The performance of the proposed OISHI and Ontology Integration framework for domains of great social and humanitarian significance, incorporating hybrid machine intelligence, is assessed using various metrics such as precision, recall, accuracy, F-Measure percentages, and FDR. The inclusion of precision, recall, accuracy, and F-measure as standard metrics is justified by their ability to evaluate the outcomes quantitatively and, in this case, the pertinence of the integrated and developed domain ontologies. FDR encompasses the number of false positives in the finally conceived ontologies and standard formulations. However, with a vantage point of ontology conception and acceptance into the domain, is used for precision, recall, accuracy, F-measure, and FDR is also computed on the same lines.

Table 1 illustrates that the four models, MSKIO, MLBOI, AOIC, and LOMSI, were chosen as the preferred baseline models for assessing the performance of the proposed OISHI. According to Table 1, OISHI has the highest average precision percentage (94.39%), average recall percentage (96.44%), average accuracy percentage (95.41%), and average F-measure percentage (95.40%). Additionally, OISHI displays an FDR of 0.06. According to Table 1's results, MKSIO achieves average precision, recall, accuracy, and accuracy-accuracy ratios of 84.43%, 84.41%, and 83.23%, respectively, with an FDR of 0.17. The MLBOI model obtains an average precision of 86.12%, recall of 88.36%, accuracy of 87.24%, and F-measure of 87.22% with an FDR of 0.14. The AOIC model results in an average precision of 88.33%, an average recall of 90.54%, average accuracy of 89.43%, and an average F-measure of 89.42%, with an FDR of 0.12. Finally, the LOMSI model has an average precision of 91.12%, recall of 93.17%, accuracy of 92.14%, and F-measure of 92.13% with an FDR of 0.09.

Table 1. Comparison of Performance of the proposed OISHI with other approach

Model	Average Precision %	Average Recall %	Average Accuracy %	Average F-Measure %	FDR
MSKIO [22]	83.23	85.63	84.43	84.41	0.17
MLBOI [23]	86.12	88.36	87.24	87.22	0.14
AOIC [24]	88.33	90.54	89.43	89.42	0.12
LOMSI [25]	91.12	93.17	92.14	92.13	0.09
Proposed OISHI	**94.39**	**96.44**	**95.41**	**95.40**	**0.06**

The exceptional performance exhibited by the OISHI model is evidenced by its outstanding precision, recall, accuracy, F-measure percentages, and low FDR value, that can be attributed to its utilization of TF-IDF in conjunction with the LDA model for topic modeling. This integration effectively extracts informative terms from the dataset of individual documents, specifically tailored to domains such as Mass Communication, Media and Journalism, Liberal Arts, and Public Policy. The TF-IDF yields highly informative terms, rare terms across the document corpus, and frequent within the document corpus. So a standard protocol is followed for discovering the informative terms, that is further enriched by applying the topic modeling to locate the relevant and yet uncovered terms to the LDA model. This is individually done for the Mass Communication documents dataset, Media and Journalism documents dataset, Liberal Arts documents dataset, and Public Policy documents dataset to conceive the Mass Communication ontology particular to the domain, Media and Journalism ontology, Liberal Arts ontology, and the Public Policy ontology.

Furthermore, the proposed OISHI model encompasses the XGBoost classifier, a robust classifier for classifying individually conceived independent domain ontologies. So parallelly, the XGBoost algorithm classifies the Mass Communication ontology, Media and Journalism ontology, Liberal Arts ontology, and Public Policy ontology separately. However, standard feature selection is made, wherein the features are selected and passed through the Semantic Network, conceived by extracting the index terms from the e-books, index terms comprising of the contents, the glossary, and the Metadata for the e-books if present. This extracted index is further used for formulation as a Taxonomy wherein the Renyi Entropy is used. The Renyi Entropy associates the index terms to formulate the Taxonomy. This Taxonomy is enriched by obtaining the entities from the LOD cloud, Wiki Data, and the Google KG API, and all these entities yielded from the pre-distinct heterogenous knowledge stores, namely the LOD cloud, Wiki Data, and the Google KG API formulate the Semantic Network and the Semantic Network is used directly used as features to classify using the Machine Learning XGBoost algorithm.

Most importantly, the classified ontologies are further utilized to measure the Semantic Similarity with that of the entities in the Semantic Network to yield the final Ontology. The Semantic Network houses a strong entity that is relevant to the domain. Apart from this, the XGBoost algorithm is mainly used because it has a feature-controlling mechanism. Instead of going for Deep Learning, auto-handcrafted feature selection takes place wherein it ensures that the out layers are not learned, and Tabu Search helps in obtaining the most optimal solution set from the feasible solution set. So, owing to all these reasons, the proposed OISHI framework outperforms the baseline models as it is knowledge-centric, encompasses hybrid Machine Intelligence, and anchors auxiliary Knowledge from standard knowledge stores like LOD cloud, Wiki Data, and Google KG API.

Regarding performance, the MKSIO baseline model must meet expectations when contrasted with the proposed model. The reason behind this discrepancy lies in the fact that MKSIO, being a multi-source knowledge integration model, utilizes machine learning algorithms that are relatively encompassing. However, ontologies are themselves used, and knowledge is also being used, but the fine-grained tuning of knowledge is absent through robust relevance computation or inferencing mechanisms. So typical similarity algorithm alone does not suffice, so the MKSIO model does not perform as expected.

In terms of performance, the MLBOI baseline model falls short of expectations when contrasted with the proposed model because the MLBOI, a Machine Learning model for Biomedical ontology integration analysis, is highly specific to the biomedical domain. However, it uses self-compilation with a deep Siamese neural network that helps in learning formal knowledge within the ontologies and text data. So, the Siamese neural network is a solid deep learning algorithm where feature selection is auto-handcrafted. These features can learn relationships, leading to out-layer-based learning or learning unnecessary data points or relationships because there is no proper feature selection mechanism. There is no auxiliary knowledge that is fed into the model. Even robust deep learning does not perform as expected.

The LOMSI model, designed as a layered ontology-based multi-source information integration approach with situation awareness, fails to achieve the anticipated performance compared to the proposed OISHI framework. The reason behind this discrepancy is the OISHI framework's adoption of ontology-driven information integration and its reliance on the LOD cloud, a valuable knowledge repository contributed by the community. However, there is no proper mechanism to fine-tune auto-drive knowledge. There is knowledge, but knowledge is obtained from third-party verification. Actual verification and reasoning for the knowledge are not done in this particular model, and a learning-based framework is absent. So, Machine Intelligence attenuation or integration of intelligence, the relevance computation mechanism with a learning model and auxiliary knowledge, is lacking.

The AOIC model, an ontology integration using clustering and a global similarity model, depends only on clustering with a robust semantic similarity model, that is acceptable to an extent. However, Machine Intelligence is absent, relevant computation mechanisms vital for knowledge derivation, segregation, and knowledge driven-reasoning is lacking in this model, and most importantly, a metaheuristic framework for achieving the results from the initial feasible solution set is also absent. Henceforth, although clustering, this model involves merging ontologies and has knowledge in terms of the ontology corpus. The Jaccard similarity model makes it weak. The RDF mapping with ontology matching is ineffective when clustering is placed instead of a robust machine-learning model. Henceforth, the AOIC model does not achieve the anticipated performance compared to the proposed OISHI framework.

The distribution of precision concerning the number of recommendations for the proposed OISHI, LOMSI, MLBOI, AOIC, and MKSOI is depicted in Fig. 3. OISHI resides at the top of the hierarchy, followed by LOMSI. The third in the scale is AOIC, and the second last in the order is MLBOI. The lowermost in the hierarchy is MKSIO. The OISHI outperforms the baseline models because it has robust relevance computation mechanisms and knowledge derivation schemes, where knowledge is not only loaded from LOD cloud, Wiki Data, and Google KG API but also reasoned, formulated as a Semantic Network and further used for reasoning and feature selection. Knowledge formulization depends upon a Taxonomy, that is also extrapolated using the Renyi Entropy and staged knowledge derivation from standard knowledge stores with Tabu Search for optimization of the initial feasible solution set and XGBoost classifier for encompassing

Machine Learning for achieving a more comprehensive degree of intelligence, makes the proposed OISHI model much better than the baseline models.

5   Conclusion

The OISHI framework has been put forth for the Ontology Integration Framework for Domains of Socio-Humanitarian Importance incorporating Hybrid Machine Intelligence. Several perspectives of Ontologies like Mass Communication, Media and Journalism, Public Policy, and Liberal Arts were generated using TF-IDF and LDA. Subsequently, a Semantic Network is formulated by classifying generated ontologies through the XGBoost classifier, extracting indices from e-books, and establishing a taxonomy using the Renyi Entropy method and a specific standard deviation measure. Furthermore, aggregate entities, a Knowledge Stack is utilized, that is formalized using resources like the LOD Cloud, Wiki Data, and the Google KG API, resulting in a formalized Semantic Network. This formalized Semantic Network is then used to calculate Semantic Similarity through a Tabu search Metaheuristic optimization approach. The ultimate goal is to formalize, refine, and integrate the ontologies. The SemantoSim measure calculates semantic similarity within the Tabu search framework, considering differential thresholds. The proposed OISHI framework has achieved impressive results, including an overall precision of 94.39%, recall of 96.44%, an accuracy of 95.41%, an F-measure of 95.40%, and the lowest false discovery rate (FDR) observed is 0.06.

References

1. Babalou, S., Algergawy, A., König-Ries, B.: SimBio: Adopting Particle Swarm Optimization for ontology-based biomedical term similarity assessment. Data Knowl. Eng. **145**, 102137 (2023)
2. Paneque, M., del Mar Roldán-García, M., García-Nieto, J.: e-LION: data integration semantic model to enhance predictive analytics in e-Learning. Expert Syst. Appl. **213**, 118892 (2023)
3. Fu, Y., Wen, P., Wu, J., Shu, Y.: Knowledge Graph-Based Policy Analysis from a Hybrid Prospect of External Attributes and Internal Characteristics Under Carbon Peaking and Carbon Neutrality Goal. Available at SSRN 4384948
4. Maghawry, N., Ghoniemy, S., Shaaban, E., Emara, K.: An automatic generation of heterogeneous knowledge graph for global disease support: a demonstration of a cancer use case. Big Data Cogn. Comput. **7**(1), 21 (2023)
5. Hnatkowska, B., Kozierkiewicz, A., Pietranik, M.: Semi-automatic definition of attribute semantics for the purpose of ontology integration. IEEE Access **8**, 107272–107284 (2020)
6. Pérez-Pérez, M., Ferreira, T., Igrejas, G., Fdez-Riverola, F.: A novel gluten knowledge base of potential biomedical and health-related interactions extracted from the literature: using machine learning and graph analysis methodologies to reconstruct the bibliome. J. Biomed. Inform. **143**, 104398 (2023)
7. Capuano, A., Rinaldi, A.M., Russo, C.: An ontology-driven multimedia focused crawler based on linked open data and deep learning techniques. Multimedia Tools Appl. **79**, 7577–7598 (2020)
8. Delgoshaei, P., Heidarinejad, M., Austin, M.A.: Combined ontology-driven and machine learning approach to monitoring of building energy consumption. In: 2018 Building Performance Modeling Conference and SimBuild, Chicago, IL, pp. 667–674 (2018)

9. Bulygin, L.: Combining lexical and semantic similarity measures with machine learning approach for ontology and schema matching problem. In: Proceedings of the XX International Conference "Data Analytics and Management in Data Intensive Domains" (DAMDID/RCDL 2018), pp. 245–249 (2018)

10. Chakraborty, J., Bansal, S.K., Virgili, L., Konar, K., Yaman, B.: Ontoconnect: unsupervised ontology alignment with recursive neural network. In: Proceedings of the 36th Annual ACM Symposium on Applied Computing, pp. 1874–1882 (2021)

11. Shrivastava, R.R., Deepak, G.: AIOIML: automatic integration of ontologies for IoT domain using hybridized machine learning techniques. In: 2023 2nd International Conference on Paradigm Shifts in Communications Embedded Systems, Machine Learning and Signal Processing (PCEMS), pp. 1–5 (2023)

12. Deepak, G., Vibakar, A., Santhanavijayan, A.: OntoInfoG++: a knowledge fusion semantic approach for infographics recommendation. Int. J. Interact. Multimedia Artif. Intell. **8**(2), 213 (2023). https://doi.org/10.9781/ijimai.2021.12.005

13. Manoj, N., Deepak, G., Santhanavijayan, A.: OntoINT: a framework for ontology integration based on entity linking from heterogeneous knowledge sources. In: Congress on Intelligent Systems: Proceedings of CIS 2021, vol. 2 (pp. 27–35). Singapore: Springer Nature Singapore (2022) https://doi.org/10.1007/978-981-16-9113-3_3

14. Gupta, S., Tiwari, S., Ortiz-Rodriguez, F., Panchal, R.: KG4ASTRA: question answering over Indian missiles knowledge graph. Soft. Comput. **25**, 13841–13855 (2021)

15. Panchal, R., Swaminarayan, P., Tiwari, S., Ortiz-Rodriguez, F.: AISHE-Onto: a semantic model for public higher education universities. In: DG. O2021: The 22nd Annual International Conference on Digital Government Research, pp. 545–547 (2021)

16. Ortiz-Rodriguez, F., Medina-Quintero, J.M., Tiwari, S., Villanueva, V.: EGODO ontology: sharing, retrieving, and exchanging legal documentation across e-government. In: Ortiz-Rodriguez, F., Tiwari, S., Iyer, S., Medina-Quintero, J.M. (eds.) Futuristic Trends for Sustainable Development and Sustainable Ecosystems:, pp. 261–276. IGI Global (2022). https://doi.org/10.4018/978-1-6684-4225-8.ch016

17. SALTON, G., YANG, C.S.: On the specification of term values in automatic indexing. J. Documentation **29**(4), 351–372 (1973)

18. Blei, D.M., Ng, A.Y., Jordan, M.I.: Latent dirichlet allocation. J. Mach. Learn. Res. **3**, 993–1022 (2003)

19. Chen, T., Guestrin, C.: Xgboost: a scalable tree boosting system. In: Proceedings of the 22nd ACM SIGKDD International Conference on Knowledge Discovery and Data Mining, pp. 785–794 (2016)

20. Foltz, P.W., Kintsch, W., Landauer, T.K.: The measurement of textual coherence with latent semantic analysis. Discourse Process. **25**(2–3), 285–307 (1998)

21. Glover, F., Laguna, M.: Tabu search, pp. 2093–2229. Springer, US (1998)

22. Wang, T., Gu, H., Wu, Z., Gao, J.: Multi-source knowledge integration based on machine learning algorithms for domain ontology. Neural Comput. Appl. **32**, 235–245 (2020)

23. Smaili, F.Z.: Machine learning models for biomedical ontology integration and analysis, Doctoral dissertation (2020)

24. Makwana, A., Ganatra, A.: A better approach to ontology integration using clustering through global similarity measure. J. Comput. Sci. **14**(6), 854–867 (2018)

25. Kim, J., Kong, J., Sohn, M., Park, G.: Layered ontology-based multi-sourced information integration for situation awareness. J. Supercomput. **77**, 9780–9809 (2021)

A Comparative Study of Machine Learning Models for House Price Prediction and Analysis in Smart Cities

Mrignainy Kansal[1(✉)], Pancham Singh[1], Shambhavi Shukla[2], and Sakshi Srivastava[2]

[1] Department of Information Technology, Ajay Kumar Garg Engineering College, Ghaziabad, Uttar Pradesh, India
mrignainyk@gmail.com
[2] Department of Computer Science and Information Technology, Ajay Kumar Garg Engineering College, Ghaziabad, Uttar Pradesh, India

Abstract. Developing any precise or exact prediction of house prices is an unsettled task for many years. It is the social as well as economic need for the welfare & comfort of the citizens. During the Covid-19 outbreak policy reforms were introduced and various businesses scaled down their workforce so prospective buyers needed to wait for the decision about the purchase of Properties. Thus it became important to provide accurate and accessible solutions to the buyers to mould their decision. The objective and aim of our research work are to provide digital-based solutions to real estate prices because of the increasing growth in online platforms that provide virtual tours. We performed a detailed study to understand the pertinent attributes and the most efficient model built to perform forecasting of the expected price. The results of this analysis verified the use of models like Linear Regression, Random forest Regression, XG Boost, and Voting Regressor as some efficient models. The model that performed fairly well as compared to other models is Random Forest with an accuracy of (98.207) while others with an accuracy of (73.12) for Linear Regression, an accuracy of (95.41) for XG Boost, the accuracy of (94.44) for Voting Regression. Our Findings in this research have advocated the idea that prices of any real estate property are governed by 2 major factors: Its Locality and Construction Composition.

Keywords: Multicollinearity · Linear Regression · bagging and boosting techniques · Random Forest Regression · Repo rates · XG Boost Regression · Voting technique · Gradient Descent

1 Introduction

During the Covid-19 pandemic, the Real estate market has narrowed its aspects considerably as we witnessed the biggest economic crashes in the past decades. Even though there was inconsistency in all markets and industries and the stock markets experienced crashes, the pricing values of houses seemed to have an unchanging effect.

Machine learning, a subfield of artificial intelligence, extracts knowledge from data using algorithms and technology. Since it would be challenging to manually process such enormous amounts of data, big data processing necessitates the application of machine learning techniques [1]. In computer science, machine learning seeks algorithmic rather than mathematical answers to problems.

Real-world problems are solved using a variety of machine-learning algorithms. The performance will be measured by predicting house prices because many regression algorithms rely on an unknown number of attributes that result in the value being predicted rather than a specific feature.

1.1 Research Questions

Q1. How has it impacted House Sales?

As a result of the aftermath of the pandemic, housing sales witnessed a drop as businesses began to cut jobs to offset sites visit by customers dropped, which impacted the sales number.

Q2. How did it impact Property Prices?

The overall cost of the project increased in addition to this there were also many delays in project deadlines and constraints.

1.2 Inspiration Drawn

The Reserve Bank of India decided to increase repo rates by 50 basis points which started impacting residential real estate and growth momentum [2]. This resulted in houses that used to be affordable being valued at absurdly high amounts and decreased house ownership. This became the inspiration for our project and research. It aims to display accurate values of houses to the customers based on the location and features of the house.

1.3 Limitations

There are many real estate websites which are responsible for predicting house prices at a particular location for buying, selling and renting purposes. But, due to a large number of sites performing the same task, there are conflicting data. There is a difference between the price of a property on different websites [3]. Due to this, the user doesn't know which one to trust, and there is no way to find out the most accurate price of a particular plot. Another problem is that the dataset we are training our model on can have different features than the one available to the user, which can make it difficult for the model to predict the actual house price.

1.4 Importance of Machine Learning in This Project

Machine Learning methods prove to be very useful in the process of General Valuations of any attribute. During this process, large sets of data related to properties can be estimated within a short period & by performing predictive analysis of future trends or events, we can forecast potential scenarios and use the predictions to take important strategic decisions [4]. In the first step, we gathered a reliable dataset that consisted of characteristics Like Lot Area, Flat Area, Year Of Renovation, Location, No. of Bedrooms/Bathrooms and their sales prices. To build our Prediction Model we have performed Linear Regression, Random Forest Regression, XG Boost Regression and Voting Regression (A combination of 2 best results of models- Random Forest & XG Boost) by implementing the following procedures gradually).

2 Related Work

Miguel Minutti [5] wrote about accounting research, in which they used regression and machine learning techniques to forecast discrete outcomes. This gave accounting researchers instructions on how to develop regression and machine-learning prediction models. Lastly, a prediction application using data from a unique SEC investigation was shown. U Bansal used an empirical examination of regression approaches by house price and income prediction, contrasted the two algorithms [6] Simple Linear Regression (SLR) and Multiple Linear Regression (MLR) and come to the conclusion that MLR performs better than SLR. Guangjie Liu completed a research study [7] using the multiple linear regression model to predict and analyse the real estate market. Their analysis outlines the elements that affected housing prices and isolates four key factors: the residents' monthly income levels, their per capita disposable income, their per capita housing spending, and the entire real estate market. Since they perform well and are less affected by overfitting than other algorithms, the ensemble-learning methods based on boosting (Gradient boosting, XG boost, and light gradient boosting) have demonstrated the best behaviour in several areas. Raul-Tomas provided examples of work done to evaluate the COVID-19 pandemic's effects on Spanish home values and to determine the most effective machine learning algorithms for predicting house prices [8]. Conclusion: All machine learning techniques outperformed the linear model based on ordinary least squares because linear models have difficulty adopting linearity over the complete distribution of data.

3 Methodology

Regression algorithms were implemented in this study's theoretical organization and practical execution. Peer-reviewed articles are used in the theoretical portion to address the research questions under study. The methodology used in this research paper is shown in Fig. 1:

3.1 Dataset Collection

We have housing prices as the target variable and various parameters that determine house prices as independent variables. There are 21614 rows and 14 columns in our dataset as depicted in Fig. 2:

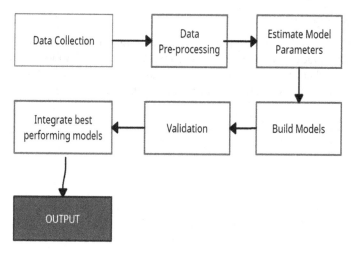

Fig. 1. Methodology

```
In [14]: data.info()

<class 'pandas.core.frame.DataFrame'>
RangeIndex: 21613 entries, 0 to 21612
Data columns (total 21 columns):
 #   Column                                     Non-Null Count  Dtype
---  ------                                     --------------  -----
 0   ID                                         21613 non-null  int64
 1   Date House was Sold                        21613 non-null  object
 2   Sale Price                                 21609 non-null  float64
 3   No of Bedrooms                             21613 non-null  int64
 4   No of Bathrooms                            21609 non-null  float64
 5   Flat Area (in Sqft)                        21604 non-null  float64
 6   Lot Area (in Sqft)                         21604 non-null  float64
 7   No of Floors                               21613 non-null  float64
 8   Waterfront View                            21613 non-null  object
 9   No of Times Visited                        21613 non-null  object
 10  Condition of the House                     21613 non-null  object
 11  Overall Grade                              21613 non-null  int64
 12  Area of the House from Basement (in Sqft)  21610 non-null  float64
 13  Basement Area (in Sqft)                    21613 non-null  int64
 14  Age of House (in Years)                    21613 non-null  int64
 15  Renovated Year                             21613 non-null  int64
 16  Zipcode                                    21612 non-null  float64
 17  Latitude                                   21612 non-null  float64
 18  Longitude                                  21612 non-null  float64
 19  Living Area after Renovation (in Sqft)     21612 non-null  float64
 20  Lot Area after Renovation (in Sqft)        21613 non-null  int64
dtypes: float64(10), int64(7), object(4)
memory usage: 3.5+ MB
```

Fig. 2. View of Dataset

3.2 Data Pre-Processing

Data used in the real world does not always have good quality content, it includes noise, and inaccuracies, and is often incomplete. It may not contain the specific attributes required and have missing or even incorrect values [9]. To improve model prediction quality, data preprocessing is required. The steps involved in this process are:

3.2.1 Outliers

An Outlier is a data point that is distant from the other data points which means its value lies outside the range of the rest of the values of data as represented in Fig. 3, points that are extreme distant in value from normal value range.

3.2.2   Removing Null Values

Data can include some invalid values, like null values instead of values that are yet to be known. These values need to be removed or replaced with other valid values. Methods to do this are either remove the row with null values. Another method to do this is to replace the null values with the mean or median of the column.

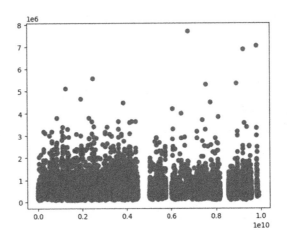

Fig. 3. Visual Representation of Outliers using a scatter plot

3.2.3   Encoding

If the dataset consists of Categorical data, the model will be unable to process them as it needs to be processed to work for numerical values. These categorical values need to be converted into dummy variables so that the models can perform training on this dataset [10]. If there is a column which includes categorical values, each distinct value needs to be converted into Binary codes for easy training on the dataset.

3.2.4   Splitting Training and Testing Dataset

The training dataset and testing dataset are the two primary components of the dataset. The model is trained on the training set, and its performance is then examined on the test set. The 'loc' function is used to carry out the functions.

- The training data is part of the data set that the machine learning algorithms are used to build the model [11]. The model learns and identifies hidden patterns in this dataset.
- Test data is simply used to validate the built models. It is used to see how the model is performing and to check the correctness of the training and testing process to know the presence of redundant or missing pages.

3.2.5   Treating Multicollinearity

Error terms w.r.to regression lines should be normally distributed(bell-shaped curve on the histogram with mean = 0) and can be made possible by variable transformation(log

X, X^2, root(X)) [12]. No Correlation between any error terms for instance time-series data correlates error terms i.e. Y(prev)-- > Y(current) is not considered in the linear regression model (X-Y relationship is considered).

Multicollinearity: (When the Correlation between independent variables is high then one of them is removed) removing multicollinearity- through VIF which means variance inflation factor Lower VIF = > lower correlation b/w independent variables while the process involves assuming one variable as dependent and other all as independent.

3.2.6   Feature Scaling (Last Stage of Pre-processing)

Scaling of feature variables or all independent variables into the same range so the model is not biased towards particular variables for prediction [13]. Since the Values in the Dataset can be in a variable range, some values might be large in the range of 10^3, while others can be of form 10^{-1}. The difference in values can affect the predicted output of input data. So, all the values need to be in a particular range so that all the values affect the predicted output equally.

Different Techniques for Feature Scaling are Standardization: In this process, the mean value of all the data is calculated. Then all the values are centred around that mean, with a standard deviation of 1. After the completion of this process, the mean of that feature is 0 and the standard deviation is 1 [14]. In this case, values are not restricted to a particular range. This can be used where the distribution of data follows the Gaussian distribution.

$$X_{Stand} \frac{X - mean(X)}{standard\ deviation(X)} \qquad X_{norm} = \frac{x - min(X)}{max(X) - min(X)}$$

Normalization: In this process, all the data is recalled so that it ends up in the range of 0 and 1. It is a scaling process which is also known as Min - Max Scaling. This is useful for algorithms that make no assumptions about the neural networks and K-Nearest Neighbors, where the data distribution does not conform to a Gaussian distribution.

4   Proposed Algorithm

Once the Data is ready to be trained, the training set is taken as input in the model. The model notices the pattern involved in the dataset, and how input is affecting the final output. Based on these observations, the Model is ready to make further predictions on the Test Dataset. The Algorithms used in this research for Model Training are:

1. Linear Regression
2. Random Forest
3. XG Boost Regressor
4. Voting Regressor

4.1 Linear Regression

For modelling the relationship between a dependent variable (often represented by "y") and one or more independent variables, linear regression is a statistical technique (usually denoted as "x") that is used [15] whose steps of implementation are depicted in Fig. 4. Finding the line or hyperplane that fits the data between the variables the best is the aim of linear regression.

Simple and multiple regression concerns can both be managed by employing linear regression. In simple linear regression, the connection that exists between the independent variable and the dependent variable is modelled using a straight line since there is only one independent variable.

The equation for this line is denoted by

$$y = A0 + A1x + \varepsilon \tag{1}$$

where A0 refers to the intercept or constant term, A1 is the slope, x is the independent variable, y is the dependent variable, and ε is the error term (or residual). Calculating the values of the coefficients that reduce the sum of squared residuals is the target of linear regression (i.e., the difference between the actual and predicted values of the dependent variable).

Fig. 4. Flowchart implementation of Linear Regression

To minimise the sum of squared errors between the predicted values and the actual values of the dependent variable, linear regression aims to estimate the coefficients of the independent variables. The method of least squares is typically used for this, which entails locating the line of greatest fit that encircles the data points. The dependent variable's value can be predicted using the calculated coefficients for fresh values of the independent variables [16]. To find the parameters of the best-fit line for multiple inputs we implemented the Gradient Descent algorithm with help of cost function curve optimization as shown in Fig. 5 and residual distribution in Fig. 6.

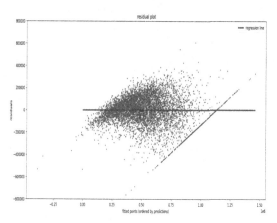

Fig. 5. Line of best fit

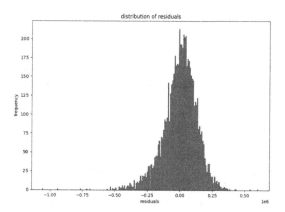

Fig. 6. Residual plot showing fitted points

On Interpretation of results of the model following observations as in Fig. 7 were made.

1. By visualization, through a horizontal bar graph of a normalized coefficient plot, we know the magnitude of coefficients i.e. up to what extent of the role the attribute pays in determining the sale price output.
2. We can see that overall grade and latitude contribute a major portion in deciding the target variable sale price [17]. This is obvious as location contributes a crucial role in determining the price of any housing property.
3. Years since renovation has displayed quite negative significance, which means customers prefer houses that are recently renovated [18].

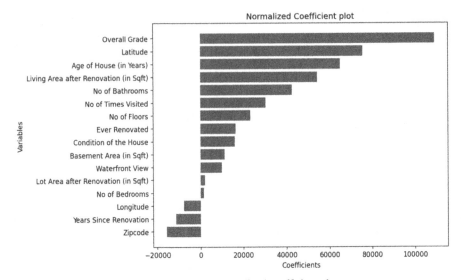

Fig. 7. Shows the normalized coefficient plot

4.2 Random Forest Regression

To address classification and regression problems, it is an ML technique that integrates many decision trees. Bootstrap sampling is used for majority classification votes an average of many decision trees that are combined and further assigned to regression. For unbalanced, missing, and multicollinear data, RF is a reliable approach. Two stages make up the analysis –

1. Choosing a sample from the main data for the training dataset as seen in Fig. 8 and then replacing it to create sub-datasets is the first stage of creating a forest. Next, using these smaller amounts of data, regression trees are created [19]. The number of variables and decision trees can be manipulated during the training phase.
2. A prediction can be made after the model has been trained. The input variables for each regression tree are first joined together. Second, the average of the predictions from each tree is used to evaluate the outcome.

A Decision Tree is a binary tree that recursively splits the dataset into parts until the data left has only one class. This data at the end is represented as leaf nodes of the decision tree [20]. The non-leaf nodes contain conditions to split the data into different datasets. If the condition is satisfied by the data sample it is shifted to the left node, otherwise, it is shifted to the right one. This continues till the dataset reaches the leaf node, which is used to assign the class label to the new data point.

The dataset is divided into numerous different datasets where rows are randomly chosen and one dataset is trained on certain features of the main dataset. After the construction of multiple datasets, the decision tree is trained on each of the datasets, where each decision tree produces a prediction on a particular data point. The final prediction as seen in Fig. 9 of the main dataset is considered after considering all the minor predictions of each of the decision trees [21]. As the number of decision trees

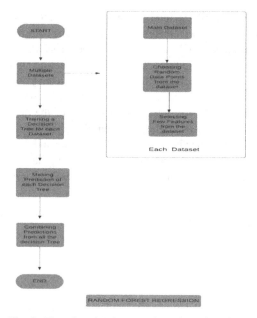

Fig. 8. Flowchart implementation of Random forest

Fig. 9. Show Visualisation of actual vs predicted prices

is more, the individual decision of each tree doesn't matter when all the decisions are combined. As there are multiple decision trees involved in this process this is regarded as a forest. It is a diverse model as it can be used for regression and classification problems both.

4.3 XG Boost Regression

Extreme gradient boosting, often known as XG Boost, is a common Machine-Learning model used mainly for regression purposes, classification, and solving ranking problems.

It is a more effective form of gradient boosting, a machine learning technique that combines decision trees as the weak learner to increase the forecast accuracy [22]. XG Boost has become well-known for its accuracy and robustness while processing intricate, sizable datasets from a variety of industries, including marketing, finance, and healthcare.

A specific variety of XG Boost that focuses on forecasting continuous variables is called XG Boost regression. Decision trees are incrementally added to a model to repair mistakes made by earlier trees. By adding the weights of the decision trees from the previous iteration, XG Boost uses gradient descent throughout each iteration to reduce the residual errors (the difference between the actual value and the predicted one) [23]. The capacity of XG Boost regression to deal with missing data, which is a prevalent issue in real-world datasets, is one of its main advantages (Fig. 10).

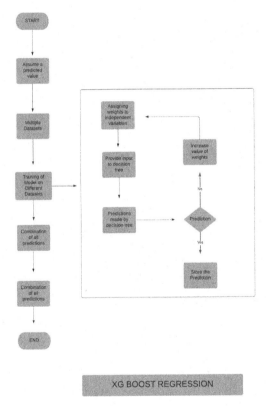

Fig. 10. Flowchart implementation of XG Boost

By leveraging the values of other known variables, the model can forecast missing values for independent variables. Due to the use of robust loss functions that are less sensitive to extreme values, XG Boost can also effectively handle outliers [24].

The ability of XG Boost regression to avoid overfitting, a major issue in machine learning models where the model fits the training data too well and performs badly on fresh or unseen data, is another important benefit of the algorithm. This is accomplished by XG Boost using regularization techniques like L1, L2, and early stopping, which stop the model from overcomplicating and overfitting the training set of data [25]. Moreover, XG Boost allows for feature selection, which enhances the model's functionality and interpretability by allowing the model to find the most valuable independent variables in the dataset and eliminate or reduce the weight of unimportant or redundant variables. In our case while plotting the relationship between the predicted price and the actual price in Fig. 11 a linear relationship was observed signifying a low rate of errors [26].

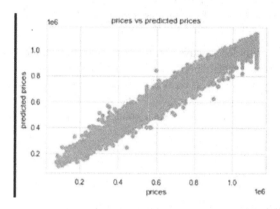

Fig. 11. Shows a graph visualization of the predicted price vs the actual price

XG Boost regression is a reliable and effective machine learning model for predicting continuous variables, to sum up. It is a preferred option in many different fields due to its capacity to manage missing data, and outliers, and avoid overfitting. Further improving the performance and interpretability of the model is its capacity for feature selection [27]. Regression issues in machine learning are effectively solved by XG Boost regression, making major contributions to the creation of predictive models, decision-making, and problem-solving across numerous industries.

4.4 Voting Regressor

An ensemble-learning technique named a voting regressor is used in machine learning to incorporate different regression models to produce more precise predictions. Each model in a voting regressor is trained using a separate subset of the training data, and the output from each model is then merged in some manner to provide the final prediction. The average or weighted average of the models' predictions is frequently used to combine the outputs of the models [28]. The voting regressor is useful when the individual regression models have different strengths and weaknesses, and the combination of their predictions can produce a more accurate and robust model.

In a voting regressor, each regression model is trained on the same dataset using different algorithms or hyperparameters to create diversity in the models. Once each model is trained, the voting regressor takes the average or weighted average of their predictions as the final output [29]. A voting regressor matches many base regressors and is an ensemble meta-estimator for the complete dataset. Then it averages the individual predictions to make a final prediction. A voting classifier could be a machine learning-based method of algorithm that can train numerous base models or estimators and predicts on the premise of aggregating the findings of every base estimator.

Types of Voting

1. **Hard voting** *entails* adding up the predictions for each category label and deciding which category label will acquire the most votes.
2. **Soft voting** *entails* adding the anticipated probabilities for each category label and choosing the one with the greatest certainty.

In our Voting ensemble, we have combined regression techniques of random forest and XG-boost (extreme gradient boosting) and compared the results to be significant and comparable to applying models as individuals [30]. Random Forest surpassed the other standalone ML models about performance. The suggested ensemble voting regression model was then generated using these basic models, weighted averages, and the results of the base models.

5 Results

After the implementation of the proposed algorithms, we observed the major factors that form most of the contribution in deciding the sale price like locational attributes and the factors that induced negative impacts like Years since the last renovation, through a coefficient plot. In addition to this, we saw which algorithms returned better results than others with higher accuracy shown in Figs. 12 and 13 up to 98%. Such algorithms were mainly random forest and XG boost based on bagging and boosting ensemble techniques (Table 1).

Table1. Model Evaluation Metrics

MODEL	Accuracy	MSE	MAE	RMSE
Linear Regression	0.7312	17249830335	99521	131338
Random Forest	0.9817	1145909573	22873	33851
XG-Boost Regression	0.9541	2879965870	39163	53665
Voting Regressor	0.9444	3484960468	41730	53665

Key Findings

1. By combining the predictions of various models, ensemble learning approaches such as bagging and boosting seek to enhance the performance of machine learning models. But how they put together the ensemble is different.

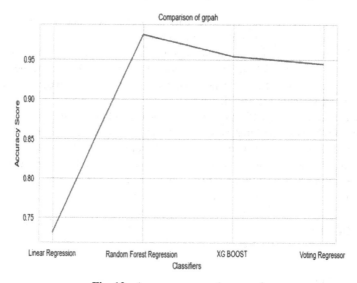

Fig. 12. Accuracy comparison graph

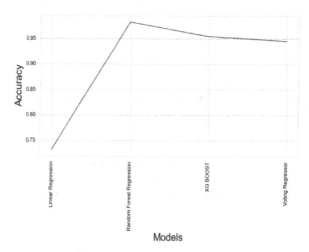

Fig. 13. Error Comparison Graph

2. By training numerous decision trees on diverse subsets of the data and then averaging their predictions, bagging, as employed in the Random Forest technique, produces an ensemble. By lessening the influence of particular noisy or outlier data points, this method aids in lowering the variance of the model and preventing overfitting. When dealing with high-dimensional data, where overfitting is more frequent, it is especially successful.

3. On the other hand, boosting, like XG boost, builds an ensemble by iteratively training weak models and modifying the weights of incorrectly categorised instances in later

iterations. This method can increase a model's accuracy, but it is more prone to overfitting and can be computationally expensive.

4. Simple linear models, such as linear regression, are frequently less complex than decision tree-based models and may be more interpretable. However, they can have limited predictive potential, especially when the correlations between characteristics and the target variable are non-linear.

5. To summarise, bagging with random forests is a good choice for machine learning problems with many features or data that is noisy or high-dimensional, whereas boosting is effective for problems with a large amount of data and more complex relationships between features and the target variable. Simple linear models can be effective when interpretability is critical, but they may not be enough for capturing more complex relationships in data.

6 Conclusion

Model Performance

We conclude that Random-Forest generally, returns to some extent comparable or probably higher prophetic performance against the linear modelling approach as Random-forest adds extra randomness to the model as it includes growing trees. One split divides a node, and then it searches for the simplest feature among a random set of options rather than trying to find the foremost vital feature. Thus, it reduces the overfitting drawback in decision trees and lessens the variance, raising accuracy. Random Forest is the best option because it is simple to tune and works well even though there are countless missing information and a lot of noise. Overfitting won't happen simply. With correct results, XG Boost is tough to figure out if they are to measure various noises. Linear Models have only a few parameters, Random Forests comprise a lot of them. Meaning that Random Forests can overfit more effectively simply than linear-regression-based models. Gradient boosting trees will be more correct than random forests. Gradient Boosting Trees can recognise complex patterns in the knowledge since we usually train them to correct each other's mistakes. The boosted trees, however, might overfit and start modelling the noise if the information is buzzy.

Feature Importance

Through techniques like Correlation Analysis, we identified the linear relationship between each feature and the target variable (house price). Features with a high correlation coefficient (positive or negative) are more likely to be important for predicting house prices. Such features included latitude, flat area, age of house etc.

7 Future Work

There are several potential areas for future work and improvement in house price prediction, including:

1. **Incorporating additional data sources**: House price prediction models could benefit from incorporating additional data sources, such as demographic data, school district ratings, crime rates, or proximity to amenities such as parks or shopping centres. This could help to improve the accuracy of the model by capturing additional factors that influence house prices.

2. **Spatial analysis:** House prices are often influenced by location, and incorporating spatial analysis techniques could help to capture spatial autocorrelation and spatial heterogeneity in the data. This could involve using geographic information systems (GIS) or other spatial data analysis tools to explore spatial patterns and relationships in the data.

References

1. Jia, J., Zhang, X., Huang, C., Luan, H.: Multiscale analysis of human social sensing of urban appearance and its effects on house price appreciation in Wuhan China. Sustain. Cities Soc. **81**, 103844 (2022)
2. Akar, A.U., Yalpir, S.: Using svr and mra methods for real estate valuation in the smart cities. Int. Arch. Photogramm. Remote. Sens. Spat. Inf. Sci. **46**, 21–26 (2021)
3. Arcuri, N., De Ruggiero, M., Salvo, F., Zinno, R.: Automated valuation methods through the cost approach in a BIM and GIS integration framework for smart city appraisals. Sustainability. **12**, 7546 (2020)
4. Varma, A., Sarma, A., Doshi, S., Nair, R.: House price prediction using machine learning and neural networks. In: 2018 Second International Conference on Inventive Communication and Computational Technologies (ICICCT), pp. 1936–1939. IEEE (2018)
5. Thamarai, M., Malarvizhi, S.P.: House price prediction modeling using machine learning. Int. J. Inf. Eng. Electron. Bus. **12**, 15 (2020)
6. Truong, Q., Nguyen, M., Dang, H., Mei, B.: Housing price prediction via improved machine learning techniques. Procedia Comput. Sci. **174**, 433–442 (2020)
7. Wang, P.-Y., Chen, C.-T., Su, J.-W., Wang, T.-Y., Huang, S.-H.: Deep learning model for house price prediction using heterogeneous data analysis along with joint self-attention mechanism. IEEE Access **9**, 55244–55259 (2021)
8. Adetunji, A.B., Akande, O.N., Ajala, F.A., Oyewo, O., Akande, Y.F., Oluwadara, G.: House price prediction using random forest machine learning technique. Procedia Comput. Sci. **199**, 806–813 (2022)
9. Karimi, Y., Haghi Kashani, M., Akbari, M., Mahdipour, E.: Leveraging big data in smart cities: a systematic review. Concurrency Comput. Pract. Exp. **33**, e6379 (2021)
10. Bilen, T., Erel-Özçevik, M., Yaslan, Y., Oktug, S.F.: A smart city application: business location estimator using machine learning techniques. In: 2018 IEEE 20th International Conference on High Performance Computing and Communications; IEEE 16th International Conference on Smart City; IEEE 4th International Conference on Data Science and Systems (HPCC/SmartCity/DSS), pp. 1314–1321. IEEE (2018)
11. Zhang, C., Zuo, J., Wu, Y., Zhang, J., Liu, J., Chang, X.: Application of combined neural network based on entropy method in smart city forecast problem. In: 2020 International Conference on Artificial Intelligence and Computer Engineering (ICAICE), pp. 378–382. IEEE (2020)
12. Ja'afar, N.S., Mohamad, J., Ismail, S.: Machine learning for property price prediction and price valuation: a systematic literature review. Plan. Malaysia **19**, 1018 (2021)

13. Shahhosseini, M., Hu, G., Pham, H.: Optimizing ensemble weights for machine learning models: a case study for housing price prediction. In: Yang, H., Qiu, R., Chen, W. (eds.) Smart Service Systems, Operations Management, and Analytics. INFORMS-CSS 2019. Springer Proceedings in Business and Economics, pp. 87–97. Springer, Cham (2020). https://doi.org/10.1007/978-3-030-30967-1_9

14. Kumar, G.K., Rani, D.M., Koppula, N., Ashraf, S.: Prediction of house price using machine learning algorithms. In: 2021 5th International Conference on Trends in Electronics and Informatics (ICOEI), pp. 1268–1271. IEEE (2021)

15. Bagheri, B., Shaykh-Baygloo, R.: Spatial analysis of urban smart growth and its effects on housing price: The case of Isfahan. Iran. Sustain. Cities Soc. **68**, 102769 (2021)

16. Cooke, P.: Silicon Valley imperialists create new model villages as smart cities in their own image. J. Open Innov. Technol. Market Complex. **6**, 24 (2020)

17. Rawool, A.G., Rogye, D.V., Rane, S.G., Bharadi, V.A.: House price prediction using machine learning. Int. J. Res. Appl. Sci. Eng. Technol. **9**, 686–692 (2021)

18. Yu, L., Jiao, C., Xin, H., Wang, Y., Wang, K.: Prediction on housing price based on deep learning. Int. J. Comput. Inf. Eng. **12**, 90–99 (2018)

19. Kang, Y., et al.: Understanding house price appreciation using multi-source big geo-data and machine learning. Land Use Policy **111**, 104919 (2021)

20. Shamsuddin, S., Srinivasan, S.: Just smart or just and smart cities? Assessing the literature on housing and information and communication technology. Hous. Policy Debate **31**, 127–150 (2021)

21. Kisia\la, W., Rącka, I.: Spatial and statistical analysis of urban poverty for sustainable city development. Sustainability **13**, 858 (2021)

22. Afonso, B., Melo, L., Oliveira, W., Sousa, S., Berton, L.: Housing prices prediction with a deep learning and random forest ensemble. In: Anais do XVI Encontro Nacional de Inteligência Artificial e Computacional. pp. 389–400. SBC (2019)

23. Ahtesham, M., Bawany, N.Z., Fatima, K.: House price prediction using machine learning algorithm-the case of Karachi city, Pakistan. In: 2020 21st International Arab Conference on Information Technology (ACIT), pp. 1–5. IEEE (2020)

24. Muhammad, A.N., Aseere, A.M., Chiroma, H., Shah, H., Gital, A.Y., Hashem, I.A.T.: Deep learning application in smart cities: recent development, taxonomy, challenges and research prospects. Neural Comput. Appl. **33**, 2973–3009 (2021)

25. Pai, P.-F., Wang, W.-C.: Using machine learning models and actual transaction data for predicting real estate prices. Appl. Sci. **10**, 5832 (2020)

26. Yazdani, M.: Machine learning, deep learning, and hedonic methods for real estate price prediction. arXiv preprint arXiv:2110.07151. (2021)

27. Lu, S., Li, Z., Qin, Z., Yang, X., Goh, R.S.M.: A hybrid regression technique for house prices prediction. In: 2017 IEEE International Conference on Industrial Engineering and Engineering Management (IEEM), pp. 319–323. IEEE (2017)

28. Jain, M., Rajput, H., Garg, N., Chawla, P.: Prediction of house pricing using machine learning with Python. In: 2020 International Conference on Electronics and Sustainable Communication Systems (ICESC), pp. 570–574. IEEE (2020)

29. Mohd, T., Jamil, N.S., Johari, N., Abdullah, L., Masrom, S.: An overview of real estate modelling techniques for house price prediction. In: Kaur, N., Ahmad, M. (eds.) Charting a Sustainable Future of ASEAN in Business and Social Sciences, vol. 1. pp. 321–338. Springer, Singapore (2020). https://doi.org/10.1007/978-981-15-3859-9_28

30. Mora-Garcia, R.-T., Cespedes-Lopez, M.-F., Perez-Sanchez, V.R.: housing price prediction using machine learning algorithms in COVID-19 times. Land. **11**, 2100 (2022). https://doi.org/10.3390/land11112100

Improving E-Governance Through Application of Hyperautomation

Sanjana Das[1]([✉]), Rajan Gupta[2] [iD], and Saibal K. Pal[3] [iD]

[1] Deen Dayal Upadhyaya College, University of Delhi, Delhi 110078, India
sanjana.20hcs4154@ddu.du.ac.in
[2] Research & Analytics Division, Analyttica Datalab, Bengaluru 560066, Karnataka, India
[3] SAG Lab, Defense Research & Development Organization, Delhi 110054, India

Abstract. E-Governance is the use of Information and Communication Technology to change governance structures or processes in ways that would be impossible without ICT. As web technology has evolved from Web 1.0, consisting of simple computer systems, to Web 4.0, involving Artificial Intelligence and the Internet of Things, so has e-governance. As a result, there has been a noticeable transformation from a digital government to an algorithmic government. However, although ICT has advanced, the impact and need for automation are prevalent. Many administrative jobs are still manual and paper-based, and technical challenges, such as legacy systems and scalability issues, persist in the current e-governance. To this end, in this paper, we aim to study the application of hyperautomation to e-governance, which helps modernize legacy systems and eliminate data silos, among other things. After performing a theoretical review of the key concepts of hyperautomation, its potential in e-governance, and two real-world public-sector use cases of hyperautomation, we find that not only can hyperautomation tackle many existing technical issues in e-governance but also open the door to previously impossible automation opportunities. We also devise a theoretical framework to demonstrate how hyperautomation can be applied to potential e-governance use-cases.

Keywords: Hyperautomation · E-Governance · Robotic Process Automation · Intelligent Automation · Algorithmic Government · scalability · legacy systems

1 Introduction

E-Governance, the use of Information and Communication Technology (ICT) to transform governance structures and processes, has evolved significantly over the years. From simple computer systems of Web 1.0 to the integration of Artificial Intelligence and the Internet of Things in Web 4.0, e-governance has witnessed a profound shift towards an algorithmic government. As we will discuss in the following section, the need for e-governance evolution lies in the fact that the development of e-governance directly impacts the development of a nation as a whole.

Despite the advancements in ICT and its potential for automation, many administrative and other tasks still rely on monotonous labour and paper-based solutions. Moreover,

F. Ortiz-Rodríguez et al. (Eds.): EGETC 2023, CCIS 1888, pp. 185–203, 2023.
https://doi.org/10.1007/978-3-031-43940-7_15

up-and-coming e-governance landscapes grapple with persisting technical challenges, such as interoperability issues, legacy systems, and scalability concerns. This paper seeks to explore how hyperautomation can offer a transformative solution to facilitate scalable automation of laborious processes and enhance existing e-governance processes. Hyperautomation is an approach that leverages a blend of cutting-edge technologies, including Robotic Process Automation (RPA), Artificial Intelligence (AI), low-code application platforms, and process mining, among others [6, 12–15, 29]. By integrating these technologies, hyperautomation enables organizations to swiftly identify, evaluate, and automate numerous processes, eliminating functional and data silos and ultimately optimizing the efficiency and effectiveness of e-governance.

In this exploratory study, we examine the current technical challenges faced in e-governance, considering the ever-evolving digital landscape. With a focus on Hyperautomation, we delve into its significance in today's digital-first environment. By analyzing case studies of Hyperautomation implementation in e-governance, we aim to unearth the potential positive effects of this cutting-edge technology. This research will shed light on how Hyperautomation can revolutionize e-governance practices, streamlining processes, enhancing efficiency, and ultimately contributing to more effective and citizen-centric governance.

Our paper investigates the following research questions.

RQ1. Study the need for hyperautomation in the current e-governance landscape.

RQ2. Discuss the key concepts of hyperautomation and show how it can improve upon current e-governance processes.

2 Research Methodology

Since Hyperautomation is still an abstract and niche term, our research methodology is purely exploratory based. We started by collecting data from various secondary sources such as government reports, websites from the Google database, and journals from google scholar manuscripts. For our first objective, we reviewed articles and papers based on the need for evolution in e-governance and the current technical challenges in e-governance. Next, we studied technology trends using journals and reports from leading technology and consultancy firms such as Gartner. We used keywords such as Robotic Process Automation, Intelligent Automation, and Hyperautomation. For our second objective, we studied various reports on Hyperautomation since there were few research papers. Websites of companies like IBM and UiPath were also used as secondary sources for Hyperautomation associated technologies. We focused on the key technologies and benefits of hyperautomation, especially in the context of e-governance operations. Using Deloitte's, IBM's, and nanonet's workflow for hyperautomation, we designed our theoretical framework for applying hyperautomation. Lastly, we reviewed two case studies of Hyperautomation in public services. We applied our theoretical framework to one of them to demonstrate how our framework can be applied to more potential use-cases. In our findings, we tie the independent benefits of hyperautomation to the solution for some of the technical challenges in e-governance, as also demonstrated by the case studies.

2.1 Framework for Research Methodology

Below is the framework for our research methodology.

Define Search Criteria for Data Collection

- Identify relevant keywords and concepts (e.g., e-governance, Hyperautomation, Robotic Process Automation, etc.).
- Determine sources for data collection (google scholar manuscripts, government reports, websites, journals, etc.).

Conduct Literature Review

- Review articles and papers on the need for evolution in e-governance and current technical challenges.
- Study technology trends using leading technology and consultancy firms' reports (e.g., Gartner).
- Explore secondary sources for Hyperautomation-related technologies and benefits.
- Identify key technologies and benefits of Hyperautomation in e-governance operations.

Scope of the Study: Data Availability

- Assess the availability and accessibility of relevant data from the selected sources.

Develop Theoretical Framework

- Design a theoretical framework for Hyperautomation application based on Deloitte's, IBM's, and nanonet's workflows.

Select Case Methodology

- Review case studies of Hyperautomation in public services.
- Choose one case study for the application of the theoretical framework.

Apply Theoretical Framework to Case Study

- Demonstrate how the framework can be applied to potential use-cases in e-governance.
- Analyze and interpret the results of applying the framework to the case study.

Data Analysis and Findings

- Tie together independent benefits of Hyperautomation to solve technical challenges in e-governance.
- Provide insights and conclusions based on the analysis.

3   Literature Review

3.1   E-Governance and Its Challenges

E-government and e-governance are two concepts that are distinguished based on the differences of their foundational terminology Government and Governance. While e-government specifically refers to the provision of services and information by the government and its agencies through ICT [1], e-governance encompasses a broader scope, involving the application of technology to various stakeholders, including the government, public sector, private sector, and other agencies [2] involved in governing a jurisdiction. According to Bannister and Connolly [2], e-governance goes beyond digitization and online processes, aiming to transform governance structures and procedures, establish new practices enabled by technology, and uphold normative qualities like transparency and integrity. We acknowledge the differentiation between e-government and e-governance, but for the purpose of this paper we consider e-government as a subset of e-governance, recognizing the need for an overarching approach that encompasses all stakeholders and the transformative potential of technology in governance processes.

The evolution of e-governance has been gradual and directly dependent on the evolution of technology. N. Bindu et al. [3] proposed a five-stage maturity model which maps this evolution from mere digitization of Government information in the form of static web pages (web 1.0) to the use of artificial intelligence algorithms (web 4.0) to promote efficient delivery of services in education, justice, transport, electricity, and assist in decision-making at different levels of the Government [4]. However, this transformation of electronic-governance has not come without its challenges. The first and foremost remains the non-uniform development and use of ICT in intra-departmental, intra-country, and inter-country governance. As emphasised in the United Nations E-Government Survey 2022 [5], the disparities in e-governance across nations, as well as their impact on different demographics, are causing a substantial digital divide and, eventually, a new kind of poverty. The epidemic of COVID-19 has exacerbated the situation. Despite forcing many e-governments around the world to leap decades into digital growth, many e-governments remain at the bottom of the development ladder. The epidemic shifted nearly all offline activities online, from virtual meetings to online service delivery (such as tax payments) to online health consultation and virtual learning platforms. As a result, people with little or no access to digital services, as well as countries with a lack of e-governance development, have been substantially overlooked in an otherwise technologically driven and linked world. In fact, during the COVID-19 epidemic, governments who were further along in their e-government developments outperformed those that were further behind [5]. Among other factors, the digital divide can be attributed to the lack of IT experts and a simple yet holistic approach to utilize different cutting-edge technologies that can be applied to existing e-governance systems in a non-disruptive manner. Some other commonly observed technical challenges in the e-governance include:

Bad Automation and Scope of Applications. In the era of web 4.0 and with the brilliant adoption of Artificial Intelligence in some areas, government agencies are still grappling with highly manual and repetitive internal processes. Many data management tasks, such as data entry, extraction, and transfer, continue to be done manually, along with monotonous jobs like invoice processing and compliance checking. Though some organizations have attempted automation, it is often haphazard and lacking organization due to the absence of a central platform to manage automation processes [6]. The lack of careful planning and monitoring leads to random automation practices that may clash with other initiatives or fail to deliver substantial benefits to the organization [6]. Furthermore, introducing ICT to processes purely for automation's sake or due to labor-intensive nature is considered bad practice, leading to wastage of resources and inefficient workflows. Thus, proper digitization and application scope identification are essential for monitoring long-term benefits and ensuring efficacy.

Lack of Centre of Intelligence and Scalability. A critical issue in e-governance practices is the lack of uniformity, starting from the organizational level. Automation solutions within government agencies often lack scalability due to the absence of a central organization-wide scheme [6]. Instead, solutions are developed in isolation for individual processes, resulting in gaps and inconsistent returns on investments. Moreover, the automation currently in place usually focuses on specific parts of processes rather than complete end-to-end workflows, further hindering scalability and integration across different functions.

Lack of Technological Integration and Data Integration. The use of various software and hardware solutions from different vendors creates a challenge of ensuring technological integration in government agencies. The lack of interoperability among these disparate technologies demands substantial efforts from IT departments, including customizing or developing interfaces, leading to time-consuming and costly processes. Consequently, the adoption of new technologies is hindered, slowing down overall digital transformation within the government. Additionally, this lack of integration results in data silos [7], where valuable information becomes confined within individual departments or systems, preventing vertical and horizontal integration as envisioned by Layne and Lee's [8] maturity model.

Legacy Systems. Legacy systems, prevalent in most public sector organizations, serve as significant assets but pose obstacles to technological integration. While these systems enable service provision and maintain critical data for public administration, they also create data and functional silos that hamper innovation. The cost of maintaining such legacy systems is substantial, as highlighted in a 2021 study by the U.S. Government Accountability [9] Office. Despite the challenges, complete removal of these systems is impractical and expensive [10], making them a significant obstacle to modernization efforts. Robotic Process Automation offers partial solutions by automating human interactions and prolonging the life of these systems. Other approaches to integrate legacy systems with new technology such as cloud applications use custom APIs to enable both the systems to communicate and exchange data with each other. However, developing custom APIs is tedious and costly. It requires API creation experts, familiarity with the technology utilized by outdated systems, adapting the legacy system to align with the API, continual enhancement, and upkeep of the customized API [11].

Evidently, the current state of e-governance practices reveals numerous gaps and bottlenecks, particularly in internal agency processes and larger public sector services. Addressing these seemingly small bottlenecks is crucial to unlocking efficiencies and reaping long-term benefits. Efficient utilization of human resources, including time, efforts, and innovation, alongside prudent management of monetary resources, is essential to achieve the expected Return on Investments. Moreover, bridging these gaps will foster uniformity in the development of e-governance within an organization, the country, and eventually, globally, contributing to a more connected and technologically advanced world. Since it is human nature to continually improve upon flaws with new inventions and technologies, it stands to reason that these challenges pave the way for a new emerging technology that could alleviate many e-governance issues. By addressing these challenges, governments can work towards narrowing the technology gap, facilitating seamless integration of innovative solutions, and ultimately enhancing the overall governance experience for citizens.

3.2 Emergence of Hyperautomation

Hyperautomation is an emerging approach that enables organizations to rapidly identify, vet and automate as many processes as possible using technology, such as robotic process automation (RPA), low-code application platforms (LCAP), artificial intelligence (AI), Digital Twins, Intelligent Business Process Management suites (iBPMS), and process mining [6, 12–15]. The term hyperautomation and all that comes with it has gained a lot of attention since 2020 due to it being listed as a top 10 strategic technology trend by Gartner [15]. Gartner highlights that the fusion of Robotic Process Automation (RPA) with Artificial Intelligence (AI) and Machine Learning (ML) is the foundational and empowering technology behind hyperautomation. This powerful combination provides the capability and adaptability to automate tasks that were previously deemed impossible to automate. See table 1. for more hyperautomation trends as predicted by leading tech companies.

Table 1. Hyperautomation trends predicted by various Tech companies.

Hyperautomation Statistics	Source
By 2024, organizations will lower operational costs by 30% by combining hyperautomation technologies with redesigned operational processes	Gartner [16]
The global hyperautomation market is expected to experience significant growth, with a Compound Annual Growth Rate (CAGR) of 18.9 percent during the period from 2020 to 2027	Coherent Market Insights [17]
Over the next three years executives expect automation to increase their workforce capacity by 27 per cent: equivalent to 2.4 million extra full-time employees	Deloitte [18]
By 2024, diffuse hyperautomation spending will drive up the total cost of ownership 40-fold, making adaptive governance a differentiating factor in corporate performance	Gartner [19]

Moreover, in Forrester Consulting's 2020 Intelligent Automation Benchmark Study, an overwhelming 67 percent of participants recognized the immense value of a "single vendor with a wide array of complementary automation technologies." This highlights a growing realization among organizations about the importance of adopting a unified, platform-based approach to automation [31]. This integrated strategy enables seamless collaboration between various automation capabilities, leading to the digitization of end-to-end business operations. Only a negligible 1 percent of respondents did not consider this integrated approach valuable.

The study's outcomes underscore the increasing awareness that integrating diverse automation technologies can be more intricate and costly than initially perceived, potentially leading to suboptimal results. As a result, organizations are now leaning towards seeking comprehensive automation solutions from a single vendor to enhance overall efficiency and effectiveness in their automation endeavors.

3.3 Components of Hyperautomation

We can see that hyperautomation in itself is not a technology, but it is an amalgamation of various technologies. Hence, we need to understand all components of it to understand it better. The core foundation of hyperautomation lies in the augmentation of RPA with Artificial Intelligence (Fig. 1).

Fig. 1. Components of Hyperautomation include RPA, Process Mining, AI, Digital Twin, OCR and iBPMS.

Robotic Process Automation (RPA). RPA is a disruptive technology that has revolutionized many industries, such as healthcare, tourism, insurance, and the likes. It is a software technology that helps build and deploy software robots that simulate human-computer interactions [20]. These software robots can accomplish many trivial tasks such as completing keyboard strokes, extracting data, and interacting with different Graphical User Interface (GUI) elements such as buttons and scroll bars, etc. Since robots do not get tired, they immensely enhance the speed and consistency of menial and repetitive tasks like filling out forms, moving files between systems, copying and pasting data, logging in applications and generating various reports [20]. Some advanced robots even undertake cognitive tasks such as language interpretation, social interactions with customers, and decision-making through the use of Machine Learning.

Hence, while these software bots indulge in monotonous, time-consuming, and energy-draining work, humans are free to work on tasks that require creative intelligence, such as innovating, collaborating with others, planning, strategizing, and more. This enhances employee engagement and leads to greater fecundity and fluidity in an organization. Moreover, RPA can be quickly installed and is non-intrusive, which speeds up digitization. It is also perfect for automating processes that use legacy systems and lack virtual desktop infrastructures (VDI), database access, and APIs [20].

During the COVID-19 outbreak, when the hiring process took a blow, one non-profit's HR staff saw their recruiting process as a possible area for automation and investigated Robotic Process Automation (RPA) [21]. They discovered that RPA could greatly improve their recruiting process through thorough documentation, beginning with automating applicant pre-screening and resume processing. This change standardised the process, boosted efficiency, and lowered pre-screening time from 20 h per recruiter to one hour per week. Annual cost reductions are expected to be $30,000 per recruiter [21]. The organisation can attract top personnel, increase results, and acquire a competitive advantage in the new normal by improving processes.

Digital Twins. In essence, a digital twin is computer software that simulates or reflects a process or physical object from the real world. Real-world data, such as sensor data or some other statistical data, is used to create efficiencies within the organization by visualizing ecosystems, predicting results for respective inputs, and identifying areas for improvement [22]. One excellent use case of digital twin can be seen in NASA.

Compared to the current generation of NASA and U.S. Air Force vehicles, future generations of aerospace vehicles will need to be lighter in mass and operate under more demanding conditions (such as higher loads) for longer periods [23]. It stands to reason that these aerospace vehicles will face unforeseen conditions in space; hence, verification and validation approaches for models must be properly developed. The certification for these vehicles will be beyond the capabilities of the current certification approaches due to the severe requirements of these vehicles. Hence, to combat the shortcomings of the current approaches, NASA is utilizing the digital twin paradigm. The digital twin will replicate the life of its flying twin to predict unforeseen scenarios from different vehicle sensor data, historical data (such as maintenance history), and fleet data, among other things. Moreover, the twin increases the safety and reliability of the vehicle by continuously projecting the vehicle's condition, remaining life, and the likelihood of mission success.

Optical Character Recognition (OCR) and Intelligent Character Recognition (ICR). With the help of optical character recognition (OCR) technology, printed text from scanned documents or picture files can be converted into machine-readable digital formats and extracted for use in data processing operations like editing and searching

[24]. Intelligent Character Recognition (ICR), a similar technology is specialized to recognize handwritten text, and interpret and convert them into digital texts for storage and subsequent analysis [24]. Simply put, OCR and ICR software facilitates the transformation of physical or digital materials into searchable formats. Text extraction tools, PDF to.txt converters, and Google's picture search feature are a few examples of this technology.

A common application where OCR is widely used is automatic number-plate recognition (ANPR) systems to recognise the numbers on licence plates. Number-plate recognition is essential in numerous applications like tracking down stolen vehicles, determining parking rates or bills for tolls, regulate entrance to safe zones, and more. OCR and ICR technology, both, have great potential in government sector applications that still process information using paper trails. For example, registered citizens' information in license registration, voting ID verification, etc., can be checked by simply scanning the card and processing the information using OCR.

Artificial Intelligence/Machine Learning Techniques. AI is the intelligence exhibited by machines to simulate human behaviours such as reasoning, planning, thinking, problem-solving, perception, and more. Machine Learning (ML), Deep Learning (DL), Computer Vision (CV), and Natural Language Processing (NLP) are some techniques under AI which are utilized for analysing large datasets among other things. Neural Networks and CV are core technologies behind various analytical computations such as voice/ face recognition, image classification, video analytics, driverless cars and the likes.

Artificial intelligence has already been incorporated in many e-governance services such as facial recognition to boost up immigration processes. Another example is of the United States Social Security Administration which is an independent agency of the U.S. federal government. The Social Security Administration (SSA) essentially determines whether a claimant is entitled to disability benefits or not [25]. The implementation to determine whether an applicant meets the criteria involves a rigorous five-step process. SSA leverages an AI model to predict the claimants with the most likelihood of qualifying for benefits at the initial application filing phase to accelerate this process. After each referral, as indicated by the model, the state Disability Determination Service (DDS) appoints a Quick Disability Determination (QDD) unit, wherein an examiner and a medical expert sign-off the claim. The AI model is even used at the hearing level to predict which claims are likely to receive benefits after being denied reconsideration. The claims with a higher chance of success are moved earlier in the queue than cases with a lower predicted probability of receiving benefits. Hence, using prediction algorithms trained on past medical findings, records, and treatment protocols, AI has helped improve and speed up the case processes tremendously.

Natural Language Processing (NLP). Natural language processing is concerned with how computers and human language interacts. It can be described as a software/machine's ability to recognise, interpret and/or produce spoken or written information [26]. This technology's goal is to equip machines with the ability to comprehend human language and make inferences from it, enabling them to process human communications (text or speech) automatically. E-governance applications usually require information be to extracted, categorized and interpreted from various sources and hence they can greatly benefit from NLP. Some of the most common application areas of NLP are document summarization, semantic text matching, topic discovery and modelling, content categorization [27] and automatic speech recognition among others. Moreover, sentiment analysis has a huge potential in the public sector, where sentiments of citizens can be analysed through diverse sources such as social media, and consequently used in some form of decision-making. Chatbots, a product of NLP, can leverage sentiment analysis to personalise conversations with users, leading to more public engagement and better government-citizen interactions.

Process Mining. Data science is applied in process mining to find, verify, and enhance workflows [28]. Organisations can use log data from information systems such as Enterprise Resource Planning (ERP) or Customer Relationship Management (CRM) to assess performance of processes and identify room for improvement. Generally, the log data is used to create a process model. From here, the entire process is looked at, and its specifics and any variances from the expected outputs are identified. Additionally, specialised algorithms can shed light on the underlying causes of abnormalities. Organizations can use process models to determine whether their processes are operating according to their expectations. If not, they can use this knowledge to change their strategy and allocate the extra resources to improve them. Usually process mining is the first step of the hyperautomation journey, since it lets an organization decided which parts or which process in its entirety will benefit from automation. Process mining can be of three types [28]:

Process Discovery. Using event log data from information systems, a process model is created without leveraging existing process models. This is the most commonly used process mining type where a new model is developed without using any previous information.

Conformance Checking. Checking for conformance ensures that the desired process model is mirrored in reality. This kind of process mining can identify any aberrations from an organization's intended model initiatives by comparing a process description to an existing process model based on its event log data.

Process Enhancement. In this subclass of process mining, an existing process model is enhanced using new data. For instance, the results of compliance/conformance checking might help the organization to identify bottlenecks in an existing process model so that they can improve that process.

3.4 Potential of Hyperautomation in E-Governance

According to Deloitte (2020), several sectors such as healthcare, insurance, tourism, travel and most importantly government are expected to experience a transformative impact from hyperautomation. They share certain characteristics that make them attractive candidates for hyperautomation. Firstly, they often have a multitude of disparate legacy systems, which hinder seamless data integration and communication. Secondly, they involve numerous complex processes and intermediary players resulting in intricate workflows and lastly, decision-making in these sectors can benefit significantly from intelligent cognitive input. It is worth noting that Hyperautomation is not a magical solution that can address all these challenges and bring e-governance to its ultimate stage of development. Rather, it is a pragmatic concept that, when implemented widely, has the potential to enhance numerous smaller processes within government systems. While hyperautomation may not be a panacea for all the existing challenges of e-governance, it can transcend traditional technologies and structures, elevating them to a newer and more efficient level.

For instance, in contrast to traditional automation which focuses on automating specific tasks on a smaller scale, hyperautomation utilizes a combination of automation tools to scale automation initiatives in an organization [12]. By providing pre-built modules through an app store, it streamlines the infusion of advanced technologies [13]. The key is to ensure that automating tools seamlessly integrate into existing technology stacks without imposing excessive demands on IT. A critical aspect of hyperautomation is its ability to serve as a versatile platform, accommodating a wide range of technologies, and ensuring smooth interoperability among automation tools.

Moreover, Hyperautomation platforms can be seamlessly overlaid onto existing technology [13] infrastructure within government agencies. This can help modernize Legacy systems and facilitate communication between systems in different departments. Hence, seamless data exchange between previously isolated systems removes data silos resulting in a holistic view of data which in turn can be stored in a central reserve. As a result, integration, and collaboration between disparate government functions (horizontal integration) and disparate levels of the government (vertical integration) will enable the creation of a one-stop shop portal for all citizen services. Additionally, decision-makers and officials can access and analyse comprehensive data sets, leading to more informed and data-driven decision-making processes.

Hyperautomation's ability to automate many administrative and paper-based tasks comes from its ability to create fluid end-to-end workflows which utilize diverse technologies. A common job of many back-office employees is to go through various citizen applications and forms, extract the relevant information from them and store it in a database for further analysis. This entire workflow can be hyperautomated using Intelligent Character Recognition and Natural Language Processing to extract relevant information (using keywords) from uploaded scans of hardcopy forms and RPA bots to store it in a database. Hence, the combined workforce of RPA and intelligence called the Digital Workforce [14], ensures data consistency and accuracy, along with the elimination of monotonous jobs.

Unlike RPA, which focuses on replicating tasks performed by humans, hyperautomation integrates both technology and human workforce [13]. This collaborative approach allows employees to engage with automation tools and software, enabling them to acquire new skills and actively participate in the automation process. As workers become more familiar with automation instruments, they can advance to using machine learning and AI-enabled decision-making, further enhancing the efficiency and intelligence of the automation process. Hence, hyperautomation helps to reinvent new jobs for government back-office workers, and in turn boost their morale and the overall productivity of e-governance processes. This in turn will have a positive effect on government-citizen relationships and citizen participation.

3.5   Workflow of Hyperautomation

The first crucial step in a hyperautomation workflow is to assess an organization's existing processes [6]. This involves identifying potential processes for automation through discussions with human stakeholders, employing process discovery tools, and leveraging digital twin technology [12].

Once identified, the process details are meticulously documented, and the processes are refined before automation to maximize the benefits [6, 12]. Then, identification and collection of the data (structured and unstructured) required for the process [12, 29] follows. Subsequently, process mining is employed to map out the potential benefits of automation, including efficiency standards and Return on Investments. Utilizing a digital twin paradigm, these benefits can be visualized and tested against various real-world input data, further enhancing the decision-making process [12].

The next critical step is to determine which technologies, such as OCR, RPA, AI, and others, will be used to achieve automation, thereby enabling the creation of a proper automation pipeline [12]. The development team then proceeds to create and implement automation solutions for the identified processes [29].

After the successful development of the automation solutions, the e-governance process is ready for deployment. Business Process Management Platforms play a pivotal role in orchestrating different processes and integrating services through a common platform, streamlining the entire workflow [12, 29].

In the evaluation stage, intelligence is harnessed using OCR, ML, and NLP techniques to facilitate analytics and gain insightful perspectives into the automated e-governance processes [6]. Moreover, Conformance Checking and Process Enhancement are utilized to ensure that the automated processes operate seamlessly according to the organization's expectations, further refining the efficiency and effectiveness of the entire system.

By combining Deloitte's [6], IBM's [12] and nanonet's [29] general workflow of hyperautomation, we have come up with the following theoretical framework for the application of hyperautomation (Fig. 2).

3.6   Case Study of Hyperautomation

Some public sector agencies have already started implementing Hyperautomation in their processes to enable efficiencies, and greater outputs. The case studies below [30] will help to concretize how hyperautomation solutions can be applied for different kinds of problem statements.

Modernizing Court Management System of Marion County, Indiana, USA

Problem Statement. Modern courtrooms in Marion County have cameras and voice recorders to record the attorneys, witnesses, and judges participating in court hearings. However, managing files of different formats and extracting information from them became tedious. It generally required a lot of human labour, specialised devices, and software to retrieve files. Moreover, the shortage of stenographic reporters in the county led the courts to hire external companies to create transcripts and proofread them using digital media files. However, this way of storing and transcription was quite inefficient

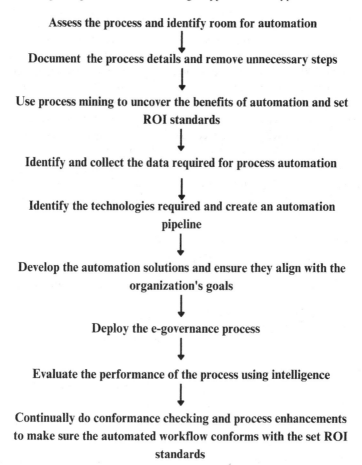

Fig. 2. Theoretical framework for application of hyperautomation.

and led to the wastage of a lot of personnel and monitory resources. To this end, Marion County took to Hyperautomation solutions.

Solution. They teamed up with TheRecordXchange (TRX), a company that works with Amazon Web Services (AWS) to help automate courtroom processes, to handle the storage and extraction of various files and manage transcription requests. TRX provides the courts of Marion Country with easy-to-use user interfaces for their automation purposes. Hosting TRX's software on AWS (SaaS) eliminates the need for bulky on-premise storage and applications. Moreover, the unlimited storage of the AWS cloud is utilized to store all data and files relating to the court hearings. TRX also provides the courts with a streaming program that allows citizens to request and access the recording of a court hearing. The most significant change was the generation of automated transcripts. TRX employs a Voice-Copy application that uses Natural Language Processing algorithms to recognize human language and create transcripts from media files. Additionally, TRX's multi-format compatible platform allowed courts to process video streams during the pandemic from different vendors, such as Cisco WebEx and Zoom. The court website is also equipped with digital commerce abilities, enabling all payments and cost estimates to be done within the site. By using the hyperautomation approach, the courts can now handle 200–300 digital requests in a month. Moreover, the automatic generation of transcripts from audio and video files relieves the pressure off the court personnel.

In the future, the county plans to take hyperautomation initiatives further by automating even the storage and retrieval of media files and making desired texts more easily searchable. These tasks will be achieved via Robotic Process Automation. Moreover, they wish to transfer every recording to the cloud, where it will get processed and categorized. This digitization will employ a combination of NLP (processing) and RPA (indexing/categorization). Finally, TRX will leverage AI-based algorithms to support context-based searching, allowing users to search for a recording or document simply by entering a word or a phrase.

Vendors Involved. TheRecordXchange (TRX) and Amazon Web Services (AWS).

Hyperautomation Technologies Used. SaaS, Cloud, NLP, RPA.

Modernizing Legacy Medicaid Systems, The Centers for Medicare & Medicaid Services

Problem. In the United States, Medicaid is a federal and state-run program that assists people with low incomes and resources with paying for healthcare. In addition, Medicaid also provides services like nursing home care and personal care. However, the current Medicaid IT systems are very old and, consequently, difficult and expensive to maintain. To this end, the Centers for Medicare and Medicaid Services (CMS) are transforming Legacy Medicaid Systems into modern systems called Medicaid Enterprise Systems (MES) by transitioning to a Medicaid IT Architecture (MITA). This modernization is what we call hyperautomation.

Solution. CMS is collaborating with Red Hat enterprise to employ hyperautomation for modernizing Legacy Medicaid Systems. To transition to a MITA architecture, installing a central Systems Integration Platform (SIP) is the first step since it enforces uniform standards and offers a shared set of APIs, data stores, and policies. Next, a legacy Medicaid module or function is selected, which is desired to be modernized. The red hat software (OpenShift) then creates a cloud-agnostic function for that legacy module. The last step is to connect the modernized module to the legacy system and turn off the legacy function. These steps can be repeated for as many modules as possible since modules are not dependent on each other. These modules can be constantly updated to cater to new Medicaid requirements leveraging Red Hat automation tools or DevOps methods. This can be thought of as a type of process mining called process enhancement, as discussed above.

Moreover, data silos have been eliminated since all the MES have a common data store. Hence, new connections and insights from this joint data can be extracted using Artificial Intelligence and Machine Learning Techniques. By employing Hyperautomation, CMS has successfully dealt with the problem of Legacy Systems, allowed monitoring and updating of processes, and used AI to gain new business insights.

Vendors Involved. Red Hat and cloud provider of choice.

Hyperautomation Technologies Used. SaaS, iBPM platform, Cloud, AI, RPA.

3.7 Application of Theoretical Framework to a Case Study

Consider the case study of the Centers for Medicare and Medicaid Services' Legacy Medicaid Systems. We will now apply our theoretical framework to the case study to visualize how hyperautomation solutions can be planned for up-and-coming use cases.

Assessment

- Identify the challenges in Legacy Medicaid Systems. As discussed previously, legacy systems suffer from the cost of maintenance, the expertise required to maintain them, and their tendency to create data and functional silos due to their non-interoperability with newer technology.
- Engage with stakeholders such as CMS and IT experts to understand the specific points for improvement.

Documentation and Refinement

- Document the process details, in this case, the Medicaid systems' structure, functioning, and limitations.
- Refining in this case study can be thought of as refining the Medicaid IT Architecture (if possible).

Data Identification and Collection

- Identify the data stored in disparate legacy systems and modules.
- The data can be stored in a central reservoir after the systems have been modernized.

Process Mining and Visualization

- Use process mining techniques to analyze existing Medicaid processes and identify areas for enhancement.
- Visualize the optimized processes using a digital twin under the new MITA architecture, ensuring the modernized modules align with CMS's requirements.
- Set ROI standards.

Technology Selection

- Identify the appropriate technologies to be used, such as Red Hat's OpenShift for cloud-agnostic functions (SaaS), central Systems Integration Platform (iBPM), AI for extracting insights from data, and RPA for automating repetitive tasks like data entry, extraction, transfer, etc.

Development and Implementation

- Develop a central Systems Integration Platform (SIP) to enforce uniform standards and provide shared APIs, data stores, and policies.
- Create cloud-agnostic functions for legacy modules, which are to be modernized, using Red Hat's OpenShift software.

- Integrate modernized modules with the legacy system and gradually replace legacy functions.

Deployment

- Deploy the modernized Medicaid Enterprise Systems, making them accessible to CMS personnel and authorized users.

Evaluation and Analytics

- Use AI and ML to extract insights from the Medicaid data and evaluate the performance of the new modules.

Conformance Checking and Process Enhancement

- Regularly conduct conformance checks to ensure modernized Medicaid systems comply with industry standards and regulatory requirements.
- Implement process enhancements based on feedback and evolving Medicaid needs.

Continuous Improvement

- Continuously improve the modernized systems based on changing Medicaid requirements using Red Hat's automation tools.
- Plan for future automation tasks, such as leveraging RPA for additional process automation, to further optimize Medicaid operations.

Hence, through the application of our theoretical hyperautomation framework to an existing case study of hyperautomation in e-governance, we can visualize how the framework can be applied to more such potential use-cases.

4 Findings

After reviewing the key components of hyperautomation, its potential in the public sector, and two case studies, it is clear that hyperautomation has many benefits for the public sector. A primary challenge for most government organizations is the need for IT expertise and employees' general lack of IT knowledge. However, with hyperautomation, a single external vendor usually supplies an integrated technological solution that can easily overlay onto existing systems. This gives the potential for e-governance development in many localities and countries that struggle with a weak IT workforce, suffer from employee dissatisfaction due to repetitive jobs, and are slow to adopt new technology since it usually means buying from multiple vendors.

Moreover, with the addition of intelligence to automation, among other things, Hyperautomation can scale automation in organisations. A central Hyperautomation platform for organisations that integrates all the different technologies at play (OCR, NLP, AI) enables the scalability of almost all scalable processes since the created automation solution is not specific to a particular process [13]. This advances the ability to identify and create dynamic automation processes. Moreover, different processes and services can also be linked [29] using this common platform (as reflected in the first use case), resulting in a truly flexible, integrated, and agile environment [13].

Hyperautomation also tackles the problems of decades-old computer systems commonly present in government agencies by integrating technologies such as RPA and Artificial Intelligence with legacy systems (as reflected in both the second use case).

Using easy-to-use intelligent business process management platforms to create scalable solutions allows organisations to automate more complex processes, drive the need for human counterparts to envision these solutions and consequently create more job opportunities. Keeping humans in the loop as and when needed is an excellent benefit of Hyperautomation, which can lead to better decision-making through a close collaboration of computers and humans (Fig. 3).

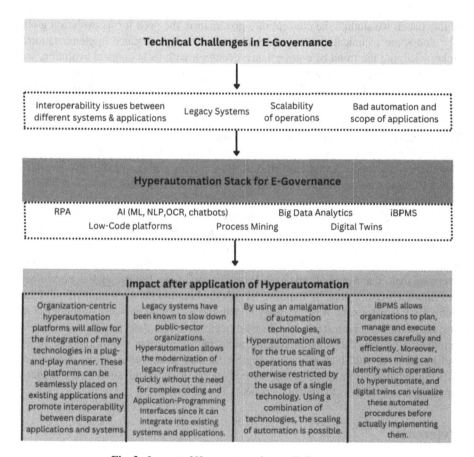

Fig. 3. Impact of Hyperautomation on E-Governance.

Not only can Hyperautomation handle interoperability between disparate systems due to technological integration, but it also moves one step further from RPA (which can handle only structured data) to handle structured, unstructured, and semi-structured data [13]. Furthermore, all this variety of data is kept in a store in the cloud for different processes to access them as and when needed.

Lastly, the business approach of hyperautomation allows for careful planning of the automation of processes through technologies such as digital twins and process mining. This avoids lousy automation practices mainly arising from simply automating highly manual processes without thinking. Instead, the goal of automation should be envisioned by making processes quicker and more efficient. Moreover, Big Data analytics and insights help to continuously learn and frequently optimize different processes and check to see if their outputs conform with the preset standards and ROI.

5 Conclusion

In this paper, we studied the concept of e-governance, the need for its evolution globally, and some technical challenges which persist in e-governance implementations. Acknowledging the trend of e-governance evolution with technological evolution, we study an emerging trend called hyperautomation. Hyperautomation is a strategy that removes functional and data silos and automates as many processes as possible using an amalgamation of technologies. These technologies include robotic process automation (RPA), low-code application platforms (LCAP), artificial intelligence (AI), Digital Twins, Intelligent Business Process Management suites (iBPMS), and process mining, among others. We discussed the key concepts of hyperautomation, its potential in e-governance, and two relevant case studies. By applying our theoretical framework to one of the case studies, we also demonstrated how hyperautomation could be applied to more use-cases.

Even though hyperautomation seems to be the next technology trend to revolutionize the automation of e-governance processes, it is not without its challenges. One of the main challenges is the resistance to the continuous creation of avant-garde technology. Employees remain sceptical and fear that technology will replace them. It is essential to ensure them that hyperautomation is bound to open more fulfilling job opportunities and improve existing jobs by requiring close collaboration between humans and their technology counterparts. It is necessary to gain the support of as many stakeholders as possible to put in a reasonable initial investment. Moreover, selecting the right hyperautomation vendor, choosing appropriate areas for automation, setting realistic ROIs, and keeping up with them are not negligible hurdles. Like technological integration, hyperautomation also requires a smooth integration of an organization's stakeholders, employees, and citizens to realize its benefits in e-governance.

References

1. http://portal.oas.org/portal/sector/sap/departamentoparalagesti%C3%B3np%C3%BAblicaef ectiva/npa/sobreprogramadeegobierno/tabid/811/default.aspx?language=en-us
2. Bannister, F., Connolly, R.: Defining e-governance. e-Serv. J. J. Electr. Serv. Pub. Private Sect. **8**(2), 3–25 (2012)
3. Bindu, N., Sankar, C.P., Kumar, K.S.: From conventional governance to e-democracy: tracing the evolution of e-governance research trends using network analysis tools. Gov. Inf. Q. **36**(3), 385–399 (2019)
4. https://www.annualreviews.org/doi/full/10.1146/annurev-lawsocsci-041221-023808

5. https://desapublications.un.org/sites/default/files/publications/2022-09/Web%20version%20E-Government%202022.pdf

6. https://www2.deloitte.com/content/dam/Deloitte/in/Documents/technology-media-telecommunications/in-hyperautomation-the-next-frontier-noexp.pdf

7. https://www.marklogic.com/blog/data-silos-state-government-agencies/

8. Almuftah, H., Weerakkody, V., Sivarajah, U.: Comparing and contrasting e-government maturity models: a qualitative-meta synthesis. Electron. Govern. Electron. Particip. Joint Proceed. Ongoing Res. Projects IFIP WG **8**, 69–79 (2016)

9. https://www.gao.gov/products/gao-21-524t

10. Abu Bakar, H., Razali, R., Jambari, D.I.: A qualitative study of legacy systems modernisation for citizen-centric digital government. Sustainability **14**(17), 10951 (2022)

11. https://research.aimultiple.com/rpa-legacy-systems/

12. https://www.ibm.com/topics/hyperautomation#:~:text=Hyperautomation%20is%20the%20concept%20of,to%20run%20without%20human%20intervention

13. Haleem, A., Javaid, M., Singh, R.P., Rab, S., Suman, R.: Hyperautomation for the enhancement of automation in industries. Sensors Int. **2**, 100124 (2021)

14. https://www.automationanywhere.com/rpa/hyperautomation

15. https://www.gartner.com/smarterwithgartner/gartner-top-10-strategic-technology-trends-for-2020

16. https://www.gartner.com/en/newsroom/press-releases/2021-04-28-gartner-forecasts-worldwide-hyperautomation-enabling-software-market-to-reach-nearly-600-billion-by-2022

17. https://www.coherentmarketinsights.com/market-insight/hyper-automation-market-3754

18. https://www2.deloitte.com/content/dam/Deloitte/tw/Documents/strategy/tw-Automation-with-intelligence.pdf

19. https://www.unisys.com/blog-post/cis/three-keys-to-realizing-expected-tco-on-hyperautomation-initiatives/#:~:text=In%20the%20report%2C%20Gartner%20predicts,next%20initiative%20become%20a%20statistic

20. https://www.uipath.com/rpa/robotic-process-automation

21. https://www.uipath.com/blog/industry-solutions/use-downtime-reimagine-recruiting-onboarding-processes

22. https://www.twi-global.com/technical-knowledge/faqs/what-is-digital-twinv

23. Glaessgen, E., Stargel, D.: The digital twin paradigm for future NASA and US Air Force vehicles. In: 53rd AIAA/ASME/ASCE/AHS/ASC Structures, Structural Dynamics and Materials Conference 20th AIAA/ASME/AHS Adaptive Structures Conference 14th AIAA, p. 1818 (2012)

24. https://www.hitechnectar.com/blogs/ocr-vs-icr/

25. Engstrom, D.F., Ho, D.E., Sharkey, C.M., Cuéllar, M.F.: Government by algorithm: artificial intelligence in federal administrative agencies. NYU School of Law, Public Law Research Paper, pp. 20–54 (2020)

26. https://www.oracle.com/in/artificial-intelligence/what-is-natural-language-processing/#:~:text=Natural%20language%20processing%20(NLP)%20is,natural%20language%20text%20or%20voice

27. https://www.projectpro.io/article/topic-modeling-nlp/801

28. https://www.ibm.com/topics/process-mining#:~:text=the%20next%20step-,What%20is%20process%20mining%3F,and%20other%20areas%20of%20improvement

29. https://nanonets.com/blog/what-is-hyperautomation/

30. Hyperautomation use case. https://papers.govtech.com/What-Is-Hyperautomation-And-How-Can-It-Help-Improve-Government-Processes-136253.html

31. https://www.kofax.com/-/media/files/white-papers/en/wp_hyperautomation-for-federal-agencies_en.pdf

Prediction of Airline Flow Using Data Analytics Methods

Beyzanur Cayir Ervural[(✉)] [iD]

Department of Aviation Management, Necmettin Erbakan University, Konya, Turkey
bc.ervural@erbakan.edu.tr

Abstract. It is very important to maintain strategic policies in the long term with reliable investment decisions. Air transport is on the agenda of all countries as one of the most important strategic sectors. For this reason, it is necessary to research the current market conditions accurately and to determine the best forecasts for the future in the investment and capacity expansion decisions to be made. Correctly designed forecasting models help strategic decisions to be taken with a low margin of error to be successful. In this study, different data analytics approaches have been developed to accurately predict air traffic with forecasting models such as multiple linear regression analysis (MLR), decision tree (DT), artificial neural networks (ANN), and times series. The obtained prediction models were compared with each other and the most appropriate model was determined in terms of margin of error.

Keywords: Prediction · airline flow · data analytics Regression analysis · Decision tree · ANN · Times series

1 Introduction

The correct execution of all operations in companies primarily depends on the development of the accurate planning and forecasting policies [1]. After the first key step is performed properly, successful results are obtained as the remaining stages of the system will proceed depending on the initial step.

In order to dominate the international arena, it is necessary to invest in air transportation and to develop in this field to a significant extent. For this reason, the aviation industry is a very prestigious and lucrative area, and it is an attractive domain where great leaders compete to get a share of the pie.

The sensitive and competitive side of air transportation makes it more privileged than other transportation modes [2]. And as it can be understood from all these explanations, air transportation should be supported with correct estimation policies and carried out with the least error and the highest profit margin.

Developing an accurate forecasting model can be cumbersome due to the dynamics within aviation management itself. Due to the distinctive natures of the aviation industry, it is essential to effort methodically on the most successful model offers. Since deviations in the prediction can be very costly for airport directors, the accomplishment of the

© The Author(s), under exclusive license to Springer Nature Switzerland AG 2023
F. Ortiz-Rodríguez et al. (Eds.): EGETC 2023, CCIS 1888, pp. 204–214, 2023.
https://doi.org/10.1007/978-3-031-43940-7_16

demand prediction model established must imitate the minimum deviation from the real data to avoid any distortion. Underestimation can lead to congestion, interruptions, suspensions and loss of customers, i.e. inadequate airport services, while overestimating passenger demand can create serious financial troubles for airport authorities.

Therefore, the accuracy of the prediction model is a very fragile and critical consideration. Turkey ranks 3rd in Europe in terms of airline flight traffic density [3]. This statistic shows how seriously Turkey takes air transport ways and is working on it.

Top ten airlines ranked according to international traffic customers. World Airline Transport Statistics showed Ryanair carried more international customers than any other airline in 2015 (Table 1), which is the world's favorite airline company by releasing at least 100,000 seats for sale across European network. Since airline flight patterns have different dynamics, quality and leadership in the sector must be sustainable. It seems that the airline company, which has been in the first place for years (Table 2), is no longer in the top ten list (Singapore Airlines and Qatar Airways). These evaluations are made with different criteria based on customer satisfaction such as family seating policies, priority boarding, children's amenities, cabin services, hygiene standards, service quality and low-cost options.

Table 1. Top ten airlines in 2015

Rank	Airline
1	Ryanair
2	EasyJet
3	Emirates
4	Lufthansa
5	British Airways
6	Turkish Airlines
7	Air France
8	KLM
9	American Airlines
10	United Airlines

In order to be at the top of the list, it is important to adapt to today's conditions and respond quickly to expectations. With accurate demand forecasting policies, the number of seats, ticket price, number of crew and new destination decisions can be precisely controlled and well managed.

In this study we aim to construct a reliable forecasting model to provide a successful prediction model using conventional prediction techniques such as multiple linear regression, times series and recently developed data analytics methods such as artificial neural networks and decision tree methods for air passenger flow forecasting in Turkey.

According to literature research, although airline passenger demand estimation studies are carried out, it is seen that there are still serious deficiencies/gaps in this regard

Table 2. The World Top 10 airlines in 2023 (announced by World Airline Awards Skytrax)

Rank	Airline
1	Singapore Airlines
2	Qatar Airways
3	ANA All Nippon Airways
4	Emirates
5	Japan Airlines
6	Turkish Airlines
7	Air France
8	Cathay Pacific Airways
9	EVA Air
10	Korean Air

[4]. It has been seen that the most frequently used methods are econometric methods. In this study, both classical and advanced methods will be evaluated together and powerful estimation models to be compared will be presented. The case of Turkey is presented by using air passenger transport data covering the 2005–2020 period.

2 Literature Reviews

Airline flow movement modeling and prediction have attracted the attention of researchers and practitioners over the last 60 years. In a general manner, passenger demand forecasting models can be categorized into three main classes: time series models, econometric methods and artificial intelligence approaches [5].

Times series models consider historical data statistics using various types such as the autoregressive integrated moving average (ARIMA) and smoothing techniques [6]. Econometric methods deal with several various variables with demand forecasting. Both approaches assume a linear relation among variables in the forecasting model.

In order to eliminate the shortage of this restricted characteristic which affect the performance of the model, artificial intelligence based models offer nonlinear and more adaptable pattern structures in complicated versions. It seems that the effectiveness of artificial intelligence methods depends on the number of observations, and well-designed data analytics patterns in machine learning content show a successful training set as well as capturing nonlinear relationships [7]. To provide more accurate forecasting models, some integrated models have been proposed to provide a superior forecasting approach.

Long et al. [8] examined demand urban air mobility from a large scale with discussing quantitative and qualitative perspectives in market demand considering most common techniques, some technical infrastructures such as potential cargo applications, shuttle services and public acceptance and emphasizing important opportunities for future research. Fildes et al. [9] provided an econometric model to predict air passenger traffic flows employing multiple error measures using autoregressive distributed lag model and vector autoregressive (VAR) model. Ghalehkhondabi et al. [10] analyzed several forecasting model from short to medium term air traffic flows utilizing econometric models with regards to multiple error measures and adding to world trade factor in the model. Xie et al. [11] applied a hybrid seasonal decomposition and support vector regression model for short term forecasting of air passenger at airports. The developed combined method outperforms than other time series models in terms of accuracy level. Suryani et al. [12] provided a system dynamic approach in order to predict air passenger demand with runaway and passenger terminal capacity constraints. The obtained results show that airfare impact, GDP, population and number of flights important parameters in identifying air passenger flow.

There are many approaches based on forecasting techniques to predict air passenger demand in the scientific literature given in Table 3.

Table 3. A summary of literature review

Authors	Goal	Method
Tang et al. [13]	making forecasts with weekly passenger traffic	machine learning model, times series model
Tirtha et al. [14]	to assess effect of COVID-19 on airline demand	a linear mixed model
Albayrak et al. [15]	to examine the factors of air passenger traffic in Turkey	a panel data estimation methodology
Solvoll et al. [16]	to make air traffic demands in Norwegian airport	a quantitative forecasting models
Sun et al. [17]	to forecast air passenger flows	a nonlinear vector auto-regression NN approach
Suh and Ryerson [18]	to predict probability of passenger volume	a statistical forecasting model
Gelhausen et al. [19]	analyze travel behavior at the German airport	co-integrated regression functions
Rajendran et al. [20]	to investigate demand of air taxi urban mobility services	logistic regression, ANN, RF and gradient boosting
Qin et al. [21]	to forecast monthly passenger flow in China	two novel hybrid methods combining
Vadlamani et al. [22]	to assess and forecast entry design of Southwest Airlines	logistic regression, decision tree, support vector machine, random forest

3 Methodology

In the following section, traditional methods and recently developed machine learning tools are explained as MLR, times series, ANN and Decision tree methods, respectively.

3.1 Multiple Linear Regression Model

Regression analysis is a statistical method that shows the link between two or more variables. It tries to comprehend the significant connection between the dependent factor and the independent factor in order to obtain information. Using MLR, we can learn the strong point of the relationship between independent variables and dependent variables. MLR operates under several key assumptions: homogeneity of variance, independence of observations, normality and linearity. The equation of the multiple linear regression analysis model is shown with the following mathematical formulation [23]:

$$Y = b_o + b_1 X_{1+\ldots} \cdots + b_n X_n + \varepsilon \qquad (1)$$

where

$$\varepsilon = \text{error rate; } b = \text{the coefficient of independent variable}$$

$$Y = \textit{the predicted value } X = \text{independent variables}$$

3.2 Artificial Neural Networks

ANNs are well-known subset of machine learning algorithms. It is basically a computational model based on genetic neural networks. ANN is an algorithm that works by merging interconnected and layered nodes [24]. ANN does not need prior knowledge between incoming and outgoing variable structures.

The main structures of ANNs are inspired by the human brain, simulating the way biological neurons pointer to each other. It adapts the incoming information according to its own structure. ANNs comprise of node layers that include an input layer, one or more hidden layers, and an output layer. Each node or artificial neuron associates to the other and has an associated weight and threshold. Each node creates its own linear regression model consisting of input data, weights, bias (or threshold), and an output (Fig. 1).

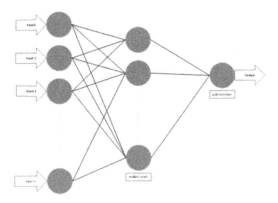

Fig. 1. ANN configuration

After the input layer is defined, weights are distributed to the related layers. These weights support checking the significance of any variable; larger ones contribute more to output compared to other inputs. ANNs can be classified into various kinds depending on their purposes, such as feedforward, multi-layer perceptions, convolutional and recurrent neural networks.

3.3 Times Series

Time series analysis is a technique based on former data, which includes methods of searching time series facts to obtain meaningful statistics and other properties of data over a period of time. The method evaluates time series data and trend analysis together to see the pattern of data such as cyclical, periodic, irregularity, stationary, and seasonality. Well-known types of time series analysis are the moving average, exponential smoothing, and trend projection [25]. The autoregression and moving average (ARMA) models are utilized in time series analysis to characterize stationary time series depend on two parameters which are the autoregression (AR) and the second for the moving average (MA).

If the related model is not stationary, then you can reach stationarity by taking a series of differences and after this transformation the model referred as ARIMA [26]. The notation ARMA (p, q) states to the model with p autoregressive expression and q moving-average expression. This model covers the AR(p) and MA(q) models, the general form of the ARMA model is given below [27]:

$$X_t = \varepsilon_t + \sum_{i=1}^{p} \varnothing_i X_{t-i} + \sum_{i=1}^{q} \theta_i \varepsilon_{t-i} \qquad (2)$$

3.4 Decision Tree

Decision Tree (DT) is a kind of supervised learning methods that can be utilized for both classification and Regression problems, however it is mostly ideal for describing classification issues. It is a tree configuration classifier in which the internal nodes symbolize the structures of a dataset, the branches specify the decision rules, and each leaf node characterizes the result. There are two nodes in a decision tree structure, decision node and leaf node. The nodes are utilized to make any decision and have several branches while leaf nodes are the output of these decisions and include no other branches.

It is a graphical characterization to provide any kind of solution to a problem/decision based on certain situations. It is known as a decision tree as it jumps with a root node that spans more branches and forms a tree-like configuration. Decision tree learning is a widely utilized means in data mining [28]. The goal is to build a model that forecasts the value of objective factor based on a number of input factors. Classification and Regression Tree (CART) is a predictive algorithm applied in machine learning that produces future predictions based on former data.

4   Application of the Methods

In this study, the prediction of air passenger flow has been implemented for Turkey between 2005 and 2020. According to the literature reviews and airline professional opinions, we firstly defined independent variables as population, exports, number of flights and number of passenger were defined as the dependent variable for air passenger flow projections. The dataset comprises 16 yearly observations. To calculate the accuracy of the appropriate models in the study, we evaluated them using various performance indicator such as mean square error (MSE), mean absolute percent error (MAPE) with the following formulas:

$$MAPE = \frac{1}{N} \sum_{i=1}^{N} \left| \frac{y_i - \hat{y}_i}{y_i} \right| * 100\% \tag{3}$$

$$MSE = \frac{\sum_{i=1}^{N} (y_i - \hat{y}_i)^2}{N} \tag{4}$$

If the MAPE value is less than 0.10, we can infer that the generated model provides a highly accurate prediction. According to the correlation analysis, the defined factors have a high and positive correlation with the number of air passenger and the obtained Pearson correlation coefficient values are over 0.60.

The sample data, the flight passenger demand of Turkey between 2005 and 2020, are collected from the Civil Aviation Administration of Turkey and Turkish Statistical Institute. The 16 observations from 2005 to 2015 are utilized for model construction phase, and the left statistics from 2016 to 2020 are measured to assess the out-sample prediction performance of the models. The data set is separated into two parts, the training set and the test set. WEKA and SPSS statistical software are applied to obtain predictive analysis.

5   The Obtained Results

As seen in Fig. 2, the passenger movement has a growing trend apart from one minor drop and one major drop. Initial drop is related to the political, economic and social pressures and then the second dramatic drop related to outbreak of COVID-19. Normalization is required for different dataset and avoid excessive deviations.

In the ANN configuration, after trying all combinations to reach ideal prediction model we determined the related parameter set as follows: ANN model includes three input layer, three hidden layer and one output layer and learning rate is 0.2 and momentum value is 0.3. The obtained MAPE value is 4.84%.

The J48 Classifier algorithm is used for tree configuration in the DT model in WEKA software. The number of iterations is set to 1000 and any randomly chosen decision tree structure is given to show the progression of the proposed RF configuration. The obtained MAPE value 4.16%.

In times series applications ARIMA (0,1,0) provides satisfactory results in terms of MAPE value (0.16). And in MLR model, adding each independent variable to the prediction model the obtained MAPE value equals to 9.58%

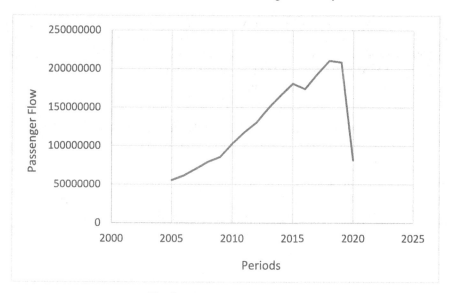

Fig. 2. Air passenger movement

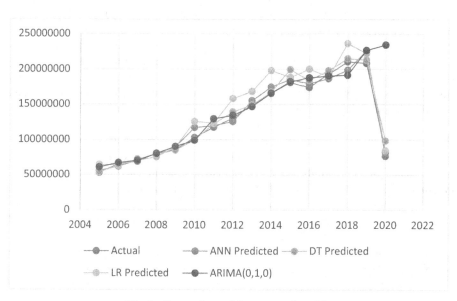

Fig. 3. Comparison of the proposed models

Prediction values for proposed models are also illustrated in Fig. 3.

As seen in Table 4 which provides the analytical results of the several forecasting methods. Machine learning algorithms outperforms the classical forecasting methods (MLR, ARIMA). The experimental results display that the DT approach has the lowest MAPE (4.16%), RMSE (7535164) and MAE (5221888). ANN gives better results than

MLR methodology with 4.83% margin MAPE, RMSE (7769419) and MAE (6272023) values. As can be seen from the table, the ARIMA (0,1,0) model provides the weakest predictive power on air traffic flow, with 16.08% MAPE value. It is clearly observed that the results of MAPE, RMSE and MAE point out that, DT and ANN can provide more consistent and reliable prediction accuracy.

Table 4. Performance criteria of the prediction models

	ANN	DT	MLR	ARIMA (0,1,0)
MAPE	0,04839	0,04164	0,0958	0,1608
MAE	6272023,68	5221888,06	12930275,49	15359091,6
RMSE	7769419,34	7535164,50	16735197,82	33049215,74

6 Conclusion

Today's most challenging and competitive means of transportation is clearly known as airlines, making a serious difference with long-term investments and improvements. The aviation sector is an invaluable power for countries and therefore most of the investments and strategic decisions are taken in this arena. Due to the different model structure in the data and the variable dynamics of the air transport system, accurately predicting passenger flows can be a challenging task. Therefore, it is important to predict the next period with a high degree of certainty with advanced forecasting methods.

In this study, sixteen years of historical information with popular machine learning algorithms ANN, DT and traditional forecasting approaches such as MLR and time series analysis were used to provide a successful airline passenger flow forecasting model. When we compare the obtained results DT predominate other prediction tools in terms of MAPE scale with 4.16%, ANN 4.84%, MLR provides 9.58% and ARIMA 16.08% subsequently. Each two advanced forecasting methods (DT, ANN) were well-designed because less than 5% error rates. From conventional methods, MLR provided a better model structure than ARIMA model.

In future studies, new determinants can be added to the prediction model with combination of other recent methods to improve performance of prediction methods.

References

1. Petropoulos, F., et al.: Forecasting: theory and practice. Int. J. Forecast. **38**(3), 705–871 (2022). https://doi.org/10.1016/J.IJFORECAST.2021.11.001
2. Air Transport, Air Transport What it is, Types & Advantages. https://www.itaerea.com/air-transport. Accessed 17 Jul 2023
3. General directorate of state airports, Havayolu Sektör Raporları (2020). https://www.dhmi.gov.tr/Sayfalar/HavaYoluSektorRaporlari.aspx. Accessed 19 Mar 2023

4. Banerjee, N., Morton, A., Akartunalı, K.: Passenger demand forecasting in scheduled transportation. Eur. J. Oper. Res. **286**(3), 797–810 (2020). https://doi.org/10.1016/J.EJOR.2019. 10.032

5. Dantas, T.M., Cyrino Oliveira, F.L., Varela Repolho, H.M.: Air transportation demand forecast through bagging holt winters methods. J. Air Transp. Manag. **59**, 116–123 (2017). https:// doi.org/10.1016/J.JAIRTRAMAN.2016.12.006

6. Samagaio, A., Wolters, M.: Comparative analysis of government forecasts for the Lisbon airport. J. Air Transp. Manag. **16**(4), 213–217 (2010). https://doi.org/10.1016/J.JAIRTRAMAN. 2009.09.002

7. Shahrabi, J., Hadavandi, E., Asadi, S.: Developing a hybrid intelligent model for forecasting problems: case study of tourism demand time series. Knowl.-Based Syst. **43**, 112–122 (2013). https://doi.org/10.1016/J.KNOSYS.2013.01.014

8. Li Long, C., Guleria, Y., Alam, S.: Air passenger forecasting using neural granger causal google trend queries3. J. Air Transp. Manag. **95**, 102083 (2021). https://doi.org/10.1016/J. JAIRTRAMAN.2021.102083

9. Fildes, R., Wei, Y., Ismail, S.: Evaluating the forecasting performance of econometric models of air passenger traffic flows using multiple error measures. Int. J. Forecast. **27**(3), 902–922 (2011). https://doi.org/10.1016/J.IJFORECAST.2009.06.002

10. Ghalehkhondabi, I., Ardjmand, E., Young, W.A., Weckman, G.R.: A review of demand forecasting models and methodological developments within tourism and passenger transportation industry. J. Tour. Futur. **5**(1), 75–93 (2019). https://doi.org/10.1108/JTF-10-2018-0061/FUL L/PDF

11. Xie, G., Wang, S., Lai, K.K.: Short-term forecasting of air passenger by using hybrid seasonal decomposition and least squares support vector regression approaches. J. Air Transp. Manag. **37**, 20–26 (2014). https://doi.org/10.1016/J.JAIRTRAMAN.2014.01.009

12. Suryani, E., Chou, S.Y., Chen, C.H.: Air passenger demand forecasting and passenger terminal capacity expansion: a system dynamics framework. Expert Syst. Appl. **37**(3), 2324–2339 (2010). https://doi.org/10.1016/J.ESWA.2009.07.041

13. Tang, H., et al.: Airport terminal passenger forecast under the impact of COVID-19 outbreaks: a case study from China. J. Build. Eng. **65**, 105740 (2023). https://doi.org/10.1016/J.JOBE. 2022.105740

14. Dey Tirtha, S., Bhowmik, T., Eluru, N.: An airport level framework for examining the impact of COVID-19 on airline demand. Transp. Res. Part A Policy Pract. **159**, 169–181 (2022). https://doi.org/10.1016/J.TRA.2022.03.014

15. Kağan Albayrak, M.B., Özcan, İ.Ç., Can, R., Dobruszkes, F.: The determinants of air passenger traffic at Turkish airports. J. Air Transp. Manag. **86**, 101818 (2020). https://doi.org/ 10.1016/J.JAIRTRAMAN.2020.101818

16. Solvoll, G., Mathisen, T.A., Welde, M.: Forecasting air traffic demand for major infrastructure changes. Res. Transp. Econ. **82**, 100873 (2020). https://doi.org/10.1016/J.RETREC.2020. 100873

17. Sun, S., Lu, H., Tsui, K.L., Wang, S.: Nonlinear vector auto-regression neural network for forecasting air passenger flow. J. Air Transp. Manag. **78**, 54–62 (2019). https://doi.org/10. 1016/j.jairtraman.2019.04.005

18. Suh, D.Y., Ryerson, M.S.: Forecast to grow: aviation demand forecasting in an era of demand uncertainty and optimism bias. Transp. Res. Part E Logist. Transp. Rev. **128**, 400–416 (2019). https://doi.org/10.1016/J.TRE.2019.06.016

19. Gelhausen, M.C., Berster, P., Wilken, D.: A new direct demand model of long-term forecasting air passengers and air transport movements at German airports. J. Air Transp. Manag. **71**, 140–152 (2018). https://doi.org/10.1016/J.JAIRTRAMAN.2018.04.001

20. Rajendran, S., Srinivas, S., Grimshaw, T.: Predicting demand for air taxi urban aviation services using machine learning algorithms. J. Air Transp. Manag. **92**, 102043 (2021). https://doi.org/10.1016/J.JAIRTRAMAN.2021.102043

21. Qin, L., Li, W., Li, S.: Effective passenger flow forecasting using STL and ESN based on two improvement strategies. Neurocomputing **356**, 244–256 (2019). https://doi.org/10.1016/J.NEUCOM.2019.04.061

22. Vadlamani, S.L., Shafiq, M.O., Baysal, O.: Using machine learning to analyze and predict entry patterns of low-cost airlines: a study of Southwest Airlines. Mach. Learn. Appl. **10**, 100410 (2022). https://doi.org/10.1016/J.MLWA.2022.100410

23. Farhadian, H., Katibeh, H.: New empirical model to evaluate groundwater flow into circular tunnel using multiple regression analysis. Int. J. Min. Sci. Technol. **27**(3), 415–421 (2017). https://doi.org/10.1016/J.IJMST.2017.03.005

24. Castellon, D.F., Fenerci, A., Øiseth, O.: A comparative study of wind-induced dynamic response models of long-span bridges using artificial neural networks, support vector regression and buffeting theory. J. Wind Eng. Ind. Aerodyn. **209**, 104484 (2021). https://doi.org/10.1016/J.JWEIA.2020.104484

25. Xin, P., Liu, Y., Yang, N., Song, X., Huang, Y.: Probability distribution of wind power volatility based on the moving average method and improved nonparametric kernel density estimation. Glob. Energy Interconnect. **3**(3), 247–258 (2020). https://doi.org/10.1016/J.GLOEI.2020.07.006

26. Cayir Ervural, B., Beyca, O.F., Zaim, S.: Model estimation of ARMA using genetic algorithms: a case study of forecasting natural gas consumption. Procedia Soc. Behav. Sci. **235**, 537–545 (2016). https://doi.org/10.1016/j.sbspro.2016.11.066

27. Shumway, R.H., Stoffer, D.S.: Time series analysis and its applications, p. 549 (2000). Accessed 17 Jul. 2023. https://www.worldcat.org/title/42392178

28. Rokach, L., Maimon, O.: Data mining with decision trees: theory and applications. In: Data Mining with Decision Trees: Theory and Applications. 2nd ed., vol. 81, pp. 1–305, January 2014. https://doi.org/10.1142/9097/SUPPL_FILE/9097_CHAP01.PDF

Author Index

© The Editor(s) (if applicable) and The Author(s), under exclusive license
to Springer Nature Switzerland AG 2023
F. Ortiz-Rodríguez et al. (Eds.): EGETC 2023, CCIS 1888, p. 215, 2023.
https://doi.org/10.1007/978-3-031-43940-7

Printed in the United States
by Baker & Taylor Publisher Services